HOW TO FLOURISH AS
A PSYCHOTHERAPIST

Books by Brett Kahr

D.W. Winnicott: A Biographical Portrait (1996)

Forensic Psychotherapy and Psychopathology: Winnicottian Perspectives, Editor (2001)

Exhibitionism (2001)

The Legacy of Winnicott: Essays on Infant and Child Mental Health, Editor (2002)

Sex and the Psyche (2007)

Who's Been Sleeping in Your Head?: The Secret World of Sexual Fantasies (2008)

Life Lessons from Freud (2013)

Tea with Winnicott (2016)

Coffee with Freud (2017)

New Horizons in Forensic Psychotherapy: Exploring the Work of Estela V. Welldon, Editor (2018)

HOW TO FLOURISH AS A PSYCHOTHERAPIST

Brett Kahr

PHOENIX
PUBLISHING HOUSE
firing the mind

First published in 2019 by
Phoenix Publishing House Ltd
62 Bucknell Road
Bicester
Oxfordshire OX26 2DS

British Library Cataloguing in Publication Data

A C.I.P. for this book is available from the British Library

ISBN-13: 978-1-912691-03-6

Typeset by Medlar Publishing Solutions Pvt Ltd, India

Printed in the United Kingdom

www.phoenixpublishinghouse.co.uk
www.firingthemind.com

To my wonderful students, past and present,
who have listened to me with open-minded affection
and with engaging challenge.

"Sie arbeiten und zeugen und verdienen, daß beide Werke gut geraten."

(Freud, 1912a, p. 119)

*["You work and you create and you deserve that
both your efforts should flourish."]*

(Freud, 1912b, p. 107)

*Professor Sigmund Freud, Letter to
Dr. Ludwig Binswanger, 16th December, 1912*

Contents

PART III

Thriving Beyond the Consulting Room

PART IV

Surviving Success

"Meine Kleine gedeiht"

(Freud, 1887a, p. 4)

["My little one is flourishing"]

(Freud, 1887b, p. 16).

Dr. Sigmund Freud, Letter to Dr. Wilhelm Fliess, 24th November, 1887, regarding the birth of Mathilde Freud

Survival May Not Be Enough

As a full-time psychotherapist, I spend much of my life seated quietly in a brown leather chair, listening to the most agonising, heart-wrenching tales of woe.

Many people would not particularly relish such a sedentary and, sometimes, burdensome profession. But I find it deeply engaging and satisfying and, over time, increasingly so, as I become more and more adept at helping my patients to live peaceful, fulfilling, even joyful, lives.

But characterological transformations do not occur magically. Psychotherapeutic work can be extremely taxing. Many of my colleagues suffer from profound stress and burn-out, and quite a number of them often lament that they never made a success of their careers. Some retired after decades in a state of deep despondency because they had never achieved their goals and desires.

In recent years, psychotherapists have become frustrated, if not frightened, because the professional marketplace has become extremely crowded, and more and more colleagues now struggle to earn a living.

In view of these challenges, how does one develop a truly rich and rewarding career in psychotherapy? How can we put a secure structure in place? How can we develop our skills and capacities and intelligence? How can we conquer our creative inhibitions? How can we derive deep delight from such painful work?

More than a quarter of a century ago, the distinguished British psycho-analyst, Dr. Nina Coltart (1993), wrote a book entitled *How to Survive as a Psychotherapist*, which certainly captured the imagination of many younger colleagues at the time of publication, myself included. This topic—survival—has remained so firmly embedded in the minds of psychotherapists that, in 2015, the British Psychoanalytic Council, in collaboration with the Association of Child Psychotherapists, actually sponsored a day-conference entitled "Life as a Therapist—How to Survive!", replete with exclamation point.

Although nothing could be more important, psychotherapy practitioners must not only survive but we must also *thrive* in order to derive true satisfaction from our work. In doing so, we not only bring comfort and fulfilment and meaning to ourselves and to our families but, above all, we become models of hope and inspiration for our patients, who scrutinise our very state of being with much intensity.

Hence, I hope that while Nina Coltart may have helped us to *survive* this challenging work, we might also wish to explore how to *flourish* as psychotherapists.

In the pages that follow, I offer a frank portrait of the life of the psycho-therapist, from cradle to grave, and I hope that these very blunt remarks will be of use to clinicians at every stage of development. Naturally, I recognise that these observations and recommendations derive predominantly from my own experience and from those of close colleagues and students. Certainly, I appreciate that there may be many other ways in which one might flourish. But for the truly enthused practitioner, this book offers some guidance on how one can undertake the *maximum*, rather than the *minimum*, in order to prosper in every respect.

PART I

Building a Secure Base

CHAPTER ONE

A Noble, Complicated Passion

Mouthwash for the Mind

Over the last forty years, I have saved many lives.

I doubt that I have rescued as many endangered souls as lifeguards or firefighters or cardiothoracic surgeons, who prevent multiple deaths every day of the week, but I have certainly done my fair share, having stopped many of my patients from committing suicide or from drinking themselves to death or from engaging in extremely dangerous sports or sexual behaviours.

Some time ago, "Mustafa", a young male, aged seventeen, arrived for a consultation in a state of extreme panic, threatening to kill himself by overdosing on aspirin tablets. He explained that he harboured a dreadful secret. This teenager looked very sweet and kindly, and from his demeanour it seemed most unlikely that he had committed murder, arson, or rape. Eventually, Mustafa confessed that he had kissed another seventeen-year-old boy at school and that, although he enjoyed this very much, he knew that he would rot in hell for all eternity.

I listened calmly and quietly as Mustafa told me all about his cultural and religious background—one which condemned homosexuality as a grave, unpardonable sin.

During the course of our conversation, this adolescent boy wept profusely, shedding what seemed a lifetime of pent-up tears. Mustafa then breathed an extremely audible sigh, relaxed his tightly clenched shoulders, and smiled with great relief, "Wow, I really thought that you would tell me that I *had* to kill myself for what I had done. Thank you for not judging me."

We discussed his sexuality more fully; and as our conversation unfolded, he seemed extremely relieved to have done so. At the end of the consultation, Mustafa reached for his coat and began to beam, as though someone had just released him from prison. He turned to me with teenage enthusiasm and exclaimed, "Gosh, this was amazing. It's like … it's like mouthwash for the mind!"

I have never forgotten Mustafa's extraordinary description of a simple psychotherapeutic encounter as "mouthwash for the mind". This pleasant, decent youngster had suffered from such long-standing feelings of dirtiness for having harboured these ostensibly ugly desires; and now, after just one short conversation, he felt clean.

Needless to say, Mustafa and I had to undertake a great many more psychotherapeutic conversations before he could begin to differentiate himself from some of the restrictive and persecutory aspects of his family background and inhabit his own sexual body and sexual mind in a much more independent manner. But that first session proved deeply cathartic, and it pleases me greatly that Mustafa did not kill himself as he had threatened to do.

Psychotherapists enjoy the great professional privilege of preventing patients from murdering themselves. But we also help people in other ways.

Often, after an extended period of psychotherapeutic work, the lives of those who consult with us will change dramatically. Addicts stop using alcohol and drugs; criminals become ethical; adulterers become faithful to their spouses; those with creative blocks and inhibitions begin to produce novels and symphonies; those who constantly spoil their relationships at home and in the office start to forge more meaningful and long-lasting intimacies; those who have neglected their bodies embrace self-protectiveness; and those riddled with depression and anxiety develop the capacity to enjoy being alive, often for the very first time.

Some patients undertake treatment for only a brief spell, as they need merely to untie a few psychological knots. But more frequently, those who seek our help will embark upon a profound piece of work over many years in order to turn their lives around in a truly substantial manner. Often, at the end of a very intensive course of psychoanalysis or psychotherapy, a patient will express deep and heartfelt gratitude.

I recently completed a multi-year analysis with a lovely patient who had worked extremely hard throughout the course of treatment (as did I), and who, on parting, shook my hand and gazed at me with teary eyes, proclaiming, "Thank you. Without you I would be dead. I never knew that one could live life in colour rather than in black and white." Another patient—a writer who simply could not put pen to paper and who, after a lengthy psychoanalysis became a most swift, accomplished, and successful professional— enthused, "Thank you, Brett, you really gave me an existence. Freud would be very proud of you." The patient, knowing of my love for Sigmund Freud, could not have offered me a more meaningful parting line, and I felt deeply moved that I had helped to facilitate a journey from sterility and misery to one of richness and engagement.

Zyklon B Gas in the Consulting Room

Although I regard the practice of psychotherapy as a noble art, designed to offer relief and compassion and insight and understanding and connection and creativity and health to our patients, undertaking such work can often be quite hellish.

As every one of my colleagues will know only too well, practising psychotherapeutically—especially for those of us who do so on a full-time basis—can be unbelievably exhausting. We wake up extremely early in the morning in order to accommodate patients who can attend only before their own working day has begun, and then we toil long hours, often until the early evening, so that we can consult with men and women who can manage appointments only after their own jobs have ended!

We sit patiently and quietly, hour after hour, listening intensively to the most horrific stories of child abuse, trauma, disappointment, cruelty, betrayal, disillusionment, illness, and death. And unlike virtually every other human worker who, when exhausted, can pop out of the office for a quick coffee break or for a telephone chat with a spouse or a friend, we remain seated—often trapped—in an atmosphere of deep grief, utilising every ounce of our brain power to decipher the complexities of the intricate, confusing, and debilitating lives of those who have come to seek our assistance.

Although we often meet patients such as Mustafa who endear themselves to us with expressions such as "mouthwash for the mind", and although from time to time a patient will thank us sincerely for having saved his or her life, psychotherapists must also endure a tremendous amount of burden, often bordering on abuse.

Our healthier patients—those on the more "normal-neurotic" end of the psychopathological spectrum—treat us with appreciation, gratitude, respect, and decency. One of my most impressive analysands—a mental health professional in her own right—attended every single session with remarkable punctuality, worked hard by free-associating honestly, spent a great deal of time in between sessions mulling over what she and I had discussed, and returned the following day to elaborate and to "work through" her anxieties and concerns. This person paid her monthly invoice in a timely fashion and often expressed deep thanks for the privilege of having sessions. Over the years, I have had quite a number of patients of this sort. But such people will have come to us with a great deal of prior psychological health upon which to draw.

As we know, not all of our analysands arrive at our offices with such internal resources. Those of our patients who grew up in more impoverished backgrounds, filled with abuse and trauma and separation and deprivation and all sorts of impingements, often harbour a great deal of rage. And as psychotherapy progresses, the sadistic underbelly of the personality becomes more and more visible and, indeed, audible. Patients begin to wail, to shout, to scream, to flail about, and to spew verbal venom, cursing their mothers, their fathers, their sisters, their brothers, their grandparents, their school teachers, their priests and rabbis and imams, their friends, their bosses, their employees, their colleagues, their fellow passengers on the bus or tube and, not surprisingly, their psychotherapist!

Angry individuals will hate us because we offer them a mere fifty minutes of confidential private time per day. They will hate us because we have not cured them of a lifetime of depression after the first consultation. They will hate us for charging a fee. They will hate us for taking a short break at Easter and Christmas. They will hate us for going away for a somewhat longer period during the month of August. They will hate us because we look just like their father or their mother. They will hate simply because they can, secure in the knowledge that we will not retaliate. Above all, they will hate us because patients know that they have struggled with a lifetime of hostility and that it must be verbalised and enacted in our presence in order for us to begin to help them neutralise such emotional toxicity.

Very occasionally, the hatred towards the psychotherapist will be fully justified. An extremely small number of our colleagues have, at times, behaved unethically. But, happily, in my experience, the vast majority of psychotherapists comport themselves with the highest degree of compassion and probity. Nonetheless, we must still endure a great deal of verbal cruelty from our more vulnerable patients who act out their early traumatic experiences in our presence.

Recently, I wrote an entire book about this very phenomenon, *Bombs in the Consulting Room: Surviving Psychological Shrapnel* (Kahr, 2019a), in which I described numerous cases of patients who had exploded in my presence, including that of an elderly brain-damaged woman who spat compulsively on the floor of my office at least 200 times during our first session, as well as that of an adolescent paedophile who kept fingering his trouser pocket, claiming that he had brought a gun into the session and that he would shoot me dead. Like most, if not all, of my colleagues, I have *so* many comparable tales of bomb-like hatred that I could include merely a fraction of those experiences in my book.

Hatred towards the psychotherapist takes many forms, and we must endure them all, and must maintain our best professional stance in order to help the patient understand the origins of such cruel thoughts. One need not be spat upon or be threatened with a gun in order to feel under siege.

I once worked with a multi-millionaire who had more money than Croesus. This person owned several homes on several different continents, as well as a private jet, priceless paintings and sculptures, and a large collection of dazzling diamond jewellery. I had worked reliably, compassionately, intelligently, and thoughtfully with this patient over a lengthy period, during which time this individual made a great deal of progress, both at home and in the office. After several years of having charged a perfectly ordinary, reasonable sessional fee, which had remained constant, I announced to the patient that, with effect from the following calendar month, I would be adjusting my sessional fee by twenty pounds—a figure which represented less than one-millionth of the patient's annual earnings. Upon hearing of my intention, the patient exploded in the most vicious anti-Semitic outburst that I have ever experienced.

Although I had never discussed my own religious background, this person reached the conclusion that I *must* be Jewish, partly because I had dared to raise my fee by the shockingly huge amount of twenty pounds sterling. The patient then began to lambast me verbally over a number of sessions, admitting to fantasies of being a Nazi officer and of taking me and my family to a concentration camp. This individual then confessed much pleasure at the thought of dropping Zyklon B gas pellets into the shower room, while watching me and those dear to me choking to death as we inhaled the poisonous fumes.

Needless to say, I experienced much private distress as I sat quietly in my consulting room chair listening to such an outpouring of cruelty, as though the Zyklon B gas erupted from the patient's mouth in the form of these incomparably nasty words. Although I experienced an immediate impulse to ask my patient to leave the office (and, perhaps, to consider never returning), I maintained my professional composure and realised that although the patient had launched a huge and painful attack, this individual had also given me an enormous gift by having dared to reveal this long-suppressed, Nazi-like aspect of the personality which had remained deeply hidden but which had seethed beneath the surface of every intimate relationship.

It pleases me to report that this patient—financially quite wealthy, but emotionally quite impoverished—eventually "worked through" this ugly episode during the psychotherapy and gradually managed to transform these cruel impulses and fantasies into words and, ultimately, into more creative endeavours. After a long period of time, the patient even apologised to me and expressed deep regret for the immense cruelty of having wished me and my family dead in this most horrific manner. Happily, both the patient and I survived the Zyklon B gas episode and this person became an increasingly kindly, decent, ethical, and honourable individual. Moreover, the patient no longer hoarded all the hard-earned financial wealth but began make liberal donations to various charities which improved the lives of people in deep distress.

Although the story of this "Nazi-like" patient has had a cheerful, reparative ending, I must confess that during the apex of the Zyklon B period, I did not enjoy going into the office at all, and I wished very profoundly that I could retrain as an accountant or as a lawyer or as a football player or, indeed, as anything which would shield me from such vicious spewing. Thus, although psychotherapy may be a noble passion that changes lives, it might also be a complicated passion that pushes us to the edge.

Friends with Oesophageal Cancer and Vascular Dementia

For those who wish to consider a career in psychotherapy, and for those who have already committed ourselves to clinical practice, we must appreciate that as we age, the work becomes both *easier* and *harder*.

Having now laboured in the psychological trenches for many decades, the prospect of meeting a chronically depressed man or a severely bulimic woman or a viciously screaming couple no longer arouses as much trepidation as it would have done at the very outset of my professional life. Over the years, I have treated many patients in such troubled states and have derived deep satisfaction from knowing that depression, eating problems, and marital aneurysms can, in fact, be cured with intelligent perseverance. I have not only seen numerous generations of patients "graduate" from successful psychoanalyses, but I have come to "own" my clinical expertise and to have acquired a much more finely tuned diagnostic radar and diplomatic style of rendering interpretations which help me to unravel complicated symptoms and characterological structures. In this respect, I would dare to describe the work as much *easier*.

But as we age, the practice of psychotherapy also becomes even *harder* at the same time. In spite of our increased gravitas and knowledge and experience and reputation and confidence, the older mental health clinician must carry the burden of working at a much deeper level.

Imagine that, during the wintertime, one begins to feel unwell and visits one's general medical practitioner for a five-minute, walk-in consultation. The physician will, in all likelihood, diagnose influenza and recommend bed rest. The general medical doctor will then turn his or her attention to the next patient and may think no more about the most recent consultee. But imagine that this flu-ridden person does not recover and must then consult a hospital physician who recommends an M.R.I. scan and soon discovers a highly advanced lymphoma which will require extensive chemotherapy.

Although one must never deploy oncological analogies lightly, I often think of the more senior psychotherapist as the psychological equivalent of the Consultant Oncologist who has the privilege and, also, the horror of treating the most advanced cases of illness at the deepest level over the longest period of time. Thus, as we progress through our careers, we develop the capacity to dig deeper into the minds and souls of our troubled patients, and consequently, we often encounter physical, sexual, and emotional traumata which younger psychotherapists might have missed. Thus, I find that our work becomes harder and harder all the time.

Not only must the psychotherapist navigate the burdens of daily clinical practice, often with very distressed and angry people, but we must do so while also having to manage and endure the ordinary challenges of life outside the consulting room. While writing this chapter, one of my oldest friends and colleagues has just died from a fast-metastasising oesophageal cancer; another dear friend and colleague has had to place his wife of forty-five years in a full-time care facility for people with vascular dementia; yet another colleague has recently lost both his mother and his father within a two-week period; and still another colleague has had to bury his only child, who died, most tragically, from a brain tumour. During this extremely painful period of time, I had to go to the office every single day in order to work intensely with my patients, and then, after work, I had to (and wished to) telephone or visit each of these long-standing friends in an effort to provide some small amount of comfort during these inevitable chapters of the human life cycle.

But as one might imagine, being a full-time psychotherapist and a nearly full-time psychotherapeutically orientated friend to many other colleagues can be exhausting; hence, I do, still, from time to time, wonder whether a career in accountancy might be easier!

I hope that I have presented a sufficiently revealing portrait of some of the delights and challenges of working as a psychotherapist. This field provides a deep opportunity to offer a humane form of psychological treatment which really can improve lives and prevent deaths. As clinicians, we derive tremendous satisfaction from having devoted ourselves to a truly meaningful and worthwhile cause. But at the same time, we have committed ourselves to a life of enforced sitting—in an era when sitting has become the new smoking—and we must endure the hatred and pain with which our patients have struggled, often for decades and decades.

So, assuming that I have not frightened off potential stellar colleagues from entering this field of professional work, how do we determine whether we have a sufficiently sensitive skin and a sufficiently sturdy spine to undertake this rewarding, but exceptionally challenging, calling?

CHAPTER TWO

Assessing One's Own Sanity

The Perfect Candidate

A career in psychotherapy is certainly not for the faint of heart.

In order to train, we must invest a great deal of time, emotion and, from a purely practical point of view, money. Of most importance, those who wish to devote themselves to psychotherapeutic work must possess an immense amount of personal mental health. Emotionally fragile people, however compassionate, should be discouraged bluntly from embarking upon this career path.

The venerable art of surgery requires men and women of steel, who do not collapse at the sight of blood. However, the art of psychotherapy demands not only an indestructible strength of character but, also, a tremendously sensitive skin. In other words, we must be sturdy without being steely, and sensitive without being soppy. In my experience, very few individuals have the capacity to be both substantial and tender, as well as robust and soulful at the very same time.

In order to practise psychotherapy successfully, we must embody a number of seminal qualities. I shall now identify merely a few of the essential ingredients required of the prospective psychotherapeutic clinician.

First and foremost, we must be supremely reliable. Dr. Donald Winnicott (1970, p. 113), the great British psychoanalyst, once defined the very essence of psychological work as *"Reliability meeting dependence"*. According to Winnicott (1968), the clinician who fails to provide reliability actually risks inflicting trauma.

As most, if not all, of our patients will have suffered from early experiences of abandonment, neglect, and disappointment at one or many points, the good psychotherapeutic practitioner must become a paragon of reliability, counteracting the impact of those early parental failures. We do so in a number of ways. Above all, we must never forget an appointment with a patient. That would be an unthinkable breach of professionalism and could, potentially, damage the prospect of a successful treatment. The competent psychotherapist must *never* oversleep, must *never* get stuck in traffic, and must *never* double-book a session. We must have had a good night's sleep in order to awaken on time, and we must leave our home sufficiently early in order to arrive at the office well in advance of the start of the session. In doing so, we demonstrate our dependability, thus creating a climate in which patients might begin to trust us with their most precious and private confessions.

Even when feeling tired or poorly, the good psychotherapist does not cancel sessions. We trudge through our working day and our working week by remaining completely available to those who seek our succour. No surgeon would ever abandon a patient mid-operation, and we simply cannot do that either. Of course, there will be times in our careers when we become extremely ill with influenza or bronchitis or, indeed, with something more sinister, and we will have to cancel one or more sessions. But, if we have already established a base of tremendous reliability, our patients will know that, at core, they can count on us, and thus they will, in most instances, tolerate our bodily infirmities.

Many years ago, I had the privilege of developing a warm friendship with the great American psychoanalyst Dr. Robert Langs—a profound and erudite theoretician of psychoanalytical technique. One of the most sagacious and prolific authors in the mental health field, Bob Langs had studied the psychotherapeutic process in tremendous detail, examining with great care which analyses worked well and which did not. I shall never forget one of our many engaging conversations, in which he underscored, time and time again, the vital role of reliability in this work. Langs even quipped, "You could be the stupidest psychoanalyst in town, but if you show up for every single session, you will have done at least eighty per cent of the work."

The proficient psychotherapist must be reliable, not only in the physical sense but, also, in the mental sense. It certainly helps to be a hugely dependable clock-watcher who remains in good health and who allocates enough time in the morning to navigate heavy traffic on the motorway. But we must also be reliable cognitively, endeavouring to remember every single seemingly insignificant detail of the patient's narrative. We lose the patient's sense of confidence and trust if we forget vital pieces of biography. The skilled psychotherapist must keep good mental notes (as well as written ones) and must mull over the details of the patient's life on a regular basis, thus truly holding that person in our thoughts. In order to do so, one needs a very good memory and a very clear mind of one's own.

In addition to being reliable, both physically and psychologically, the perfect psychotherapeutic candidate must be not only empathic and compassionate but, also, extremely well-educated and intelligent. Deciphering the complex vicissitudes of the patient's history requires a sharp set of mental skills and, also, a capacity to think in symbolic terms.

Dr. Bertram Karon, an American psychologist, once treated a severely schizophrenic man in a psychiatric hospital who suffered from hallucinations of snakes coming out of his mouth. The patient agonised, "'You swallow a snake, and then you stutter; you mustn't let anyone know about it'" (quoted in Karon and VandenBos, 1981, p. 38). Most psychiatrists and psychologists untrained in psychotherapy and psychoanalysis would regard such a psychotic symptom as little more than a confirmation of the patient's severe mental illness. But Dr. Karon, a very savvy clinician, observed that, whenever this man spoke about the hallucinated snakes in his mouth, he would also burble, simultaneously, in Latin. Karon became intrigued and wondered how on earth his patient—a chap from a humble background in Detroit, Michigan, with a meagre education—could possibly speak in Latin; and with shrewdness, he discovered that his patient had, many years previously, served as an altar boy in church. Thinking symbolically, Dr. Karon then enquired whether a priest had ever inserted his penis into the patient's mouth. Extraordinarily, Karon had speculated correctly that this adult schizophrenic patient who hallucinated about snakes in the mouth had, as a youngster, once suffered enforced fellatio from a priest. Suddenly, such a seemingly bizarre psychotic outburst began to make a very great deal of sense.

If Bertram Karon had responded to the patient's terror about snakes in the mouth with a pedestrian comment such as, "Oh, dear, that must be very painful", or "You must be very scared by the snakes", this really would not suffice. We might win a few small points for demonstrating our concern, but at the end of the day, the patient will be cured *only* if we have fully deciphered the secret meaning of the communication. The successful psychotherapist must listen not only with care and compassion, but must also investigate the deeper, unconscious layers of the patient's narrative. We cannot engage merely on the surface level. And such listening and deciphering requires a great deal of cognitive capacity. Thus, the ideal psychotherapeutic candidate must be a man or woman of a very particular type of intelligence, crowned by the ability to think in symbolic, rather than concrete, terms.

In addition to reliability and intelligence, we must also have "worked through" our own vulnerabilities sufficiently in order to create space for the patient to become the sole focus of the session. Narcissistic psychotherapists who constantly interrupt the patient with their own stories—however relevant these might seem—will, in my experience, damage their analysands. Similarly, envious psychotherapists will be so burdened with their own hatred towards their patients that they will not be able to concentrate efficaciously.

The ideal psychotherapeutic candidate must be a person of great internal wealth, and must, also, possess a tremendous capacity to tolerate being used and even verbally abused by the patient. In order to achieve such a state, we will need to have grown up in a profoundly emotionally healthy household, facilitated by truly loving caregivers, or, we will have had to undergo our own very successful experience of psychotherapy or psychoanalysis.

Pathological Motivations

Although being reliable, thoughtful, sensitive, compassionate, intelligent, and sufficiently non-narcissistic will be of huge help to the prospective psychotherapist, such personal qualities may not be quite enough to sustain an aspiring clinician across the long journey of professional formation. Even the most seemingly healthy and robust of incipient psychotherapists must scrutinise his or her motivations as fully as possible, so that we may undertake the huge demands—indeed *burdens*—of psychotherapeutic work for the *right* reasons rather than for the *wrong* ones. Too often certain well-meaning and ostensibly healthy individuals embark upon psychotherapeutic training for very complex, even murky, reasons.

What might be a suspicious, even pathological, motivation for entering this profession?

In 1929, Dr. Smiley Blanton, an American psychiatrist, travelled to Vienna, Austria, in order to undergo psychoanalytical treatment from Professor Sigmund Freud. During one of their conversations, Freud spoke about the thorny question of motivation for training in mental health. "'Do you know why psychiatrists go into their specialty?" he continued. "It is because they do not feel that they are normal, and they go into this work because it is a means of sublimation for this feeling—a means of assuring themselves that they are really normal. Society puts them in charge of the mentally abnormal, and so they feel reassured"' (quoted in Blanton, 1971, pp. 46–47). Although we might assume that the psychiatrist ought to be reasonably "normal" and that the patient will probably be somewhat "mad", Sigmund Freud challenged this stereotype, noting that many sane people struggle with an underbelly of psychological illness, just as many insane people possess areas of great strength and creativity.

In view of Sigmund Freud's sage observation, prospective candidates must first ensure that they do not enter the mental health profession in order to feel normal by projecting their "mad" parts onto their patients.

Not only do future psychotherapists often gravitate towards this work in order to indulge the fantasy of being the "sane" ones, many do so in order to master the early childhood trauma of having grown up with depressed mothers and fathers. Having had the opportunity to work psychoanalytically with numerous trainee psychotherapists and other mental health professionals, I can confirm that many of the people who gravitate to this field have had very fragile parents who often turned to their own children for emotional support. Thus, quite a number of psychotherapy practitioners actually began "treating" patients at the tender age of one and two, listening carefully as their parents burdened them with their own sorrows and fears.

Years ago, Dr. Irving Weisberg, a psychoanalyst in New York City, told me a very witty riddle. Dr. Weisberg quipped, "Do you know why people become analysts? It's because most analysts failed with their first two patients." In other words, having endeavoured, albeit unsuccessfully, to provide emotional comfort to Mummy and Daddy, many will have embraced psychological work in order to sublimate the desire to help their parents.

One might argue that, having had an early experience of being good listeners, the children of the depressed might grow up to become extremely adept at practising psychotherapy, and this may well be the case in certain instances. But every prospective clinician must be vigilant that he or she has entered the psychotherapeutic profession as a result of careful thought, rather than as the inevitable re-enactment of a certain childhood template.

Other people embark upon psychotherapeutic training as a rationalisation for undertaking their own personal treatment. Over the years, I have heard many candidates boast, "Oh, I don't really *need* to be in therapy. I'm only doing it because it's a requirement for my course." And still others have become attracted to the prospect of training because they have forged a very powerful identification with their own psychotherapist and wish to *become* their therapist, much as a little child wishes to follow in the footsteps of a mother or father.

Whatever the motivation might be, it remains the responsibility of both the prospective applicant as well as his or her training psychotherapist to scrutinise the urge to enter this field as fully and as comprehensively as possible.

Irrespective of our deepest unconscious reasons for wishing to become psychotherapists, the profession has put many protective barriers in place in order to prevent truly unsuitable candidates from embarking upon this extremely demanding work. First of all, most of our training programmes require potential applicants to undertake at least one year of personal psychotherapy prior to an admissions interview. One might regard this stipulation as the psychological equivalent of the well-known British school exam, the General Certificate of Secondary Education, or its American counterpart, the Scholastic Aptitude Test—the bare minimum requirement for applying to university. Thus, if a very psychologically unsuitable person enthused about the prospect of training while undergoing therapy, one would hope that the treating psychotherapist might find a diplomatic, yet clear, way in which to express some concerns about such a plan.

Additionally, most training programmes offer certificate-level entry courses for prospective candidates. Thus, those who wish to consider applying for full psychotherapeutic training will often enrol on a year-long certificate in order to obtain a good sense of what the profession requires. Such courses offer the potential candidates an opportunity to learn about the demands of clinical work in a full and frank manner, thus allowing them to consider and to *reconsider* their plan. Simultaneously, these introductory courses afford the faculty a privileged glimpse into the minds of the certificate students; therefore, if an especially fragile person, known to the staff, should subsequently submit a formal application for the full clinical training, the senior members would already have considerable evidence as to the potential candidate's suitability or lack thereof.

But, assuming that one has undertaken at least a year of preparatory personal psychotherapy or psychoanalysis, and has applied oneself to this process with diligence and seriousness, and assuming that one has completed an introductory course and has acquitted oneself well, impressing the faculty as a reasonable, if not promising, student, does that really mean that one should forge ahead with an application?

Can We Afford to Train?

Each of us must think through our potential career choice in psychotherapy with exquisite care, not least as the financial cost will be considerable.

Compared to the ancient disciplines of medicine and the law, the art and craft of psychotherapy might best be described as a young profession, still in its infancy; hence, students will struggle to obtain grants from government agencies in order to pay for their training and qualification programmes. In my experience, nearly 100 per cent of all psychotherapeutic trainees have had to fund their own education without any bursaries.

Whereas other courses of study require only basic tuition fees, psychotherapeutic trainings insist—and rightly so—that apprentices embark upon an extended period of personal psychotherapy or psychoanalysis throughout the duration. In fact, most training programmes require potential students to have begun their personal analysis prior to application; and many candidates will continue with their intensive psychoanalysis after they have completed their course. And this can be a most expensive process.

As a young student in this field, I underwent a five-times-weekly psychoanalysis, on the couch, with a truly brilliant psychoanalyst who taught me an inestimable amount and who facilitated my development in so many ways, for which I shall remain eternally grateful. But I had to pay a significant fee for many years, and I worked extremely hard and managed my finances very carefully in order to do so. Not everyone wishes to make such an investment or has the confidence that such an investment will reap sufficient dividends.

At the present point in history, psychotherapy training has remained a private concern; and although a few university departments have begun to sponsor courses in psychotherapy and psychoanalysis, the increasing privatisation (and consequent rise in fees) of many institutions of higher education in the United Kingdom, as in the United States of America, has prevented quite a number of worthy individuals from training.

In an ideal world, our governments would recognise the importance of subsidising the training of solid psychotherapists, so that our growing army of practitioners would be able to contribute to the alleviation of widespread mental distress and mental illness. Fortunately, with persistent lobbying and education, politicians have become increasingly aware of the work we undertake. Not long ago, I had the privilege of addressing a meeting in the House of Lords at the Palace of Westminster, and I found the peers who attended to be extremely thoughtful and engaged, and deeply keen to encourage future generations of mental health practitioners (Kahr, 2013b, 2013c).

But until such time as we become properly funded and supported, prospective applicants should be under no illusion as to the sheer costs of training.

In terms of assessing our own motivations and our sanity, we must, at least at present, also assess our ability to afford the significant financial burden of training in psychotherapy. Not only will we have to invest in our own personal psychoanalysis or psychotherapy, but we will also have to pay clinical supervision fees to the mentors who will help us scrutinise the details of our work with patients, often on a line-by-line basis. Eventually, we will need to hire or purchase a consulting room—no mean feat in central London or Manhattan or other large cities. Moreover, while devoting so many hours to training and personal psychotherapy, we will not always be able to sustain a full-time job elsewhere.

Of greatest importance, we must be very mindful of the fact that even if we manage to pay our training costs without amassing loans and debts, we cannot assume that we will find gainful employment upon graduation, at least not straightaway.

In Great Britain, the public sector sponsors only a tiny number of paid positions for fully qualified psychotherapists, and very few "newbies" will ever succeed in obtaining such rare, coveted posts. Consequently, many who have completed their training must aspire to open a private practice (or "independent practice" as it has now become known increasingly). And, as any seasoned psychotherapist will explain, building up a successful private practice requires years of dedication and skill and ability and, also, patience.

Not only might it take a decade or more to develop a robust roster of clients and consultees, we must also remember that, by and large, those who can afford a full professional fee will often be very reluctant to consult a young, newly qualified practitioner. If a barrister or a professor of endocrinology or a film star wishes to undertake psychotherapy for the alleviation of private anxieties, such a person would, in all likelihood, seek out a mental health professional who has come highly recommended by a family physician or by another trusted source. Many recently qualified psychotherapists who have not yet developed a professional referral network must, therefore, consider offering sessions at more reduced fees from the outset, in order to accommodate patients who earn more ordinary wages. I do not mind admitting that when I opened up an office, my first patient—a profoundly intellectually disabled individual on state benefits—could not afford to pay me any money at all. For five or six years, I treated this man free of charge. Eventually, I introduced a token fee of twenty pence per session. Even the most frugal individual cannot support himself or his family on such a tiny amount of money. Thankfully, I had income from my public sector work and from my lecturing post. But it would be naïve to assume that we will be able support ourselves immediately from our private practice endeavours.

Thus, we should not proceed down the long path towards qualification unless we have assessed not only our sanity but, also, our financial situation with considerable vigilance.

In summary, for those with a serious interest in pursuing a psychotherapeutic career, we must approach the field slowly, carefully, and judiciously with, perhaps, at least a few pounds sterling or dollars already in the bank for a rainy day.

CHAPTER THREE

On Marrying a Library

Bibliophilia Psychotherapeutica

I shall now reveal a very shameful secret about our profession.

The vast majority of clinical psychotherapists do not read.

Having met literally thousands of psychotherapeutic colleagues over the decades, I regret to report that, although most practitioners distinguish themselves as warm-hearted and compassionate people, very few have mastered the literature of books and chapters and essays on psychotherapy and psychoanalysis, let alone on the related disciplines of psychology, psychiatry, and psychopathology, with any degree of seriousness or comprehensiveness.

The failure to read deeply, widely, and systematically can, alas, in no way be regarded as a new phenomenon among mental health professionals. As long ago as 1933, the great Swiss analytical psychologist, Dr. Carl Gustav Jung, lamented to his German colleague, Dr. Gustav Richard Heyer, that many of their medical colleagues had read far too little and that those who did so concentrated on short articles, rather than on full-length works. And more than forty years later, Dr. Anna Freud (1975, p. 195) wrote to her Cuban-American colleague, Professor Humberto Nágera, that, to her great regret, "Neither students nor their teachers have any appreciation of past work anymore. They are going further and further away from it in the present."

In my experience, those who do study the publications in our field—contemporary articles as well as old classics—have an infinitely greater prospect of flourishing in every respect, not only in terms of obtaining work but, of even greater importance, of curing our patients. The well-read psychotherapist not only inspires confidence in our potential institutional employers, but those of us who have immersed ourselves deeply in the professional literature will have internalised a rich collection of thoughts and ideas, of recommendations and techniques, of understandings and insights, which will help us to treat our patients more successfully.

The truly adept psychotherapist—no matter how empathic and sensitive and soulful—must also become a scholar. Once we have decided to pursue a career in this field, and once we have determined that we might well be quite sane and solid, with the prospect of becoming even more so through our own personal psychotherapy or psychoanalysis, the cunning student must now devote himself or herself to a deep and detailed examination of the publications of our foremothers and forefathers and of our contemporaries.

I began reading the psychological literature during my adolescence, and I have never stopped. I still read compulsively, suffering as I do from an advanced case of *bibliophilia psychotherapeutica*, sometimes known as "Karnacitis", named for Karnac Books—Great Britain's only psychological bookshop, founded in 1950 (Kahr, 2005, 2006a, 2006b, 2014, 2017d). For reasons that I do not quite understand, most colleagues have never embraced the publications in our field quite so fully and have never succumbed to the bibliographical urge. This surprises me, as Sigmund Freud and, indeed, most of the early psychoanalytical practitioners immersed themselves deeply in reading, to great effect.

As a young trainee, it always saddened me tremendously that my teachers and supervisors never required us to read more than a few short journal articles per week, in preparation for the forthcoming lecture or seminar or case discussion. For example, when I trained in couple psychotherapy at the world-famous Tavistock Marital Studies Institute, part of the Tavistock Institute of Medical Psychology, our theory instructor never assigned more than one essay at a time. To be fair, my fellow students and I did read that particular text with great care and we discussed it in tremendous detail. But I found this approach to learning rather unsatisfying, and so I supplemented my curriculum intensively out of hours. I could never understand why we should read only one brief clinical or theoretical paper at a time, rather than the entire *oeuvre* of all the great thinkers.

I concede that not all of my colleagues will share my zest for reading *in bulk*. Some might argue that having digested a short essay written by Melanie Klein, which one would then discuss extensively with an experienced teacher, would be more useful than gorging on her complete works, but I do not agree. And neither would the rest of academia. If one matriculated to study literature or history, one would be required to read the entire university library, rather than only the odd paper here and there.

Granted, psychotherapy, unlike literature and history, might best be described as an "experiential" profession. Some would argue that, rather like medicine, one cannot learn psychotherapy by immersing oneself in books. We must plunge ourselves into the consulting room with real patients and then struggle to understand the process directly, discussing it afterwards with an experienced clinical supervisor or with a training therapist. Naturally, I would agree with this attitude, and I have certainly learned an enormous amount from direct clinical contact and from careful supervision and training. But I have also learned hugely from sitting in a library, *reading* and *reading* and *reading* and *reading*, and even taking notes, absorbing the key findings of those who have preceded us, in as scholarly and systematic a fashion as possible.

In my experience, the very best clinical practitioners have devoured the literature microscopically, and bring not only their own wisdom with them into the office each day, but also, the very best of Sigmund Freud, Carl Gustav Jung, and Alfred Adler, as well as Karl Abraham, Sándor Ferenczi, Otto Rank, Ernest Jones, Abraham Brill, Theodor Reik, Franz Alexander, Anna Freud, Melanie Klein, Donald Winnicott, Ronald Fairbairn, and a host of hundreds of other great thinkers and theoreticians who, collectively, created the very foundations of our profession.

Most clinical psychotherapists have a very good grasp of the reasons why our patients have become emotionally unwell. After all, we listen quietly and carefully, session after session, and we learn much about some truly painful histories. Furthermore, most clinical psychotherapists know a very great deal about how to treat our patients, by offering regular, reliable appointments, by deciphering the unconscious meanings of the free associations and dreams and fantasies of our patients, and by tolerating the powerful "Zyklon B-style" hatred which often emerges in the midst of sessions. Do we really need to be scholarly "geeks" as well, who can spot historical errors in a printed bibliography at a moment's notice? Will it really be necessary for us to have read Sigmund Freud's analysis of Michelangelo Buonarroti's statue of Moses (Anonymous [Sigmund Freud], 1914; Freud, 1914b)? How on earth will that help us with our patients? Must we actually devote an hour to the study of Karl Abraham's (1917a, 1917b) thesis about the secret meaning of premature ejaculation? What relevance might that have for our work with females? Must one really have digested Melanie Klein's (1925a, 1925b) little paper on the origin of tics in children? How will that assist us in our work with adults? And even if we do take the time and trouble to engage with these essays, do we really have to read them in the original German?

Although I know many academic *historians* of psychoanalysis who have consumed all of these aforementioned papers and who have written compendious tomes about these progenitors of our profession, I can think of very few *clinical* colleagues who could, at short notice, offer a reliable summary of any of these seminal texts. Most would defend themselves and claim that they have done very well over the years in spite of never having read Abraham on premature ejaculation, and this may well be true. But, in my estimation, the psychotherapist who studies the literature in depth will have a much better chance of "reading" his or her patient properly— fully and comprehensively—taking account of every little footnote of biographical data.

It may be that those who have the capacity to differentiate between Sigmund Freud's (1926) first theory of anxiety and his second theory of anxiety, or to memorise all the mechanisms of defence adumbrated by Anna Freud (1936), or to recite Donald Winnicott's (1949) list of the eighteen reasons why mothers hate their babies, may suffer from an advanced case of *bibliophilia psychotherapeutica*, and may fail to appreciate that not everyone needs to be well versed in these matters. After all, very few medical doctors will have read the complete works of Hippocrates in ancient Greek, and yet they all know how to save lives just fine. Do psychotherapists really need to become historical scholars as well? Might that not be rather excessive?

I certainly concede that a mastery of the ancient and modern psychotherapeutic literature may not be the *sine qua non* of our professional solidity. But having worked in this field for a very long time, I can certainly report with confidence that those clinical colleagues who have impressed me most, and to whom I have referred copious patients over the years, and whom I have engaged to teach and supervise, have all read the literature with *profondeur*! Thus, if one really wishes to flourish, one must tackle the vast library of bibliophilic treasures to which we have ready access.

Additionally, for those who wish to position themselves on a "flourishing track" towards success and engagement and fulfilment in psychotherapy,

I strongly recommend that one begins to read as much as possible *before* embarking upon one's training and before establishing oneself in practice. Although I still read a very great deal, I have infinitely less free time to do so now that I have responsibility for my clinical caseload. Therefore, I deeply encourage prospective psychotherapy colleagues to absorb a good foundation of the professional literature sooner rather than later.

Curling Up with Sigmund Freud

My *bibliophilia psychotherapeutica* developed at an early age, and I must admit that as time has progressed, this condition has become much more intense. By reading the professional literature, I consider myself not only better educated and better prepared to undertake treatment with patients but, moreover, I become stimulated and engaged, as though I have taken my mind to the gymnasium for a good workout. Perhaps above all, I find that reading the publications on psychotherapy and psychoanalysis has allowed me to feel as though I really do belong to a venerable tradition of clinicians and researchers. I experience myself as part of an ancient professional family, and that, I must confess, brings great gratification.

For those who might appreciate the potential benefits of being afflicted with *bibliophilia psychotherapeutica*, or for those who have already contracted this condition, I shall now offer a brief, but detailed, set of recommendations of some very key texts.

In my estimation, one cannot find a better tour guide than Sigmund Freud. Although many people—even psychotherapists—revile Freud as an old-fashioned male chauvinist who claimed that women suffer from penis envy, I have come to know a very different man. For me, Sigmund Freud deserves our long-term gratitude as the person who challenged the cruelties of late nineteenth-century psychiatry and who provided a systematic and humane alternative, namely, the talking cure. During Freud's youth, most psychiatric physicians dismissed their patients as little more than neurotic malingerers and time-wasters, and often despatched the wealthier ones to spas across central Europe, while hospitalising the poorer ones in wretched lunatic asylums, chaining them to walls, and even beating them. Freud, by contrast, offered his patients a very comfortable couch on which to recline, and he positioned himself out of sight and listened quietly to their narratives of abuse and trauma, thus facilitating a cathartic reaction and an immediate reduction in symptomatology (Kahr, 2018c).

Of course, Freud, like all human beings, had a shadow side, and he could often be quite vicious and intolerant towards some of his colleagues and frustrated by some of his more challenging patients. But on the whole, he devoted his life to the study of the meaningfulness of the mind and to its cure by exclusively psychological methods. As a mere adolescent, I fell in love with Sigmund Freud, and that love has only grown with time.

For those who wish to embark upon a careful programme of reading and study, I advise that one might begin by immersing oneself in the range of well-written books on the history of psychiatry, thus contextualising the work of Freud more fully. I particularly recommend *A History of Medical Psychology* by Gregory Zilboorg and George Henry (1941) and, also, *The History of Psychiatry: An Evaluation of Psychiatric Thought and Practice from Prehistoric Times to the Present* by Franz Alexander and Sheldon Selesnick (1966), which, though often regarded as somewhat outdated, if not completely passé, really capture the essence of Freud's radical contribution. For contrast, I might consider the more contemporary book, *A History of Psychiatry: From the Era of the Asylum to the Age of Prozac*, written by Edward Shorter (1997), a Canadian-based scholar, who, though quite anti-Freudian by temperament, actually presents a rather damning portrait of biological psychiatry. Thereafter, I would imbibe several good biographies of Freud himself, as well as some of the stalwart histories of the psychoanalytical movement. In this respect, I would encourage colleagues to read, in particular, the three-volume classic biography by Ernest Jones (1953, 1955, 1957), the works of Paul Roazen (1969, 1975, 1990, 1993, 1995, 2001), the hefty tome by Peter Gay (1988), and the broader histories by George Makari (2008) and Ernst Falzeder (2015) for starters. For those who wish a more playful, yet also serious, approach to the father of psychoanalysis, I would dare to suggest my own efforts to engage young students, namely, *Life Lessons from Freud* (Kahr, 2013a) and, also, *Coffee with Freud* (Kahr, 2017a).

Once one has absorbed a good foundation in the cultural and historical background of Freud's works and in the detailed scope of his biography—both personal and professional—I would then attempt to master his compendious original writings. It might be fun to begin by reading several volumes of his correspondence with disciples. The letters between Sigmund Freud and the Italian psychoanalyst Edoardo Weiss—not very lengthy—might be a good starting point (Weiss, 1970; Freud and Weiss, 1973).

Having thus acquired a good contextual grounding, I would then immerse myself fully in Freud's published writings. For those who can read German, I recommend the original editions, as Freud wrote with such consummate style. But for those who must digest Freud in English, one can do no better than read the excellent translations by James Strachey, assisted by Anna Freud, Alix Strachey, and Alan Tyson, and published in the famous twenty-four-volume set known as *The Standard Edition of the Complete Psychological Works of Sigmund Freud* (Freud, 1953a, 1953b, 1953c, 1953d, 1955a, 1955b, 1955c, 1955d, 1957a, 1957b, 1958, 1959a, 1959b, 1960a, 1960b, 1961a, 1961b, 1962, 1963a, 1963b, 1964a, 1964b, 1966, 1974). Although some authors have criticised these translations (e.g., Bettelheim, 1982, 1983; Ornston, 1981, 1985a, 1985b, 1988, 1992a, 1992b, 1992c), and although other scholars have prepared different editions and translations, the Strachey version contains such wonderful editorial material that one would be hard pressed to find a better set of texts.

It might seem rather daunting to begin at the beginning and to plough through all of these volumes sequentially, although several of my students and colleagues have done so to great effect. For those who wish to dip into these books more gingerly, I strongly recommend that one might commence with the early text *Studien über Hysterie* (Breuer and Freud, 1895a)—the *Studies on Hysteria* (Breuer and Freud, 1895b)—which Freud co-authored with his older medical colleague Dr. Josef Breuer. This remarkable work contains the best overview of the talking cure, plentifully illustrated with engaging case histories, including that of "Anna O" (Breuer, 1895a, 1895b) and, my own favourite, "Katharina" (Freud, 1895a, 1895b), the account of a young woman whose hysteria developed in the wake of sexual abuse. After digesting these compelling, almost novelistic, accounts, I would next tackle Freud's (1901a, 1901b) delightful text on the unconscious meaning of slips of the tongue, slips of the pen, and other seemingly trivial errors, namely, the monograph known in English as *The Psychopathology of Everyday Life: Forgetting, Slips of the Tongue, Bungled Actions, Superstitions and Errors* (Freud, 1901c). To my mind, this extraordinary classic provides the best insight into the art of deciphering unconscious material, reminding us constantly that every little detail, no matter how ostensibly insignificant, possesses a much deeper and, often, more sinister meaning. Freud's work on slips has helped me in my clinical work far more than any other book that I have ever read.

With these foundational tomes in place, any prospective candidate will have acquired a good platform from which to tackle the rest of Freud's works, as well as everything else ever written in the history of psychotherapy and psychoanalysis!

My Three Favourite Reading Rooms

It will not be at all surprising that I absolutely worship libraries. Indeed, whenever possible, I much prefer to read in a library than at home or in the office or on the train or on a beach. Working in a library provides one with access not only to the specific books that one requires at any given time, often in the original language or in the first edition, but it also offers its users thousands upon thousands of other books that one cannot discover readily simply by googling! To become a fine scholar and to master one's subject truly, one must also become an accomplished browser of library shelves. In doing so, we afford ourselves the opportunity of stumbling upon all sorts of wonderful, often unexpected, gems.

Although I have had the privilege of using libraries and archives all around the world, I have three very special institutions that I visit more than any other, all based in central London, and it gives me great pleasure to recommend them to fellow psychotherapists or to psychotherapists-in-training who live in the United Kingdom and to those from other countries who may wish to make a pilgrimage to this side of the pond from time to time. The first two require a paid-up membership subscription—well worth the investment—while the third does not.

For those wishing to romance some great libraries, I would begin by joining the world-famous London Library in St. James's Square, founded in 1841, which boasts a collection of over one million books in approximately fifty-five languages, published between the sixteenth century and the present day. As a scholar, I find the London Library utterly indispensable. Although it does not have the largest collection of books on psychoanalysis, its history collection remains almost unparalleled and thus offers an incomparable opportunity to borrow volumes relevant to the cultural background of psychotherapeutic work. Thus, if one wishes to examine John Bowlby's and Donald Winnicott's concerns about the impact of the evacuation of children to the countryside during the Second World War (Bowlby, Miller, and Winnicott, 1939), one has no shortage of great texts which provide all the information that one would require to understand this chilling chapter in British history. Every single room within the London Library provides education and joy simultaneously, but I particularly recommend the seats in the basement, surrounded by innumerable bound volumes of old periodicals, as that area of the library, in particular, ensures a great deal of solitude.

I also warmly recommend the Members' Library of the Royal Society of Medicine, located on Wimpole Street. This remarkable institution—also a lending library—offers readers a unique collection of books, periodicals, pamphlets, drawings, archives, and related materials from across many centuries. Psychotherapeutic scholars will particularly enjoy the extensive collection of nineteenth-century European medical journals, which offer an unparalleled glimpse into the context in which Sigmund Freud and his colleagues created a radical alternative to traditional psychiatric treatments. Here, too, I find the basement stacks the most private, in spite of the harsh fluorescent lighting and the piles of dust!

Finally, for those who do not wish to pay any subscription fee at all, one must rush to the Wellcome Library, located on the second and third floors of The Wellcome Building on the bustling Euston Road, which contains the most wonderful stock of medical history books—for reference only—including an extensive psychology collection. I have spent thousands of happy hours at the Wellcome Library, and I particularly encourage users to arrive early in order to nab a table at the very back of the upstairs level, in the psychoanalysis section itself.

According to the ancient Greek historian Hecataeus of Abdera, the great ancient Egyptian library in Waset—better known as Thebes—bore an inscription which scholars have translated, variously, as "Clinic for the Soul" or as "Healing-Place of the Soul". Libraries can indeed bring much healing pleasure, and they do help us to mend the battered souls of our patients. By embarking upon a flirtation and, ultimately, a marriage with one or more libraries, one will become much more likely to flourish as a psychotherapist in every respect.

CHAPTER FOUR

The Joys and Pitfalls of Training

A Child in a Sweet Shop

Nowadays, the psychotherapeutic landscape has become so extensive that prospective students have literally hundreds of training routes from which to choose.

I often wish that psychotherapists and psychoanalysts worldwide could agree upon a standard curriculum, in the way that physicians and lawyers have done. For instance, one cannot qualify as a medical doctor without having studied anatomy, physiology, pathology, and so on. But the curricula of different psychotherapy training programmes vary so enormously that no two clinicians will graduate with anything approximating the same education.

When psychoanalytical ideas first began to penetrate the British Isles in the very final years of the nineteenth century and, more particularly, during the earliest years of the twentieth century, those wishing to develop their skills in psychotherapy had only a tiny number of training options. In 1913, the Medico-Psychological Clinic of London opened, which offered opportunities to study Freudian ideas (e.g., Boll, 1962; Raitt, 2004), as did the London Psycho-Analytical Society, a forerunner of the British Psycho-Analytical Society. Not until 1924 did the British Psycho-Analytical Society inaugurate a formal training body, the Institute of Psycho-Analysis, whose earliest graduates included Dr. Donald Winnicott (Kahr, 1996).

Back then, those wishing to undertake a comprehensive psychoanalytical training in the United Kingdom could do so only at the Institute of Psycho-Analysis, which remained, for many years, the sole provider of such an educational programme. But as the twentieth century unfolded, numerous other organisations developed, which sponsored training programmes in such diverse branches of psychotherapy as individual psychoanalytical psychotherapy, marital psychotherapy, family psychotherapy, group psychotherapy, parent–infant psychotherapy, child psychotherapy, adolescent psychotherapy, psychoanalytical organisational consultancy, music therapy, art therapy, dramatherapy, dance-movement therapy, and many more strands besides.

I remember that, round about 1983 or 1984, the pioneering British psychiatrist and psychotherapist, Dr. Robin Skynner, delivered a lecture at the Warneford Hospital in Oxford, where I then worked, and I went to hear him speak. The warm-hearted Skynner, quite a senior figure in the field, and a progenitor of both family therapy and group analysis, reminisced about his early years as a trainee. His teachers in psychiatry at the venerable Maudsley Hospital in London told him that if he wished to have a successful career, he would need to complete the Diploma in Psychological Medicine (the D.P.M.), offered by the Royal Medico-Psychological Association (the precursor to the Royal College of Psychiatrists) and, moreover, that he should undertake the training at the Institute of Psycho-Analysis. Skynner delighted in telling the audience in Oxford that he had no desire to work in academic psychiatry and therefore did not pursue the advanced qualification of the D.P.M., and that, likewise, he did not wish to sit all day behind a couch, and so he never trained as a psychoanalyst. Instead, he allowed himself the freedom to develop his own burgeoning interests in family systems and groups; and consequently, he became one of the founders of both British family psychotherapy and British group psychotherapy.

I have related this tale about Robin Skynner as representative of the fact that one need not follow the traditional or elitist path. A truly creative person can draw upon a whole range of trainings and can utilise his or her knowledge and experience and abilities to forge new canvases within the field of mental health. Had Dr. Skynner undertaken the very same training as his mentors had done, he might never have helped to develop either the Institute of Family Therapy or the Institute of Group Analysis, both of which remain, to this day, extremely well-regarded organisations in these pioneering arenas.

Prospective psychotherapists often consult me and ask for advice as to which course would suit them best. I always struggle to offer the most helpful response, as I have friends and colleagues who have graduated from virtually every psychotherapy training programme in Great Britain, some of whom adored their formations, while others detested their studies. Indeed, I have come to the conclusion that it seems to be far *less* important *which* training one enrols upon than whether one has a fine and stable mind and access to good teachers, clinical supervisors, and mentors. Some of the least impressive people in our field have graduated from some of the more historically established trainings, while some of the most inspiring practitioners have qualified from some of the more recently formed institutions.

In the United Kingdom, training programmes change in nature all the time. For instance, when I undertook my education, I had to pursue completely separate courses at different institutions in order to qualify in both the practice of individual psychotherapy and in marital psychotherapy. But, in recent years, Tavistock Relationships—the nation's leading training programme for couple psychotherapists—has begun to offer a combined course in *both* individual *and* couple psychotherapy. Students now have the privilege of being rather like children in a sweet shop, often overwhelmed by too much choice.

One might benefit, therefore, from speaking to representatives from numerous institutions in order to find out more about the various training programmes, many of which now offer "open days" in which one can meet the teaching staff and ask questions about the formal requirements. Those hoping to train should talk to as many colleagues as possible in order to canvass a range of opinions, as trainings change in calibre over time. Quite some years ago, I taught psychotherapy at an organisation which, during that period, boasted some very impressive faculty members who published extensively and who lectured all round the world. Alas, during the last quarter of a century, most of that pioneering generation of teachers has either moved to other positions, or retired, or died, and, sadly, the current crop of instructors—very few of whom have made original contributions to the field—offer their students a much less impressive programme.

From my perspective I regard it as far more important as to who one is rather than where one trains.

Exhausted, Frazzled, and Scrutinised

Over the years I had not only the pleasure and the privilege but, also, the burden of having completed a number of different mental health trainings in various fields, all of which contributed hugely to the development of my psychological skills. I remain grateful that I had the energy and the passion (and the youthfulness) to undertake such educational experiences, and I worked very hard indeed. I found these trainings not only intellectually and clinically rigorous but, also, quite physically demanding, having had to start my days extremely early.

While training at the Tavistock Centre in North London, I seemed to spend a very great deal of time on my bicycle. At the crack of dawn, I would ride from home to my private consulting room in Hampstead in order to see one or two patients; then I would hop on my cycle once again and race down Fitzjohns Avenue to the Tavistock Clinic in nearby Belsize Park, about ten minutes away, in order to treat several patients there and to attend clinical seminars. In the midst of all of this, I would dash out of the building every day and would cycle to visit my own training analyst who worked from a nearby consulting room. Then I rode back to the "Tavi" for further appointments, before speeding uphill to Hampstead High Street yet again, in the early evening, to see some more private patients. I only wish that I could be as physically fit today as I simply *had* to be during those training years.

In retrospect, I really cannot complain, as many other clinicians had far more demanding travelling routes and far more challenging timetables. Many years ago, I had the delight of meeting a very genteel and inspiring psychoanalyst, Dr. Ismond Rosen, one of the stars of the British mental health scene during the 1960s and 1970s and beyond. Rosen not only pioneered the study of sexual deviations, but, as a talented artist, he also found time to produce the most magnificent sculptures. In the 1950s, while training, Rosen had to endure some incredibly long days. He would leave his home quite early and dash into central London in order to treat his first patient at 8.00 a.m. Then, he would speed his way to Chelsea, in central South-West London, for his daily 9.15 a.m. training analysis session with Dr. Ilse Hellman, one of the disciples of Anna Freud. Thereafter, he raced to the Maudsley Hospital in South-East London, where he worked with psychiatric patients, before returning to central London by 5.00 p.m. in order to treat yet another private psychoanalytical patient. Afterwards, Rosen would attend an art class at the Regent Street Polytechnic—thankfully not too far from the psychoanalytical clinic—before returning to the Institute of Psycho-Analysis in nearby New Cavendish Street on several evenings per week, for seminars which never ended before 9.45 p.m. (Freeman, 1992). Eventually, Dr. Rosen returned home … shattered, no doubt; but still, he harnessed enough energy to sculpt, sometimes until midnight (Rosen, 2016).

Although my daily timetable might seem rather debilitating, and Ismond Rosen's even more so, I know of other colleagues who had to endure far greater obstacles while training. Years ago, I collaborated on a project with a very talented clinician who lived in south-western Sweden, and who, in order to qualify as a psychoanalyst, had to take the ferry every day— Monday to Friday, inclusive—from his home in Malmö to Copenhagen, in nearby Denmark, as he lived infinitely closer to the Danish psychoanalytical institute than to the Swedish one, situated in Stockholm, many more miles away! For those of us with a passion to study psychotherapy or psychoanalysis, we must do what we must do, however tiring this might be.

But travel and timetabling may not be the only challenges, indeed pitfalls, of the training experience. As we have already indicated, the majority of mental health practitioners must fund ourselves; hence, the financial burden of course fees, personal analysis, supervision, textbooks, train tickets, not to mention the occasional daily round-trip ferry ride to Denmark, will be not inconsiderable.

Furthermore, training provides us with many other hurdles. One must remember that, throughout the course of study, most conscientious psychotherapy students will undergo personal therapy, which can be a very emotive experience, which challenges our understanding of our minds, our bodies, our parents, our spouses, our children, our friends, and our colleagues. And this can often be painful. Additionally, we must navigate the demands of working with some very troubled patients in public mental health settings who will often project their most psychotic or sadistic parts onto us or into us, and this, too, can prove quite difficult.

Additionally, we must often tolerate the fact that no matter how prestigious or well known our training institution, we will all bear the burden of interacting with some truly mediocre and uninspiring teachers and colleagues. Frequently, the very best clinicians will have full practices and will not always be available to deliver lectures or to lead seminars. Moreover, some of the most experienced clinicians will be too exhausted from having taught Freud for decade upon decade and will, therefore, often farm out their teaching to their own protégés, some of whom may not be particularly adept or knowledgeable or charismatic. Having read Freud from the age of sixteen or thereabouts, I often had to grit my teeth quietly during student seminars as I had to listen to some uninspiring colleagues pontificate quite badly about Freud, frequently committing many historical errors in the process. I sometimes had the impression that these well-intentioned teachers had only just read Freud's case histories for the first time on the night before the seminar!

But whatever we might think about our teachers, these men and women will determine our professional futures. Throughout the course of study, trainees must never forget that they remain under constant scrutiny by their seminar leaders and supervisors. After all, the training committee holds the responsibility for evaluating each candidate carefully, in order to protect the general public from potentially poor practitioners. Thus, each of us will be examined microscopically, and we must work very hard to make a good impression in terms of timekeeping, professionalism, open-mindedness, preparedness, and strength of character. And we must never forget that our teachers will often become sources of referral in years to come and, in all likelihood, will not send patients to those trainees who have failed to impress sufficiently.

Recently, I had the opportunity to serve as the tutor to three students from the same training cohort, each of whom worked with me quite closely during the same four-year period. I came to regard these three individuals as honest, ethical, and decent people. Nevertheless, nowadays, I refer patients to only *one* of these three former trainees. Although I did my very best to prepare them as thoroughly as I could, I never send patients to Mr. A., because, in spite of his commitment to the training, I found him quite arrogant on a regular basis. Likewise, I do not refer any patients to Dr. B., whom I found to be quite a kindly person, but who, in spite of a great deal of supervision, continued to make rather pedestrian interpretations to her patients, and did not quite have the aptitude to decipher deep unconscious meanings with sufficient panache. Mrs. C., however, the third of my students, distinguished herself as a reliable and dedicated trainee who read extensively, who attended numerous supplementary conferences and workshops, who never missed a seminar or a clinical supervision, and who had begun the training already rather sane. Of greatest importance, Mrs. C. demonstrated a great felicity for unravelling the unconscious causes of the complex symptomatologies of the hospitalised individuals with whom she worked. I have had the pleasure of having sent many, many patients to her, and she now has a full, thriving clinical practice.

Legitimate at Last

Happily, in spite of the many burdens and costs and vulnerabilities and pitfalls of the training experience, those who do have the stamina and the good humour to survive will be richly rewarded in a multitude of ways. First and foremost, sturdy and accomplished candidates will enjoy the privilege of graduating from a training and of obtaining a substantial qualification in the art and science of psychotherapy, which will entitle them to registration with one or more national bodies, such as the British Psychoanalytic Council, or the United Kingdom Council for Psychotherapy, or the British Association for Counselling and Psychotherapy, or the Register of Psychologists Specialising in Psychotherapy of the British Psychological Society, or the Faculty of Medical Psychotherapy of the Royal College of Psychiatrists; and such a qualification will permit one to practise in the United Kingdom. Our colleagues in other countries will be able to register with comparable organisations. Thus, by having completed one's training, one has the right to earn a living and, of even greater importance, to devote one's life to the alleviation of psychological distress and mental illness.

Not only will the training permit us to practise in a legitimate manner, but it will facilitate a rich canvas of possibilities in our professional spheres and, also, in our personal lives. For instance, we should never underestimate the potentiality for meeting some very special, lifelong friends through the qualification process. Only last night, I had the delight of dining with a colleague with whom I had trained at the "Tavi" more than thirty years previously. She and I supported one another with good humour and good cheer throughout our long clinical formation, and she has become a reliable friend in every respect. In fact, we have grown up together, and our spouses have become quite friendly as well. We had the loveliest supper, reminiscing about the old days as students, sharing interesting learning points with one another about our current professional situations, and providing great emotional support as we navigate the complex vicissitudes of the ageing process. We have assisted one another career-wise over many decades, referring patients, extending lecturing invitations, serving on committees together, discussing complex clinical situations (including a forensic case of stalking, which proved rather frightening), and much more besides.

Forging friendships through the training process may be one of its most wonderful and essential by-products.

I also had the privilege of developing deeply enriching social relationships and collegial comradeships not only with various peers but, also, with some of my teachers, several of whom became lifelong mentors. Certainly, when I enrolled on one or other training course, I had no idea at the time that some of my seminar leaders would one day be dancing at my wedding—quite literally!

Studentship on a psychotherapy course also permits us to embrace our considerable base of knowledge and to find our "voice" in life. By having completed a training, we develop quite extensive expertise; and with creativity and support, we can apply that learning in a number of enriching arenas.

For instance, after I completed my training in marital psychotherapy (a field now known more commonly as "couple psychotherapy"), I developed a growing knowledge of the psychological complexities of marital and sexual life; and after years of having worked with couples, I eventually received an opportunity to undertake a large-scale, transnational study on the nature of adult sexual fantasies, with a particular emphasis on the way in which private fantasies often challenge the security of marital relationships. Having internalised the clinical experience of working with couples psychoanalytically, through my intensive six-year training at the Tavistock Marital Studies Institute, I became the Principal Investigator of the British Sexual Fantasy Research Project, in which context I had the privilege of assembling an international database of over 25,000 adult sexual fantasies, exploring their traumatic origins. This work resulted in the publication of two books, *Sex and the Psyche* (Kahr, 2007a), an analysis of the British data, and *Who's Been Sleeping in Your Head?: The Secret World of Sexual Fantasies* (Kahr, 2008), a revised and expanded version of the former book, which analysed the American data. This research also formed the basis of two separate television programmes, which helped to educate the general public about the deeper psychological roots of sexual behaviours and fantasies; and through this work, I received numerous opportunities to travel the world in order to lecture on this compelling subject.

I cite this research project as just one example of the ways in which each of us has the capacity to transform an area of specialisation into a creative array of possibilities, whether through writing, teaching, lecturing, broadcasting, or many other routes besides.

But in spite of the tremendous advantages afforded by good training, our careers will not flourish without constant nurture and support throughout the post-qualification period. Let us now consider the very vital role of maintaining and developing relationships with mentors, both inside and outside our training institutions.

CHAPTER FIVE

Cultivating Brilliant Mentors

Dis-identifying from Disappointing Tutors

Young students today may not recognise the name of Professor Ralph Greenson. During the 1950s and 1960s, few psychoanalysts in the United States of America had as prominent a profile. One of Anna Freud's most warmly regarded colleagues, Greenson ran a lavish private practice on the West Coast and treated many Hollywood superstars, including Frank Sinatra and Marilyn Monroe (Kelley, 1984, 1986; Freeman, 1992; Farber and Green, 1993; Spoto, 1993). Of most importance, Ralph Greenson (1967) published a remarkable textbook on *The Technique and Practice of Psychoanalysis: Volume 1*, which became a veritable bible for decades to come.

Among his many professional contributions, Greenson (1968) wrote a sterling paper, now little cited in the literature, entitled "Dis-Identifying from Mother: Its Special Importance for the Boy", in which he elaborated upon the challenge faced by young male children, in particular, of growing up in such close identification with the mother and then having to face the task of *dis-identification*, in order to develop a more masculine sense of self. Drawing upon the work of Sigmund Freud (1931), Greenson underscored that the boy must find a way to retain the best of mother, while also forging an identification with father.

Just as the little child must constantly navigate the art of identification and, also, dis-identification from parental figures, so must the incipient psychotherapist as well. As inexperienced, naïve youngsters in training, we arrive at the clinic with zestful eagerness, ready to take on board all the wisdom of our teachers. I shall never forget that, many years ago, I asked a group of my own trainees what sort of career they fantasised about in years to come. One of my students—a very sweet young woman—made us all giggle when she replied, "If I ever manage to I grow up, I want to become *you*, Brett!" (Needless to say, I told her not to!) Certainly, the urge to engage in a full-scale identification with our training therapists, our clinical supervisors, and our seminar leaders remains quite powerful.

I strongly recommend that every trainee psychotherapist and every newly qualified psychotherapist should, actually, work very hard to identify with his or her teachers while, at the same time, reserving the right to dis-identify as well.

Shortly after I had embarked upon one of my trainings as a very young man, I attended some seminars on psychoanalytical technique, delivered by Dr. X., a very senior, venerable psychoanalyst who had worked in the profession for aeons and who held very high office. I knew that I would learn a great deal from this man. One day, we began to discuss the "niceties" of the clinical session, which included an examination of such seemingly unimportant matters as whether one smiles at the patient upon first greeting, and whether one offers one's hand for a convivial shake. In any other professional situation, most of us would not hesitate to smile at a new customer and grasp this person's hand, but in the psychoanalytical field, each of us must be careful that we do not overwhelm our new analysands with too much friendliness. A depressed patient, for instance, might find a generous, unrestricted smile rather provocative, whereas a sexually abused patient might become quite frightened at the prospect of immediate bodily contact, however symbolic or restrained. My teacher, Dr. X.—an "old school" psychoanalyst—told us that, under *no* circumstances should we *ever* smile at our patients, nor should we *ever* extend a hand.

As a polite young student, I took diligent notes but, I must confess, I had my doubts about the recommendation to refrain from smiles and handshakes entirely, not least as virtually all the patients who arrived at my consulting room greeted me with a benign smile and a willing hand upon entering my office for the first time. I canvassed the opinions of numerous senior colleagues and I spoke about this dilemma with many of my fellow trainees. It seems that virtually *everybody* disagreed with Dr. X., myself included. Sigmund Freud also disagreed, because I eventually discovered that he extended his hand to patients at both the beginning *and* at the end of every single clinical session (e.g., Grinker, 1940; Kardiner, 1977; Roazen, 1995).

The smiling and handshaking conundrum remained on my mind constantly, as I struggled to find the best way to welcome patients into my consulting room. Eventually, I settled upon offering what I have come to regard as a rather British "soft" smile, as opposed to a very broad one. And as for the handshake, I decided that I would, as any other professional might, extend my hand at the start of the first consultation, unless I knew, in advance, or could ascertain from the patient's body language, that she or he feared simple physical contact tremendously, perhaps as a result of a history of gross sexual traumatisation. This system has worked quite well, and, to the best of my knowledge, I have never had a problem in this respect (Kahr, 2006b).

Many years after I participated in Dr. X.'s seminars, I came to meet several of his former training patients, all of whom had undergone lengthy periods of psychoanalysis on his couch. Two of Dr. X.'s one-time analysands had already developed a reputation for being rather cruel and contemptuous colleagues, disliked and gossiped about by large numbers of people. Another one of Dr. X.'s patients—quite a kindly man—told me that although he had enjoyed a good analysis, Dr. X. ruined the experience for him on the last day of treatment. When I raised my eyebrows with concern, this gentleman explained that, after ten years of analysis, he and Dr. X. parted; and in the final session, the patient extended his hand to Dr. X., who refused to shake, underscoring that this would be a breach of classical technique. The former patient told me that Dr. X.'s refusal to touch his hand after a decade of intimate, life-changing conversation had actually spoiled the lengthy analysis for him quite bitterly.

Having learned about this complicated incident, I came to appreciate, only too clearly, that although senior teachers and colleagues often have a great deal of crucial information to share with younger students, we must never idolise our "tribal elders", and each of us must exert the right not only to identify with their fine qualities but, also, to *dis-identify* from their less impressive parts.

Sometimes, we struggle to dis-identify from good mentors whom we find quite honourable and decent and even inspiring. During my training in marital psychotherapy, I attended a lengthy year-long course taught by a wonderfully experienced and deeply gracious woman whom I had long admired. A senior marital psychoanalyst, she had a great deal of experience to impart, and she did so quite liberally. But in spite of these fine qualities, this much older woman comported herself with a certain air of what I can only describe as "prissiness"; and even though she considered herself a classical Freudian, she never, ever mentioned the word "sex", even when speaking about couples. One day, in a seminar, one of my young colleagues presented a marital case which he had assessed and, on the basis of his report, the members of the discussion group—myself included—became very curious about the sexual life of this particular couple, who slept in separate bedrooms. One of us wondered aloud whether our colleague had actually dared to ask this couple about their sexual history in a direct fashion, which seemed quite reasonable, especially as large numbers of spouses struggle with all sorts of sexual conflicts ranging from infidelity to divergent sexual fantasy constellations, to sexual anaesthesia, and so on. Our teacher, the warm but prissy marital psychoanalyst, burst out, "I never, *ever* ask couples about their sexual lives unless they introduce the subject first. If I spoke first about sex, that would be an intrusion and an invasion of their privacy."

Instinctively, each of the young students in the seminar disagreed with our esteemed teacher. All of us had grown up in the so-called "post-sexual liberation" period, as had virtually all of our couple patients, and we had no difficulty raising the subject of sexuality in a gentle and professional fashion. But our teacher disagreed, perhaps, in part, due to her age and her innocence, in spite of her psychoanalytical training. After the seminar ended, all the students sat around chatting, and we all agreed that we would be perfectly willing to speak to couples about their erotic lives directly; indeed, we could all see the need for doing so, in spite of our seminar leader's warning. In this regard, I have followed my own clinical judgement, rather than the forbidding injunction of my teacher, and I believe that I have done so to good effect. In fact, I have come to discover that if we do *not* raise the subject of the sexual life of a couple in the first or the second assessment session, many couples become unnecessarily inhibited, unable to discuss their intimate relationship for fear that the psychotherapist might be quite Victorian!

So, in choosing one's mentors, students must exert the right to embrace the practices of their teachers wholeheartedly but, also, must be authorised to disagree when necessary.

A Most Inspiring Lecturer from Mendoza

Throughout my professional lifetime, I have enjoyed learning from some truly amazing instructors: university lecturers, teaching assistants, course tutors, seminar leaders, clinical supervisors, case consultants, clinical directors, team leaders, and so many more, not to mention my own training psychoanalyst. Many of these great men and women had studied with some of the foundational figures in world psychoanalysis, and some could trace their own analytical lineage back to Sigmund Freud. I owe such gratitude to so many of these wonderful mentors, and I will single out just a few of the many kindly people who had taken me under wing.

When, during the late 1980s, I embarked upon a training in forensic psychotherapy at the Portman Clinic in London, I had the deep honour of studying with the director of the course, the formidable and inspiring Dr. Estela Welldon. Born in Mendoza, in Argentina—home of the best Malbec wines—she had trained under Professor Horacio Etchegoyen (1986, 1991), the leading South American psychoanalyst of his day, a man who would eventually come to author the most comprehensive textbook on clinical technique of all time. Thereafter, Estela undertook further training with Dr. Karl Menninger, in Topeka, Kansas. Menninger (1968), who had met Freud in person, held the distinction of being the most influential American psychiatrist of the middle years of the twentieth century, and he became a true pioneer of forensic psychoanalysis, well known for his classic book, *The Crime of Punishment*. This man inspired Estela greatly. After her time in Kansas, she emigrated to Great Britain and eventually became Consultant Psychiatrist at the Portman Clinic, a specialist psychoanalytical service which provides treatment for offender patients who committed crimes ranging from genital exhibitionism and rape to paedophilia and arson. Estela established the world's very first training programme in forensic psychotherapy, designed to help her students offer more humane methods of working with dangerous patients; and I had the privilege of being among the first to undertake her course.

As a young man in my twenties, I found Dr. Welldon rather intimidating at first, because she knew so much, and I knew so little. As someone who specialised in group analysis, she, unlike many of her colleagues, did not allow seminar participants to sit silently in the background; Estela forced us all to engage quite actively and to become visible, spirited members of the group. As the youngest of the trainees by far, I had infinitely less experience than anyone else in the room, and I had virtually nothing to contribute. But Estela kept calling upon me to offer some views. Although I wished, at first, to curl up and hide, this amazing woman refused to let me do so, and consequently, she helped me to find my voice.

When the course ended, I received my diploma and carried on developing various strands of my forensic work. Unlike many of my colleagues, I had never intended to practise full-time in the forensic mental health field. Consequently, Estela and I could easily have gone our separate ways. But I knew that I wanted to maintain a link with this brilliant psychotherapeutic leader; and so, I found ways to remain in close contact. I had recently joined the editorial board of a very small academic psychology journal which had, at that time, only just begun publication; and with a certain temerity, I invited Estela to write an article. She could readily have refused, as she had many other professional commitments, but she consented most warmly and graciously. I, too, could have remained bashful, and could have refrained from soliciting a contribution, thinking that a famous psychiatrist such as Estela would be too busy to pen a short essay. In fact, we both seized the opportunity, and from that point, our teacher–student relationship began to change into one between an older and a younger colleague.

Not long thereafter, I received an offer to edit a monograph series on forensic psychotherapy from the psychoanalytical publisher Karnac Books, and I agreed to do so, happily, but only if Estela Welldon could be appointed as the Honorary Consultant. The publisher cheerfully agreed to my request, and I believe that Estela enjoyed the invitation—a recognition that one of her baby students had begun to make his own small contribution to her field of expertise. Over the decades, our little library of forensic psychoanalytical titles has grown in size, and we have published some clinically rich books on a whole range of subjects from paedophilia (Socarides and Loeb, 2004), to murder (Doctor, 2008), to child sexual abuse (Corbett, 2016).

From there, my relationship with Estela grew and grew. I invited her to appear on panels and at conferences, and she extended similar invitations to me. Over time, a social friendship also developed, and our two families became increasingly intertwined. Across more than four decades, Estela Welldon has become one of the most significant figures not only in my professional life but, also, in my personal life. We have referred patients to one another, we have consulted on cases together, we have conducted clinical interviews together, we have created projects together, and so much more. But of greatest importance, we have become good friends and we have looked after one another during pleasant times and during times of challenge, especially as we have grown older.

Recently, I had the great delight of editing a book as a surprise gift for Estela's eightieth birthday. In secret, I commissioned a group of several former Welldon students to write tributes for a "Festschrift"—a collection of essays examining her work. Together with these talented colleagues, we produced a volume entitled *New Horizons in Forensic Psychotherapy: Exploring the Work of Estela V. Welldon* (Kahr, 2018a), which we presented to Estela at a private party and which we then launched, more publicly, in cooperation with the International Association for Forensic Psychotherapy, at the Freud Museum London.

Estela Welldon certainly qualifies as one of my most brilliant mentors. She encouraged me to find my voice and to use it fully and effectively, just as she does with her own magnificent voice. In this respect, she will always be one of my most influential teachers. Each of us needs tutors of this type, and one must work hard to ensure that these relationships grow beyond graduation.

A Great Teacher Under Whom I *Never* Studied

We must consider ourselves very fortunate if we have had the opportunity to enrol on courses or on training programmes staffed by very inspiring tutors. But one need not be formally registered as a student in order to learn from some particularly remarkable people. I have had the unbelievable good fortune to have received several full-scale educations from quite a number of amazing teachers under whom I never studied officially.

Once again, I find myself deeply reluctant to single out any one particular individual, because I have had so many great mentors both inside the classroom and, also, outside. But I will speak briefly about the memorable Dr. Valerie Sinason, under whom I never studied in a formal capacity, but who has taught me such an immense amount about psychoanalysis and psychotherapy and traumatology.

In 1987, I attended the eightieth birthday party of the venerable psychoanalyst and developmental psychologist Dr. John Bowlby, whom I had met several years previously, having invited him to lecture at the University of Oxford. Dr. Bowlby and I had maintained a pleasant correspondence in the interim, and hence, I relished the opportunity to participate in this special birthday conference, held at the Zoological Society in London.

Valerie Sinason, then a child psychotherapist at the Tavistock Clinic, organised this event and served as chairwoman of one of the sessions; and I found her warm style so pleasant and delightful that I fell in love with her instantly and I yearned to find a reason to speak with her. As she had a great many tasks to attend to on the day, I certainly did not intrude upon her then, especially as she had to look after the ageing Dr. Bowlby. But some months later, our paths crossed at a conference at the University of East London. On that occasion, I approached Valerie directly, as I needed a new clinical supervisor for one of my adult cases, and I wondered whether she might be able to assist me. To my chagrin, Valerie had not, at that point, completed her training in adult psychoanalysis and, very honourably, she told me that she could supervise only the treatment of children. Nevertheless, she kindly recommended another colleague to whom I could turn and even made some telephone calls on my behalf.

Undeterred, I knew that I wished to forge a relationship with Valerie, and so, when I set up a monthly public lecture series on "Psycho-Analysis and Child Abuse" not long thereafter, I invited her to deliver one of the talks. Within a matter of moments, we soon discovered that we both shared a love for the work of Lloyd deMause (1974), the American historian of child abuse, and our conversation became quite animated. I believe that I took Valerie out to lunch as a means of thanking her for her inspiring lecture; and our collegiality and our friendship grew from that point onwards.

Eventually, Valerie Sinason invited me to present the case history of one of my disabled forensic patients before the Mental Handicap Workshop at the Tavistock Clinic, which she chaired, and in time, I became a long-serving and grateful member of both the Mental Handicap Workshop and the Mental Handicap Team, and eventually received a formal appointment as Valerie's deputy, taking responsibility for the organisation of the Tavistock's disability psychotherapy training courses. Not long thereafter, Valerie and I collaborated with two of our distinguished colleagues—Dr. Patricia Frankish and Professor Sheila Hollins (later Professor the Baroness Hollins) to form the Institute of Psychotherapy and Disability—an organisation designed to promote psychological treatment for patients struggling with intellectual and physical disabilities.

Subsequently, over the years, Valerie and I have lectured together, we have generated projects together, and we have lobbied together. Above all, we have become firm friends and I remain a deeply grateful student, even though I cannot *formally* claim Dr. Sinason as my teacher.

Psychotherapists who wish to create a secure base for themselves in this profession cannot do so in isolation. We must embrace the tutelage of brilliant mentors. But we must also invest a great deal in the *cultivation* of these mentorships. They will not simply fall into our laps!

PART II

The Art of Prospering

CHAPTER SIX

Perpetual Pupils

Training Never Ends

So … after years and years of long, hard, expensive work, you have now qualified as a psychotherapist. I offer my deepest congratulations, as we really need good people in this field of endeavour. I earnestly hope that someone will have thrown a party in your honour or that you have done so yourself, as all of our new graduates deserve proper recognition.

It might well be a great relief that we need no longer attend evening seminars or write up transcripts of sessions for our supervisors. And it may be a huge delight that we will have no further substantial course fees to pay or voluntary work to undertake in hospitals or mental health centres as part of our clinical placements or internships.

But, although we will have received a passing grade on the final qualifying paper, and although the training committee will have given its blessing for us to proceed to registration, this does not mean that studentship has ended completely. In order to be a truly accomplished psychotherapeutic practitioner, we must become lifelong students.

Qualification certainly enhances our sense of legitimacy and potency and affords us the satisfaction of knowing that we have completed a substantial piece of work. But qualification, per se, will not guarantee that we become successful, flourishing psychotherapists. Decades ago, one my oldest friends, Ben, with whom I attended university, finished his medical training and qualified as a member of the British Medical Association and as a registrar of the General Medical Council. That very evening, some chums and I took Ben out for a celebratory supper, and as we toasted our friend on his great achievement, he looked at us and giggled, "Yesterday, I wasn't allowed to call myself a doctor. But today I am a doctor. And it's odd, because I don't know anything more about medicine today than I did yesterday." This observation has remained in my mind over many long years, and it has particular relevance for the newly authorised psychotherapist.

Even the most rigorous of trainings will not necessarily prepare us for all the clinical challenges that we will encounter in the consulting room on any ordinary working day.

Recently, I treated ten patients, back-to-back.

The first patient told me that she had screamed at her husband louder than ever before. The second patient informed me that his son had just been diagnosed with a fast-metastasising cancer. The third patient explained that he had cheated on his wife with a prostitute and that he had contracted a sexually transmitted disease. The fourth patient—an actress—lamented that she had to attend an important movie screen test on the day of her father's funeral and felt guilty that she had agreed to this audition. The fifth patient had received a threatening letter from a social worker, concerned about domestic violence in the home. The sixth patient admitted to profound death wishes towards one of her children. The seventh patient had just committed an unethical act at work and expressed great terror at being caught by the boss. The eighth patient had just become involved in an ugly custody dispute during divorce proceedings. The ninth patient wept profusely after discovering a malicious article about herself posted on the internet. And the tenth and final patient of the day admitted that, at the age of fifty-three years, she had decided to become lesbian, in spite of a lifetime of reasonably, if not very, satisfying sex with men.

In thinking about these "top-line" summaries of ten intricate, moving, and complex clinical sessions, I realised that my various trainings, to which I had devoted years and years and years of study and hard labour, had provided me with only the most *minimal* preparation for navigating such conundrums. I hope that I managed to be helpful to all ten of these patients, but I do know that if I succeeded, I did so *not* because of my training but, rather, because of all the knowledge and experience that I acquired from my post-qualification readings and seminars and collegial discussions. Often, the best training experiences occur only after our formal training has ended!

Once we have registered with one or more of our professional bodies, each one of us will be required to complete a certain number of hours of further training, known in the United Kingdom as C.P.D.—continuing professional development—and in the United States of America as C.E.—continuing education. Our registration organisations will require us to document these further educational experiences on a regular basis. Some of our professional organisations insist that we attend for a minimum of forty hours of C.P.D. per annum. This seems most worthy. But from my observations, the flourishing psychotherapist will undertake not forty hours but, rather, four hundred hours, if not four thousand, each year, thus immersing himself or herself truly in the experience of being a proper, grown-up practitioner.

So, what might be the best ways to educate ourselves after we have *already* completed our formal education?

How to Be a Medieval Monk

It will come as no surprise that I strongly advocate reading books and journals in a much more considered and serious manner than ever before. I can only reiterate that, in my experience, the most accomplished clinicians have all obtained a significant mastery of the professional literature.

Whenever I attend dinner parties with fellow psychotherapists and other mental health professionals, colleagues often discuss their reading materials, and I would estimate that, on nineteen occasions out of twenty, my comrades will chat, predominantly, about the latest contemporary novels that they have just read on holiday. While I enjoy a good work of fiction as much as the next person, and while I appreciate that fine literature often provides us with rich characterological portraits which will be of interest to every practising psychotherapist, most works of fiction do not teach us very much about the treatment of drug addictions, or about the handling of the erotic transference in borderline patients, or about the complex vicissitudes of dissociative identity disorder. At the risk of being finger-wagging, I believe that psychotherapists read too many novels and not nearly enough psychological textbooks.

Let me ask each and every reader of this chapter some very painful and probing questions. Please answer as honestly as possible.

1) Have you read Sigmund Freud's (1900a) masterpiece, *Die Traumdeutung*, known in English as *The Interpretation of Dreams* (Freud, 1900b, 1900c)? Have you read it in full, and could you, at gunpoint, provide a detailed summary of the seminal third chapter, in which Freud describes his theory of dreams as the fulfilment of wishes, and of the classic seventh chapter, in which he explicates his now legendary topographical model of the mind?

2) Have you read any of the principal works of Melanie Klein in full? For instance, have you studied her first book, *Die Psychoanalyse des Kindes* (1932a), published in English as *The Psycho-Analysis of Children* (1932b), and if so, can you pontificate about her vision for a fully psychoanalysed world without neurotics or criminals, discussed at the very end of the book? Have you read Klein's (1957) swansong, *Envy and Gratitude: A Study of Unconscious Sources*, and can you provide a developmental map of the transformation of primitive envy across the life cycle?

3) Have you read Donald Winnicott's two landmark volumes of clinical psychoanalytical essays, written predominantly for colleagues, namely, *Collected Papers: Through Paediatrics to Psycho-Analysis* (1958) and, also, *The Maturational Processes and the Facilitating Environment: Studies in the Theory of Emotional Development* (1965), and can you provide a reliable account of his theory of development from absolute dependency towards independence?

4) Have you studied the latest edition of the *Diagnostic and Statistical Manual of Mental Disorders: Fifth Edition. DSM-5™*, published by the American Psychiatric Association (2013)?

5) Have you consulted any histories of the psychotherapy profession in order to contextualise your work more fully? (e.g., Ellenberger, 1970).

6) Have you read any of the groundbreaking studies on the role of child sexual abuse in the genesis of psychotic states (e.g., Read and Hammersley, 2005; Read and Gumley, 2008)?

7) How many journals do you peruse on a regular basis? Do you subscribe to the *British Journal of Psychotherapy* or to *Contemporary Psychoanalysis* or to *Psychoanalytic Dialogues*, and if so, do you read these publications consistently?

If you have scored 100 per cent, please telephone me at once! If you have received a more modest score, then I recommend that you allocate some regular time for *structured* study.

Many psychotherapists read in a "dipping" manner, browsing a few pages of Jung here, a few pages of Fairbairn there. Very few, in my experience, read in a systematic manner. The good psychotherapist must become, at times, something of a medieval monk, absorbing the professional literature in a well-programmed fashion, by candlelight if necessary, into the small hours of the morning. For instance, if one really wishes to acquire a good grasp of a certain theorist or of a particular area of psychopathology, one must absorb not one, but many, textbooks in that field.

I often recommend to my students that it might be helpful to begin by engaging with the complete works of Melanie Klein during the forthcoming summer holidays, in part because of the relatively modest and manageable size of her literary output. While Freud, Jung, and Winnicott each produced a huge corpus, which requires years of study, Klein (1932a, 1948, 1957, 1961) wrote only four books, and one could readily begin to digest those in chronological order during the month of August. One could then read Phyllis Grosskurth's (1986) magnificent biography of Klein, which one will struggle to put down: a wonderful way of meeting Klein as a woman, as well as Klein as a theoretician and clinician. I would supplement those four classic volumes by reading Hanna Segal's (1964, 1973) sturdy guide to Klein's psychoanalytical work and, also, Robert Hinshelwood's (1989) scholarly dictionary of Kleinian terminology. If one devoted each forthcoming summer to an intensive reading of just one major thinker within the field of psychotherapy or psychoanalysis, one could, within only a decade, acquire a considerable mastery of the work of our key progenitors.

If I had to recommend ten great psychoanalytical giants with whom I would enjoy spending ten successive summers, I would recommend the following, albeit not necessarily in this order: Sigmund Freud, as well as Karl Abraham, Franz Alexander, Michael Balint, Sándor Ferenczi, Anna Freud, Ernest Jones, Carl Gustav Jung, Melanie Klein, and Donald Winnicott. For those with longer life expectancies, one might devote the ten summers thereafter to the works of Edmund Bergler, Wilfred Bion, John Bowlby, Helene Deutsch, Erik Erikson, Ronald Fairbairn, Frieda Fromm-Reichmann, Margaret Mahler, Wilhelm Reich, and Theodor Reik.

It might, perhaps, be helpful to read these giants in book form, rather than in online editions. In my experience, one really needs to curl up with a text in one's hands—preferably in a first edition—in order to absorb this knowledge slowly and carefully and, also, to reserve the right to make careful marginal annotations in pencil, should that be of help. As a teacher,

I know that those who read online, ravaged by the flashing of lights and the pinging of emails, do not digest material quite as successfully.

If reading in bulk does not come naturally, then do not fear. One need not do so in total isolation. I strongly urge those so inclined to form a study group or a book group so that such reading can be undertaken collaboratively with cherished colleagues.

In addition to reading, it might be pleasant to listen to some podcasts. Virtually all psychotherapeutic and psychoanalytical organisations boast a website nowadays, and some have accumulated an impressive archive of excellent recorded talks. In particular, I recommend the webinars offered by Confer—the United Kingdom's premier mental health conference organisation—as well as those produced by the Freud Museum London. More recently, I have discovered the American podcast series called *New Books in Psychoanalysis*, part of the "New Books Network", which I strongly endorse, as well as the delightful conversations on *Shrink Rap Radio*, created by the intelligent and warm-hearted American psychologist, Professor David Van Nuys.

Recent graduates may also wish to consider undertaking additional postgraduate clinical supervision. After I qualified, I remained in weekly, private supervision for many years with one of my most inspiring teachers, and this experience, though time-consuming, provided me with a remarkable expansion of technical knowledge and finesse. So, please do choose a supervisor … and choose wisely. Many psychotherapists prefer to study with rather mediocre people so that they do not feel at all envious or threatened or, indeed, challenged. I recommend that one might wish to consider a formidable supervisor who knows *much* more than you do!

As most psychotherapists spend many hours each day sitting in complete silence, offering the occasional brilliant interpretation to their patients, the majority of us have few opportunities to use our voices fully and properly; thus, for colleagues with an even greater hunger to progress, particularly those who wish to develop their skills in teaching, lecturing and, also, in mental health broadcasting, I heartily recommend—quite seriously—a course of singing lessons to enhance one's vocal dexterity and diaphragmatic control. Having a rich and resonant speaking voice not only helps us to garner invitations as guest lecturers, but good vocal tones also contribute to a more tenderly attuned atmosphere within the consulting room itself.

Swimming in Organisations

The aforementioned activities, whether systematic reading of the literature, or private supervision, or even singing lessons, involve no more than one or, at most, two people. Because the practising psychotherapist spends so much time in a small, quiet room with one patient at a time, each of us needs the stimulation of a wider community of people. Consequently, I recommend that, although much of our continuing professional development work will take place in the quietude of our home or office, or in the consulting room of our clinical supervisor, we also have a great need to undertake further learning within the context of a larger collegial group.

For those graduates with a sense of vision and ambition, I recommend that one might take time to consider embarking upon further formal training in a complementary psychotherapeutic modality such as child psychotherapy or couple psychotherapy or group psychotherapy or organisational consultation. Although additional training will require a very great deal of hard graft, younger colleagues, in particular, might develop an appetite to become as well trained and as deeply experienced as possible.

As a very young man, I had already trained in both psychology and individual psychotherapy, and I never intended to expand my horizons beyond that point, as I had more than enough to keep me busy. But during my time working for Valerie Sinason in the Mental Handicap Team at the Tavistock Clinic, I had the opportunity to offer consultations to the mothers and fathers of our severely or profoundly intellectually disabled patients. The burden of caring for handicapped children often proved very painful indeed for the often good-willed parents and, consequently, many of these couples needed psychological assistance. Having conducted one or two sessions with parents, I realised that I knew very little about the delicate and challenging art of couple work; hence, I shared my concerns with Valerie, my very helpful and understanding boss. She and I worked in the Child and Family Department on the second floor of the "Tavi", situated just a stone's throw from the Tavistock Marital Studies Institute, located on the third floor. Pointing her finger upwards, Valerie intoned, "The marital people are just above us, and they are the warmest people in this building. You should walk up that staircase and ask them for supervision." To my delight, the gracious Christopher Vincent—a long-serving and gentlemanly clinician—interviewed me and kindly arranged for me to receive supervision and to participate in clinical discussion seminars. I enjoyed the experience so much that, after roughly a year of this very rich education as a Clinical Associate, I decided to apply for the full marital training and have remained involved with the organisation ever since.

Although I could happily have avoided completing a further psychoanalytical training, it pleases me greatly that I did so, because this experience opened up vast new canvases for me and prompted me to undertake the British Sexual Fantasy Research Project, which resulted in many publications, speaking engagements, and even radio and television appearances, not to mention a large number of referrals of sexually troubled patients who had read my books and who wished to arrange for treatment.

Of course, not everyone will have the energy or the capacity to undertake a second or third complete training. But for those with an appetite to learn even more, it might be useful to know that virtually all of the psychotherapy training programmes offer foundation courses or one-year-long courses at diploma level which permit us to obtain a further qualification or an additional piece of education, without having to devote another four or five or six years to formalised study. Many higher education facilities even offer part-time postgraduate degrees in a raft of subjects, some of which lead to a clinical qualification and some of which do not. Irrespective of which route or routes one will pursue, it can be very helpful to engage in further study within an institutional context, not least as we will meet many new colleagues and teachers who will constitute a rich professional community and who will often serve as a helpful source of referrals.

We might also note that, nowadays, many of the training organisations have begun to offer "advanced standing" to senior candidates. In my day, anyone wishing to complete the couple psychoanalytical training had to start at the very beginning, irrespective of how much previous study he or she had already undertaken. But today, qualified individual psychotherapists and psychoanalysts will receive credit for their prior learning and can complete the training in half the time, thus making a further substantial educational experience more manageable than ever before.

Above all, we should throw ourselves into our organisations with gusto, rather like talented swimmers who do more than stick merely a toe into the ice-cold water. Once we have embarked upon a post-qualification training, we should work hard to become well acquainted with the other members of the organisation; and we should offer our services to that institution and might make suggestions for new activities and projects. Organisations always need good people to service committees and to provide teaching.

So, it certainly helps to make our skills and abilities known to the senior members.

I realise that my campaign to promote further education among psychotherapists might seem somewhat persecutory, especially for those who, having just qualified, may well be, by this point, extremely tired! Please remember that, above all, the good psychotherapist must be a well-nourished person in every respect, so, in between reading the complete works of Sigmund Freud in German, please do spend time with your loved ones, please do travel the world, please do play the violin, and please do go to the gym. As Donald Winnicott might have recommended, the good-enough psychotherapist must be able to love well, to work well and, of course, to play well.

CHAPTER SEVEN

Attracting Referrals

The Art of Advertising

In olden days, health care professionals—medical practitioners, in particular—could not advertise their services. The British Medical Association considered all publicity quite gauche, even unethical. When, during the Second World War, the British Broadcasting Corporation engaged the services of a physician, Dr. Charles Hill, Secretary of the British Medical Association, to address the nation about health matters such as diet, during a time of severe nutritional rationing, he had to be introduced on air solely as the "Radio Doctor".

Similarly, when Dr. Donald Winnicott, the eminent psychoanalyst—also a medic by training—appeared regularly on the radio, the British Broadcasting Corporation did not identify him, likewise, by name, for fear that such exposure would offer him an unfair advantage over his colleagues. Consequently, Winnicott became one of the most secret celebrities of the mid-twentieth century (Kahr, 2015b, 2018b).

But today, in the twenty-first century, health care professionals operate under no such restrictions. Indeed, virtually everyone seems to have a website, a Twitter account, and goodness knows what other types of technologised forms of contact with unlimited numbers of people.

What then might be the ideal type of public profile for the contemporary practitioner of psychotherapy or psychoanalysis?

I suspect that I may not be the best person to advise on this particular topic, as I belong to a pre-computer generation, and I do not have my own personal website as many younger colleagues do. However, even if one does not maintain a website, anyone who belongs to an organisation, whether a clinic, a university, a group practice, or what have you, will benefit from an online profile, as nowadays every single institution must have a web presence which ought to be updated constantly.

I must confess that I do not have a strong view about whether a psychotherapist should maintain a solo website. At every level, this seems perfectly reasonable in our culture. But whether a website will help one to attract referrals and whether a website will inspire confidence, I cannot say. Although a judiciously designed website may not hurt a practice, and might even help it, in my experience, most patients who attend for psychotherapy have come via a considered recommendation from a health care professional. Therefore, even if one hires the fanciest designer to create the most magnificent and engaging internet presence of all time, this may not impress prospective patients.

Sometimes, a website can be counterproductive. Quite often, very inexperienced, newly qualified psychotherapists will list all the psychological illnesses and symptoms which they *claim* to treat very successfully. One psychotherapist boasted on her website that she can cure all of the following conditions: addiction disorders, anger management, anxiety disorders, attention deficit disorders, bereavement, chronic pain, debt stress, depression, family issues, low self-esteem, memory difficulties, mood disorders, obsessive–compulsive disorder, panic attacks, phobias and fears, relationship issues, sexual issues, sleep disorders, trauma, as well as lesbian, gay, bisexual, and transgender issues, not to mention abusive relationships and intrusive thoughts. While I certainly cannot comment on the clinical dexterity of this practitioner, such "advertising" strikes me as deeply ineffective in the long run, as I doubt that I would ever refer prospective patients to someone who presents in this fashion, claiming expertise in everything. After all, would one rush to consult a general medical practitioner who listed on his or her website a special concentration in all of the following body parts: head, face, eyes, ears, neck, shoulders, chest, abdomen, arms, wrists, hands, fingers, pelvis, legs, thighs, ankles, feet, toes, hair, brain, heart, lungs, liver, kidneys, pancreas, bile duct, genitals, and so forth? Such advertising strikes me as both ridiculously boastful and quite naïve at the same time.

Thus, I would urge all newly qualified practitioners to exert great care before launching a website and to seek feedback from a range of colleagues of different ages and statures within the profession as to the best way of advertising one's services.

We must also be cognisant of the fact that those prospective patients who approach colleagues through a website or through email often *never* become ongoing, long-term patients. Such individuals may well be uncertain whether they wish to undertake psychotherapy in the first place and, if so, which sort of psychotherapy they might find useful. Thus, I know of many colleagues who receive innumerable enquiries via a website, but as soon as the patient discovers that one's location might not be ideal or that one's fee might be just a few pounds more than anticipated, these people flee into the night. In my experience, many of the most serious patients approach us through a proper referral channel, rather than through window-shopping.

So, where do our patients actually come from?

My Last 500 Patients

Psychotherapy patients arrive at our doorsteps via a multitude of routes. Often a colleague or a teacher will recommend a potential patient to us, but sometimes, prospective clients will undertake their own researches and will find us through copious googling on the internet. On quite a number of occasions, patients themselves do not know the origin of the referral; and from time to time, an individual will explain, somewhat vaguely, "Oh, I got your name through a friend of a friend. I can't remember that person's name."

Some psychotherapists maintain very specialist practices and receive virtually all of their referrals from the same source. For instance, I have a very cherished colleague who works extensively with couples undergoing divorce. This psychotherapist has cultivated warm relationships with a small number of family law firms, and has offered seminars to innumerable solicitors; consequently, approximately ninety per cent of this practitioner's patients come through the same tiny cadre of lawyers, many of whom find themselves overwhelmed by the emotional chaos of their divorcing clients.

Other colleagues, particularly younger, computer-friendly ones, have subscribed to any number of online "Find a Therapist"-type services and sometimes receive more referrals than they can possibly navigate. I have never subscribed to any of these online referral networks, so I cannot comment about them directly, but I do know from many of my supervisees and students that a large percentage of the potential patients who trawl these sites will send out emails indiscriminately to a whole gaggle of psychotherapists simultaneously, often looking for just the right person at just the right time of day or night and at just the right fee. So, if a psychotherapist offers a 5.30 p.m. slot, many of these window-shoppers will reply by email or by text, "Sorry, I can only manage 5.45 p.m. Thanks anyway." Or if the psychotherapist sets the fee at £100, the prospective patient will write back, "Sorry, I was looking for a shrink who charges no more than £95."

Although future psychotherapy patients have the right to be ambivalent, a clinician who wishes to flourish and to maintain a solid, sturdy practice must have access to strong and reliable referral sources who pass on those patients who really *do* want to work and who really do wish to, and need to, commit to the intensity of ongoing psychological treatment.

In preparation for the writing of this chapter, I undertook an audit of my own private practice in order to ascertain how each prospective individual, couple, or family had first contacted me. I have created a table of the sources of referral of the last 500 patients who approached me for consultations, which I offer on the next page.

I hope that the following information will be of some sober use to fellow psychotherapeutic workers.

Interestingly, the vast majority of patients who have approached me for a consultation or for ongoing psychotherapy or psychoanalysis—whether once-weekly, twice-weekly, thrice-weekly, four-times-weekly, or five-times-weekly—contacted me after a recommendation from a *colleague within the mental health profession* with whom I have had a lengthy association over the years and who knows the nature and quality of my clinical work, having either spoken to me, having listened to me presenting papers at conferences, or having taught me directly or having been taught by me. Thus, 16.8 per cent of my patients came from older colleagues, and another 14.8 per cent of them came through recommendations by my contemporaries (and increasingly, by my younger colleagues). A further 10.8 per cent arrived at my office through a recommendation from my clinical supervisees who know of my level of competence and professionalism from first-hand experience; and 9.2 per cent found their way to me through my students. Thus, of the 500 patients in this sample, more than half of them—258 referrals, to be precise—entered my private practice through personalised endorsements from other mental health workers who have a direct experience of me and of my work. An additional 83 referrals—as many as 16.6 per cent—had come through mental health institutions at which I had held posts; thus, I would include these as collegial referrals as well. Therefore, strictly speaking, 341 patients out of a sample of 500—fully 68.2 per cent—had found their

Table 1. Sources of Referrals

Referring person or agency	Number	Percentage
Senior colleagues	84	16.8
Institutional referrals	83	16.6
Contemporary colleagues	74	14.8
Former supervisees	54	10.8
Former students	46	9.2
Unknown source	30	6.0
Former supervisors	20	4.0
Former patients	16	3.2
General reputation	15	3.0
Social acquaintances	14	2.8
Media colleagues	11	2.2
Public lectures	8	1.6
Publications	8	1.6
Former teachers	6	1.2
Psychiatrists	6	1.2
Websites of membership bodies	5	1.0
Miscellaneous health care professionals	4	0.8
General medical practitioners	3	0.6
Google search	3	0.6
Overseas colleagues	3	0.6
Lawyers	2	0.4
Newspaper articles	2	0.4
Radio appearances	2	0.4
Websites of non-membership bodies	1	0.2
Total	**500**	**100.0**

way to my consulting room through the collegial network. Creating a super-duper website with all the bells and whistles might well be helpful but, in my direct experience, nearly 70 per cent of the income from my professional practice has come to me through very specific recommendations from knowledgeable, trusted sources. Perhaps if one learns nothing else at all from this book, one will take serious note of this data and will come to appreciate that our reputations rest substantially in the hands of our fellow mental health workers and that, in consequence, we need the richness of a wide and good-hearted network.

We cannot rely on only one or two or three generous colleagues, because, at some point, these individuals will retire, or move to the countryside, and will eventually die off. We need, without doubt, a large community of fellow workers of all ages who have the potential to replenish our referrals.

Interestingly, the more glamorous, flashy methods of developing a reputation (e.g., listing one's name on a website, media appearances, publications)—though real and proper—produce far fewer referrals than a well-informed endorsement from another psychological professional.

It might be worth mentioning that some 3.8 per cent of my patients came to me via the recommendation of *former* patients. I should state categorically that I never have, and never would, work with someone who might be a friend or colleague of a patient currently undergoing treatment. Our patients or clients need to know that our offices remain safe havens, far away from the intrusions of their family members, friends, and co-workers. But, over the years, a very "ancient" patient—in other words, someone whom I had treated long ago—might well recommend me to an acquaintance. Sometimes, the former patient will ring me in the first instance to ask whether it would be possible to send "Mr. X." or "Mrs. Y." in my direction. In such situations, I would accept the referral only *after* I have had an extensive conversation with my old, one-time patient to see whether that person might ever wish to return to treatment in the future. In most instances, such former patients will already have undertaken a substantial piece of psychological work, will have completed their analyses, and then, years later, will feel sufficiently able to recommend me.

Approximately 2.8 per cent of my patients came to me on the advice of social acquaintances. I would never treat the friends of my close friends, as that seems too intimate and would involve me and my family boycotting social gatherings within our own circle. But if I happened to meet someone briefly at a dinner party, with whom I did not intend to socialise further, and if that person wished to make a recommendation to one of his or her acquaintances at some time in the future, I would, in all likelihood, consider accepting such a referral.

Interestingly, only a mere 1.0 per cent of patients had found me through the websites of my professional registration bodies. One wonders, therefore, whether our registration organisations have positioned their websites as effectively as possible. Funnily enough, some years ago, I did receive a referral through the website of an organisation in which I do *not* maintain membership. This professional association had listed some of my publications on its website and, apparently, the title of one of my books had intrigued a particular prospective patient who thus found me through a rival institution.

Answering the Telephone

Assuming that we have begun to develop a wide and reliable group of potential referrers, we will soon receive requests for consultations from patients or clients of every age, gender, and cultural background. Nowadays, many psychotherapists accept referrals electronically and enjoy receiving text messages or emails or mobile telephone calls out of the blue from prospective patients. I must admit that, as someone who would describe himself temperamentally as a "nineteenth-century man", I do not use electronic devices at all in my clinical work. I provide my colleagues and my patients with an old-fashioned landline telephone number, complete with answering machine, and everyone knows that if they wish to contact me, they have but to pick up the telephone and leave me a message.

Although this may seem a very dinosaur-like approach to the running of a professional business, especially since every single physician's office, dentist's office, lawyer's office, and accountant's office uses modern technology, why on earth have I not joined the twenty-first century?

From my perspective, I regard psychotherapy as so exceptionally private and confidential that I do not wish to correspond with patients electronically, as email addresses can be hacked, and messages can be passed along unwittingly. Indeed, an experienced colleague recently sent a sensitive email to the wrong patient, by "accident", and this technological error caused some unpleasant ripples for all parties concerned.

I prefer the old-fashioned approach of direct human contact. No one else has access to my telephone answering machine, and my patients have my assurance of complete protection in this respect. Of even greater importance, I have come to appreciate that people will often use emails and text messages as rather quick, even cheap, modes of communication. The psychotherapist, by contrast, wishes to encourage a calm, paced, thoughtful, and extended style of talking and listening; therefore, I find that emails and text messages set the wrong tone for the way in which I hope psychotherapeutic conversations with patients will unfold. In brief, I consider the direct, non-technologised approach much more containing, both for me and, above all, for my patients.

I do appreciate that I represent a tiny minority, and I would never insist that my supervisees adopt the "no email" approach to conducting a clinical practice. I share my own experience on this occasion simply for the consideration of my readers, so that each young, up-and-coming practitioner can think about the whole range of possible options.

Whether we run a nineteenth-century office or, by contrast, a twenty-first-century one, I would, however, urge my comrades to answer telephone calls or emails as expeditiously as possible. This may seem an all too obvious recommendation but, in my experience, many psychotherapists, who *should* be pillars of reliability and dependability, fall far from the mark.

Quite some time ago, I received a telephone call from a potential new patient, whom I shall call "Hester". She rang and left a message on the answering machine, asking to see me. I called her back a short while later on that very same day. We spoke briefly, and then we arranged an appointment for the following week. Hester attended for several preliminary consultations, and it soon became clear that she wished to (and needed to) embark upon a full five-times-weekly course of psychoanalysis. We began to work together most reliably, and this woman remained in treatment for more than eleven years. To my surprise, shortly after we began our first session, Hester exclaimed, "I am so grateful to you for seeing me, Professor Kahr." I nodded appreciatively, whereupon Hester then told me, "You know, before I came to see you, I really needed help desperately, but I didn't know whom I should see. So, I went onto a website, and I found the telephone numbers of *six* different psychotherapists in North London and I left messages for *all* of them. But, believe it or not, you are the *only* one who rang me back."

Hester's "bombshell" rather astonished me. I would never have imagined that as many as five fellow psychotherapists would somehow manage to leave a prospective patient dangling in this way. But since that time, I have encountered similar stories of neglectful colleagues who, for some mysterious reason, do not prioritise professional telephone calls. I find this quite extraordinary, as I simply cannot leave my office at the end of a working day until I have returned each and every clinical call. Thus, although it may seem far too obvious, the flourishing psychotherapist must become the epitome of reliability and must respond to all enquiries in an extremely timely fashion.

When returning a telephone call from a potential new patient, I always try to do so when I have a gap of at least fifteen or, preferably, twenty minutes to spare, as speaking with a patient in the first instance might take some time, not least arranging a mutually convenient appointment and providing clear directions to my consulting room. Often, I will return such calls at the very end of the working day. Obviously, if a client should happen to telephone and leave a message late at night, I might not receive the message until the following morning, at which point I shall respond to the call at that time. I check messages during the evenings and always before bedtime, in case an emergency should have arisen, and I always ring in for my telephone messages at weekends and during holidays, even on Christmas Day. A psychotherapist must be eternally vigilant. Our patients deserve no less.

CHAPTER EIGHT

Managing Money

Under-Charging and Over-Charging

In order to succeed as a psychotherapist, we need a great deal of sanity, an extensive amount of training and supervision, and a substantial ability to unravel the origins of a patient's psychological distress. Hundreds, if not thousands, of my predecessors from Sigmund Freud onwards have written copiously about the way in which we establish a treatment, and about how we decipher unconscious material, as well as render interpretations, work through complex biographical data, and facilitate a successful termination. I shall not attempt to repeat a century of readily available clinical wisdom in the confines of a short guidebook.

I do, however, wish to offer some thoughts about the complicated and often taboo subject of finance in relation to psychotherapy, as this topic rarely receives adequate attention. In my experience, many colleagues refuse to talk about either the setting of a fee, or its management, in our professional work. Sometimes practitioners will avoid discussing money because of a sense of shame that their own fees might not be as impressive as those of their fellow psychotherapists; similarly, other clinicians will not mention financial matters to colleagues for fear that they might evoke envy due to the high fees that they charge. And although money constitutes a very ordinary part of the daily life of virtually every adult human being in the Western world and beyond, many psychological workers regard the subject as something that should never be broached outside the consulting room.

I shall never forget that, many years ago, my dear colleague Jane Ryan, the founding Director of Confer—the mental health conference bureau and supplier of continuing professional development—organised a special one-day seminar for clinicians on the psychoanalysis of money. Surprisingly, although Jane hosted a very well-attended and engaging conference, which garnered numerous accolades from participants, she also received an anonymous letter lambasting Confer as "vulgar" for having mounted a public event about such a private matter. As I have served as the Academic Adviser to Confer for many years, Jane showed me the letter. Although the cowardly author did not sign his name, he did post this angry missive from his clinic address, and the envelope bore the stamp of that institution. It did not take long to discover the identity of the author as a very envious person with a very tiny private practice. It seems that, simply by mentioning money, one risks evoking the wrath of certain individuals.

Nevertheless, I shall now pass along something of the knowledge that I have accumulated over the years in the hope that this will be helpful to colleagues, as we simply cannot flourish in psychotherapeutic practice unless we can also pay our monthly bills and put food on the family table.

Setting a fee might best be described as an art form in which none of us has received any training. Consequently, very few practitioners charge precisely the same fee as one another. Furthermore, very few psychotherapists set the same fee for each and every patient. This has always surprised me. For instance, if one visits a private dentist for a teeth-cleaning, the receptionist will demand precisely the same amount of money from each patient for that particular service. I very much doubt that either the patient or the receptionist would haggle. Sometimes, a dentist will charge a high fee across the board, and as a consumer, one will probably pay the fee on that occasion but will also reserve the right to choose a different dentist in future should that particular fee prove to be unmanageable or cause too much resentment. Furthermore, as most people have their teeth cleaned by a dental hygienist only very infrequently, few patients will ever launch into huge objections.

But fees in psychotherapy evoke a very different reaction, in part, because, unlike the dentist, we insist on meeting with our patients every single week or, on occasion, even more frequently than that. Hence, committing to ongoing psychotherapy or psychoanalysis represents in many ways a much more substantial commitment than the occasional teeth-cleaning.

Moreover, because of the "loving" or "caring" nature of psychotherapeutic work, many patients develop a regressive fantasy that we, as professionals, have really become honorary mothers and fathers who look after the fragile souls of our patients with tenderness and concern. Thus, when we present patients with bills for our services, we often evoke much disgruntlement for having dared to insist upon a fee in the first place.

Perhaps, one day, psychotherapy will become recognised as such an indispensable service that governments all around the world will employ millions and millions of psychotherapists at a fixed rate, thus abolishing the need for independent practices. But until that utopian day arrives, the need for self-financed private psychotherapy remains very high, and somehow, each practitioner will have to find a way to charge a professional fee with clarity and conviction.

In my extensive experience of working with young clinical trainees and with newly qualified practitioners, I have come to appreciate that freshly launched psychotherapists often make one of two mistakes: either they will undercharge severely, or they will overcharge. While neither approach to the setting of a fee will result in world catastrophe, those who fail to establish a more median fee at the outset of their careers will often find themselves in great difficulty.

The under-chargers deserve our deep thanks, because we all depend upon colleagues who will agree to work with patients at very modest fees, well below the market rate. Under-chargers can sleep soundly at night, knowing that they have not succumbed to the evils of capitalism, and that they can, therefore, provide psychological relief for those patients who have few financial resources. But under-chargers, however virtuous, must also recognise the potential risks to themselves, to their patients, and to the profession at large. First of all, if one sets a very low fee for each and every patient, one will struggle mightily even to pay the rent on one's consulting room, let alone one's general living expenses; and this represents not social justice or charitableness but, rather, pathological masochism. Furthermore, at the outset of one's career, a newly qualified clinician might be only too delighted to have a few patients who will provide us with much-needed experience, but unless one receives proper remuneration over time, one will become deeply resentful at not being reimbursed for such potentially exhausting and potentially multi-year work.

By setting a very, very low fee, one also runs the risk of doing a disservice to the patient. Many of our customers can actually afford a full professional fee, but due to their own internal sense of impoverishment or their own greediness, they will often claim that they cannot pay more than £10. Thus, the psychotherapist who instantly agrees to a low fee may, at times, find himself or herself colluding with the more aggressive or deprivational components of the patient's mind, and one should be aware of this as a possibility. Furthermore, someone who specialises in undercharging may also damage the public reputation of the profession by presenting the field of psychotherapy as a denigrated one. A private neurosurgeon would not operate upon someone's brain for only £40. He or she would charge thousands of pounds for doing so. And although one cannot make a direct comparison between the work of the psychotherapist and that of the surgeon, we must remember that we have spent as many years in training as the neurosurgeon has and, moreover, that we will have funded our training entirely by ourselves, whereas medics, by contrast, had, for many decades, received subsidies from the British government.

Those who wish to acquire basic clinical experience or who wish to provide for the mental health needs of men and women lacking in financial resources must be encouraged to do so. As I indicated in Chapter 2, I treated many of my earliest patients for absolutely no money at all, and, in a radical moment, I began charging one of my first patients twenty pence per hour! As our careers progress, we can certainly preserve space for one or two "low fee" clients. But to run an entire practice by undercharging might be quite risky at every level.

Overcharging, likewise, presents the practitioner with a wide set of potential problems. An over-charger runs the risk of losing virtually all of his or her patients in the first telephone conversation. (And be advised that many patients, if not most, will enquire about the fee prior to the first consultation).

As we age and as our professional reputation develops, we will begin to charge higher fees than we had done previously. This seems only fair and proper. But once again, we must be careful that we do not set such a high fee that only a member of the British Royal Family or a Russian oligarch can afford our services. We must also appreciate that patients will often gossip about the fees of various colleagues. On more than one occasion, I have had a patient tell me that "Dr. So-and-So" had asked for £500 for a first consultation. This patient—fully outraged—refused to pay that amount of money, and hence came to see me and spent much of the session insulting this high-charging colleague. Thus, extremely hefty private fees might ultimately become the subject of semi-public discussions. Young practitioners, in particular, must be cautious about setting too high a fee, as that will infuriate older colleagues who might regard one's youthful temerity in doing so as a grandiose act of gumption, and this will not help endear one to more senior practitioners who might otherwise become very good long-term sources of referrals.

Some over-chargers do not consider their fees to be unreasonable. Often, such people will have demonstrated considerable competency, if not brilliant innovation, in the field, and regard their robust charges as perfectly reasonable. Sigmund Freud, for instance, set a very high fee which rose steadily over time, with inflation, but grew, also, with the expansion of his reputation. In 1909, Freud charged one of his patients 40 *Kronen*—the equivalent of ten American dollars (Roazen, 1995)—but, by the 1920s, he had raised his fee to $20 per hour, and then to $25 (Blanton, 1971; Roazen, 1995). His British patients paid one guinea after the Great War, and then, over the next years, his fee climbed to two guineas (Roazen, 1995) and, ultimately, towards the end of his life, to three guineas (Ritholz, 1938) and, sometimes, as high as six guineas (Molnar, 1992). Freud charged far greater fees than his colleagues (e.g., Menaker, 1989), but many might argue that, as the founder of psychoanalysis, he deserved these financial rewards.

Should we, therefore, all charge the same middling fee? Some of our colleagues would agree that this might be the fairest way to offer privatised psychotherapy. Naturally, setting fees remains a matter for each individual, but we must also consider the market rate.

I often advise my new trainees that they should maintain as open a mind as possible when first establishing a practice, and that it might be helpful to identify a minimum figure, below which they simply will not work. In this way, one protects both oneself and, also, the patient from any untoward resentment or even hateful feelings. For instance, if one receives a referral from a distinguished senior colleague who wishes to place a low-fee patient, and if one wishes to acquire the experience of treating such a case, one may accept the referral, but must exert the right to insist upon one's minimum fee. A newly qualified person might agree to work with the patient for £20 per hour, but if the patient balks, we do not have an obligation to lower the fee to £5. We should certainly be entitled to run our own businesses.

Collecting Fees

In order to operate a financially sound psychotherapeutic practice, each clinician must attend to the collection of fees in an extremely ethical and reliable fashion. Billing on a regular basis, perhaps on the first day of each new calendar month or on the last day of each month, provides the patient with a clear and predictable timetable. Having established such a structure, one must never vary the arrangement; indeed, we must treat the rendering of our bills with the very same reliability as our sessional timekeeping. Such regularity underscores both the financial seriousness and professionalism of the arrangement and, also, permits the patient to plan his or her own cash flow as carefully as possible.

As a "nineteenth-century psychotherapist", I prefer to hand a printed invoice directly to my patients at the end of the session hour, at the start of each new calendar month, setting out the fee for the previous month's appointments. Some colleagues will post invoices to their patients or will send them by email, but I prefer to keep all communications between me and my patients confined to the privacy and the immediacy of the consulting room whenever possible.

It pleases me to report that approximately ninety per cent of all psychotherapy patients pay their bills with reasonable, if not excellent, promptitude. The vast majority have never "acted out" at all in relation to their financial commitment to the psychotherapeutic process. Occasionally, one will encounter patients who, for whatever reason or reasons, will either delay in paying their monthly invoices or will disappear and fail to settle their accounts. In my experience, those who behave cruelly to their intimates (e.g., family members, partners, and colleagues) tend to be at much higher risk of perpetrating a version of that cruelty by neglecting their psychotherapy invoices.

Sometimes, a very long-standing, loyal, well-meaning person might not pay his or her bill immediately, but will do so within two or three or, even, four weeks. In such instances, I will not, on the whole, comment upon this passage of time, unless the question of money happens to emerge directly or indirectly in the patient's material during a session. In virtually all cases, the busy, travelling executive will settle his or her bill in due course, and I would not, with such individuals, chase them up. Nor do I mark my invoices, as some colleagues do, "All fees must be paid within seven days of receipt", which I find rather stringent. I prefer the more trusting and gentlemanly approach.

But sometimes, our more aggressive patients—especially those with an already documented forensic history—will behave dishonourably and will simply evade payment. In such circumstances, one has the right to seek collegial counsel, whether supervision or consultation with one's professional body, to determine the best way to recoup one's fees. Some colleagues will underscore to the patient that treatment cannot continue until he or she settles the outstanding bill; some colleagues will write a formal letter, insisting that payment be made within seven or ten working days; other colleagues will instigate legal proceedings, often through the small claims court, if necessary.

Most psychotherapists do not enjoy becoming tough or hard-hearted in terms of collecting fees, especially as we know that failure to settle the account often stems from a re-enactment of early childhood traumata and from a sense of being cheated of parental affection and protection. Nonetheless, whatever the roots of the patient's non-payment, the psychotherapist has established an ongoing contract for his or her professional services, and we must not be suckers! We certainly have a right to receive payment for the sessions that we have provided.

Sometimes, the non-payment of fees by patients represents an expression of the patient's ambivalence towards the psychotherapist for not having "cured" him or her in record time. Naturally, the self-scrutinising clinician must always consider the possibility that he or she has actually provoked the patient's reluctance to pay. But in my experience, most of the occasional non-payers have a long-standing history of emotional or physical cruelty, and we must be prepared for the possibility that such dynamics will be repeated, unconsciously, within the context of the consulting room.

Financial Planning for the Future

In order to flourish as a psychotherapist, we must be well fed and watered, and must have a roof over our head. We must also ensure that our immediate family members will be cared for as well. And while retirement may seem a very long way off for newly qualified members of our profession, I can speak with assurance that the decades really do fly by very quickly. Each of us must, therefore, be canny.

Unlike corporate employees or state employees who belong to a pension scheme as part of their contract, independent psychotherapists work entirely for ourselves, and our patients, however decent and appreciative, will not support us in the final chapters of our lives. We must, therefore, create our own pension plan, whether through savings, or investment, or property, or through some other means.

Although I have no qualifications in finance or in economics and cannot give direct advice on such subjects, I can, however, urge the self-employed psychotherapist to seek a very sturdy and attentive accountant, with whom one can begin to discuss such matters. One might also wish to consider consulting a financial adviser who can assist with the setting up of a private pension.

I know many psychotherapists who enjoy their work so richly that they boast to me that they will never, ever retire and that they hope to continue treating patients into their seventies, eighties, and even into their nineties. One of the great British psychoanalysts, Marion Milner—a disciple of Donald Winnicott—died at the age of ninety-eight years; and although *mostly* retired in her nineties, I can reveal that, until her death, she did continue to offer sessions to a long-standing patient, whom she had first begun to psychoanalyse some fifty-five years previously.

Happily, our profession does not prohibit elderly psychotherapists from consulting to patients. But we certainly cannot be grandiose and presume that we will, automatically, be alive in our seventies, eighties, and nineties, and that we will be both physically capable and compos mentis.

A short while ago, one of my long-standing colleagues—only seventy years of age—entered a nursing home, suffering from Alzheimer's disease. Her plan to continue treating patients into her nineties could not be realised. Another colleague, however, worked with patients well into his mid-nineties, rather like Marion Milner. Remarkably, this man had remained in excellent health, with a clear memory, and proved very useful to his patients until, at ninety-six years of age, he began to forget appointments and, also, neglected to deposit his cheques from patients into his bank account. Regretfully, he had to stop work completely, and did so rather abruptly.

Personally, I do *not* recommend that we should aspire to provide sessions for our patients when in our tenth decade. For those of us who have the good fortune to live a long life, we might wish to enjoy some retirement! In fact, although patients might benefit hugely from the wisdom of an octogenarian, a nonagenarian, or even a centenarian psychotherapist, we must be careful that we do not put our patients in a vulnerable position by dying on them in the middle of treatment! That might be quite a gross burden to place upon men and women who may already have sustained deep losses throughout their lives.

Whether we retire at sixty-five years of age or at ninety-five years of age, we will need some money to sustain us. Thus, careful financial planning in a profession that can, at best, attract only a comparatively modest income, should be very much in our thoughts.

CHAPTER NINE

The Promotion of Expertise

Flagrant Exhibitionism or Neurotic Inhibitionism?

Over the decades, I have worked with many people in the entertainment industry, whether performers, directors, producers, or writers. These creative men and women often struggle with intimacy, with addiction, with meaningfulness, and with a host of other human anxieties and conflicts. They also possess a remarkable resiliency and many of these outward-facing people really do know how to impress other people with their skills and abilities and talents.

"Anthea", a very beautiful and accomplished actress, received rave reviews from her teachers at drama school. She knew that she possessed the capacity to make an audience cry. Brimming with unbridled confidence, and eager to forge a successful career, Anthea wrote to every single talent agency in London, bombarding them with headshot photographs and with copies of her curriculum vitae until she found someone who would represent her and would secure auditions for her. Anthea always appeared *early* for every single audition with a casting director, having memorised her script fully the night before. She comported herself with tremendous professionalism throughout and, in due time, Anthea had become acquainted with numerous film and theatre directors, all of whom found her captivating. Before long, Anthea had established herself so firmly in the entertainment industry that, as time unfolded, she took more and more responsibility for the shaping of her own career. Unlike other performers who sit at home by the telephone in the misguided hope that their agent might ring at any moment with an offer to play *Hamlet* in the West End or on Broadway, Anthea decided to generate her own projects. She refused to remain in a passive position; instead, through her psychotherapeutic treatment, she became increasingly aware of her own internal potencies and capacities, and she developed a truly active state of mind.

In many respects, psychotherapists have a great deal to learn from Anthea, this forward-thinking actress.

I know of too many psychotherapists who, however well-qualified, experienced, and kindly, have virtually no patients. Most of these colleagues sit by the telephone, waiting—often in vain—for a prospective referral. Such people exist in a pathologically passive state of mind, rather than in a healthily active one.

Unlike Anthea, mental health professionals do not work in such a public arena. On the contrary, we sit in an extremely private room, shielded from the glare of the media. Our patients rely upon our discretion, and they would not be particularly thrilled if photos of us appeared in newspapers and magazines on a daily basis. In view of this, how do we promote our expertise in order to have a meaningful and gratifying professional career, while also preserving our discretion?

Back in the year 2000, my old friend and colleague Ivan Ward, the long-standing Director of Education at the Freud Museum in London, very kindly commissioned me to write a small volume for the book series which he edited, "Ideas in Psychoanalysis", published by Icon Books. Ivan knew that I had worked for many years in the forensic mental health field, and he asked me whether I would write a short tome about exhibitionism. It may not be widely appreciated, but more men (and, also, women) commit acts of genital exhibitionism than any other sexual offence. Having worked with a number of genital exhibitionists over the years, I already had many thoughts on the subject, and I responded to Ivan's invitation with gusto.

Throughout my book on *Exhibitionism* (Kahr, 2001), I focused pre-dominantly on the actual forensics of this sexual crime, explaining why people felt impelled to expose themselves in such a concrete manner. But I wrote not only about the way in which exhibitionism constitutes a legal offence, but, also, about how it can be understood as a form of psychological characterology. One need not drop one's trousers to be an exhibitionist. Anyone who hogs the microphone at a conference or who talks only about himself or herself at a dinner party might very well be a psychological exhibitionist of one sort or another.

Happily, most psychotherapists do not suffer from psychological exhibitionism. In order to be an accomplished clinician, one must yield space to the other—to the *patient*—and not spend the entire session talking about oneself. But because we play merely a supporting role, rather than a starring role, in our daily work, we often inhibit ourselves unnecessarily and destructively outside the consulting room. Indeed, many psychotherapists struggle with what I have referred to as *"psychological inhibitionism"* (Kahr, 2001, p. 63), which, I suspect, might often serve as a defence against our own wish and need to exhibit ourselves and to be seen and recognised.

Although the flagrantly exhibitionistic psychotherapist will win few, if any, friends, neither will the neurotically inhibitionistic psychotherapist.

For those of us who have acquired years and years of hard-earned professional expertise, we do ourselves and the community at large a great disservice by hiding in the shadows. Thus, before a psychotherapist can reap the rewards of his or her abilities, each of us must first conquer our own pathologically inhibitionistic tendencies.

I would argue that the highly inhibited psychotherapist, who struggles to lecture in public or to set up new projects, will not only damage his or her own potentiality, but might, also, undermine patients as well. As every clinician will know, our patients or clients engage in a process of identification with us, and look to us for guidance, not only in terms of ethics and reliability but, also, in terms of style. Thus, the psychotherapist who has no public voice or outward reach might be a very disappointing role model for those who already feel notably inhibited or restricted by life.

Over the years, through googling, my patients have discovered that I have written various books and articles, and that I have delivered numerous public lectures. Many have told me—quite often, in fact—that they admire my capacity to be not only so attentive inside the consulting room but, also, sufficiently creative outside the office as well. Some have indicated that they feel inspired and that my public presence has given them hope that they, too, might one day conquer their writer's block or other forms of inhibitionism.

Consequently, in order to promote our expertise as clinicians, we must first adopt a state of mind in which we can take *ownership* of such expertise without shame or guilt.

Generativity versus Stagnation

As a young first-year undergraduate, I had the good fortune to read a masterwork of psychology, namely, Professor Erik Erikson's (1950) classic book, *Childhood and Society*. Erikson had trained as a psychoanalyst in Vienna back in the 1920s and 1930s, having undergone a personal analysis with Anna Freud; and after his emigration to the United States of America, he became one of the most seminal psychoanalytical thinkers of the mid-twentieth century. It has always saddened me that very few students nowadays—especially in the United Kingdom—engage with the work of this remarkable man.

In his *opus classicus*, Erikson crafted his now famous eight-stage model of human development from infancy to old age. He referred to the seventh stage, the apotheosis of the middle years, as a conflict between *generativity* and *stagnation*. The healthy, creative, productive person with a strong ego structure and with good infantile foundations will be able to become highly generative, producing rich and rewarding achievements. But, alas, the less stable person with a more fragile, inhibited, or compromised ego structure will succumb to the miseries of stagnation, unable to be generative and fertile.

I find Erikson's developmental model a source of great inspiration and of huge relevance to each practising mental health worker. Once we have trained, and once we have launched into our adult lives as clinical practitioners, each of us will have to navigate this complex struggle between generativity and stagnation. Alas, in my experience, many colleagues succumb to disappointment and failure, unable to harvest the full fruits of their lengthy careers. Thus, the average psychotherapist suffers from the aforementioned psychological inhibitionism and from an Eriksonian stagnation, causing tremendous resentment, envy, and even depression.

Although the consequences of inhibitionism and stagnation can be severe and debilitating, Erikson offered little insight into how we can overcome these traps, short of turning back the clock and reliving our lives with a more inspiring set of parents. Still, we must work to push ourselves into a more fruitful mode of creativity, and we must allow ourselves to be encouraged by our kindly mentors. As I have already indicated, one needs *brilliant* mentors—not *mediocre* ones—to serve as deep sources of inspiration and aspiration.

With a core of sanity, with an embrace of perpetual studentship, with an advanced case of *bibliophilia psychotherapeutica*, and with bold mentors serving as our protective shields, we will have all the raw ingredients needed to pursue interesting projects which will better position us to enjoy our lives in the psychotherapeutic field.

In order to conquer the toxicity of inhibitionism and of stagnation, every good psychotherapist must become a veritable *project manager*. In other words, each of us must conjure up projects and plans on a regular basis and begin to collaborate with colleagues and with organisations to bring these schemes to life.

As a young student of psychology, matriculated at the University of Oxford, which offered absolutely no instruction in psychoanalysis what-soever, I became increasingly frustrated. I had two choices: I realised that I could either swim in bitterness, lambasting my professors and lecturers for their lack of imagination and for their stupidity in embracing behaviourism rather than Freudianism, or, I thought, I could mount my own special interest group on psychoanalysis in an effort to enrich my soul and to share some of my growing enthusiasm for psychodynamics with the wider community.

On a whim and a prayer and with absolutely no financial support or formal institutional backing, I decided that I would organise a weekly lecture series for members of the university and that I would invite dis-tinguished practitioners from all over the world to deliver talks on psycho-analysis. Back then, we had no computers or emails or mobile telephones. I had only a small electric typewriter at my disposal, and so I sat down at my desk and posted a smattering of letters to some of the most eminent psychoanalysts in the world, explaining my situation, and extending a warm invitation to speak.

To my delight and surprise, the famous American psychoanalyst, Dr. Muriel Gardiner, who had trained in Freud's circle in Vienna, and who had the good fortune to be independently wealthy, wrote back at once. She had studied at the University of Oxford during the 1920s and had found it a stuffy place, and she had not particularly enjoyed her time there. But now, more than half a century later, Dr. Gardiner wished to have a better experience, and so agreed to travel to Oxford to speak and even offered to pay for her own flight. In her youth, this dynamic woman had met Freud personally and, in later years, she came to assume the responsibility of caring for Freud's (1918) famous Russian patient, Sergéi Konstantínovich Pankéev, better known as the "Wolf Man". The generosity of Muriel Gardiner's letter absolutely flab-bergasted me. I deeply appreciated her kind offer to travel to Great Britain, and I arranged a special lecture for her in the large theatre of the university's Department of Experimental Psychology on South Parks Road—perhaps the first time a Freudian psychoanalyst had ever set foot in such an anti-Freudian building. To my utter surprise and delight, more than 100 people attended, and thus, I launched the Oxford Psycho-Analytical Forum.

Over the next few years, I had the privilege of inviting such distinguished visitors as Dr. John Bowlby, Dr. Ronald Laing, Dr. Hanna Segal, Dr. Robin Skynner, and numerous others from England, France, Germany, and the United States. Although younger than most of these distinguished people by some forty, fifty, or sixty years, I maintained ongoing correspondences with many of them until their deaths, and I felt a deep sense of warmth and encouragement. Some of these remarkable personalities gave me hope that, one day, I might forge a home within the mental health community, for which I remain eternally grateful.

I offer this anecdote as a small example of what one might undertake, irrespective of whether one has received a grant or a formal invitation to do so. In truth, we need only a little bit of passion and a little bit of *internal* authorisation.

On Stage at the Royal Opera House

Often, we never quite know how our exciting projects will materialise.

In 2007, during my tenure as Chair of the Society of Couple Psychoanalytic Psychotherapists—the membership body of graduates of the Tavistock Centre for Couple Relationships—a group of colleagues and I wished to mount a large-scale event to popularise the genre of couple psychoanalysis among members of the general public. At that time, in London, very few people in Great Britain wished to train as couple mental health professionals, and thus, we hoped that by publicising our work more fully, we might be able to generate some enthusiasm for this type of work.

To my delight, we managed to acquire the Linbury Studio Theatre at the Royal Opera House in Covent Garden, on a Sunday evening, and we hosted a sell-out fund-raising event for approximately 400 people, entitled "Couples in Counterpoint", in which five musical theatre stars of the West End stage performed classic songs about the psychology of romantic relationships, with four senior couple psychotherapists, seated on stage left, offering commentary about the deeper, unconscious dynamics of marriage. We had so many requests for tickets that we simply could not accommodate all those who wished to attend. In the end, the evening proved to be a huge success, raised a lot of money for our professional organisation, and even attracted glowing reviews in several of the leading broadsheets (Kahr, 2007c). Never in my life could I have imagined that I would have the opportunity to spend an evening on stage in the studio space of the Royal Opera House, along with my cherished colleagues Christopher Clulow, Pauline Hodson, and Helen Tarsh, not to mention stars of such shows as *Les Misérables* and *The Phantom of the Opera*!

How on earth did this unusual, but impactful, musico-psychological evening emerge?

Let us work backwards.

Obtaining the use of the studio at the Royal Opera House, for *free*, does not happen very often. But, one year previously, I attended a dinner party at the home of my colleague Pauline Hodson in Oxford, where I met a charming married couple, who had donated a great deal of money to the Royal Opera House. These philanthropists had also undergone psychoanalysis and had found the process useful. I almost did not attend this meal—a train-ride away—as I felt tired and unwell on that occasion, on the verge of coming down with influenza; but I forced myself onto British Rail nonetheless, and in the end, I had a lovely time. I also forged an ongoing rapport with the couple—both warm and convivial family-orientated people—who offered to help our little professional organisation. And so, when I became Chair of the Society of Couple Psychoanalytic Psychotherapists, I invited the husband to lunch in London, and discussed our plans to develop our professional body. Before long, he obtained the Linbury Studio Theatre space for us without any charge!

I then contacted a dear friend, theatre director Lisa Forrell—herself the daughter of a psychoanalyst, Mildred Forrell—who not only loves the arts but, also, has a profound respect for depth psychology. As someone steeped in theatre, having directed numerous West End plays, Lisa knows hundreds of great actors and singers, and she agreed to cast our little evening, "Couples in Counterpoint", and to rehearse the company.

So, how did I come to know Lisa Forrell?

She and I met through a wonderful woman, Susan, Lady Hollick, a great patron of the arts, whom I first encountered at a Thanksgiving dinner party hosted by Dr. Susie Orbach, one of the world's most gifted psychoanalytical theoreticians and clinicians. Knowing of my interest in music and theatre, Susie pointedly sat me next to Lady Hollick, with whom I became quite friendly, and she, in turn, suspected that I would enjoy the company of Lisa Forrell and so arranged a gathering.

And how did I come to meet Susie Orbach?

I have known Susie for decades. Many years ago, I launched a series of public lectures on the theme of "Psycho-Analysis and Child Abuse", and I sent copies of the programme, by post, to every mental health professional in the north-west London area. The vast majority of colleagues ignored the programme, too busy with their own projects, no doubt; but Susie Orbach telephoned me upon receipt of the flyer to express her appreciation and her interest. We began to chat, but we had no further contact at that time. Some months thereafter, through my forays in teaching, I met a Jungian analyst who asked me whether I knew Susie Orbach. I explained that, although we had spoken briefly on the telephone, she and I had not met in person. This Jungian analyst told me that she thought that Susie and I might enjoy one another's company, and so she invited us both to dinner. I fell in love with Susie within minutes—seconds, perhaps—and over the last thirty years, we have become lifelong friends.

I hope that this backward-reconstruction of our night at the opera will confirm that creative projects rarely materialise out of thin air. They develop through a bit of bravery, a bit of boldness, a bit of passion (perhaps a *lot* of passion), and through the creation of, and use of, a warm community of colleagues with whom one can collaborate.

In writing this section, I realise the important role that creative lunches and dinners have played in the genesis of a very large number of projects. I received an invitation to write for Penguin Books during the course of a pleasant lunch; I received a commission for my first television documentary over a convivial dinner at the home of a producer; and so forth. As psychotherapists, we must, inevitably, spend a great deal of our time in consultation with patients, not eating lunch or dinner but, rather, listening and interpreting and processing all the painful stories that we hear on an hourly and daily basis. But when we leave the consulting room, we must endeavour to socialise as broadly as possible and find ways to bring our various social networks together for collaborative purposes. In doing so, we can better conquer our psychological inhibitionism in a non-exhibitionistic way, and we can begin to transform our Eriksonian stagnation into true generativity.

CHAPTER TEN

Patients as Persecutors and as Privileges

The Prevention of Burn-Out

For those intent on flourishing beyond the training years, we must, as I have already indicated, find ways to prosper. As I have also explained, in spite of having graduated from one's training, every good psychotherapist must also become a perpetual student and true scholar of the literature. Furthermore, each of us must maintain a wide array of colleagues who will come to appreciate the quality of our clinical work and who might be in a position to send us referrals. Additionally, we must charge appropriate professional fees so that we can support ourselves (and, also, our loved ones). And we must claim our specialist expert capacities and not be too shy about them.

In the preceding four chapters, I have offered a glimpse of my own thoughts and views on the art of prospering. But no matter how many lectures we organise, no matter how many writing invitations we receive, no matter how many fees we collect, no matter how many cups of tea we may have taken with John Bowlby, we must, above all, find a way to enjoy the slow, demanding, often painful, and frequently frustrating day-to-day work with our patients.

As we know, clinical practice can be extremely emotionally burdensome, even debilitating. We must, therefore, engage meaningfully with the very special nature of this work so that it will not destroy us.

I could, of course, write a whole chapter full of tips and techniques for remaining refreshed. Naturally, it helps to have breaks throughout the working day, if possible. It might be of use to take a walk at lunchtime or during the afternoon. It might be a good idea to have a decent night's sleep. It might be of great value to lead a rich social life and to cultivate one's hobbies and interests. We hardly need to read a book to remind ourselves of the benefits of leading a full, well-rounded professional and personal life.

But instead of recommending that we should spend our Saturdays at the British Museum or at the Empire State Building, or our Sundays watching a film with the family—however lovely such activities might be—I wish to propose that burn-out can be staved off *not* by having fun outside working hours, but, rather, by doing our job as well as possible, so that we will derive the tremendous satisfaction of actually curing our patients.

Over the years, I have met innumerable colleagues who have suffered from emotional exhaustion, but I have also met many who have *not* succumbed to the evils of burn-out. I have spoken to students and senior practitioners alike who have felt shattered after having worked with only two patients in a day, and I have met others who seem to be refreshed and exhilarated, even after having treated ten patients back-to-back. It may be that, no matter how many trips we have made to galleries and stately homes, and no matter how many holidays we have enjoyed with our loved ones, the burdens of psychotherapy result not from the workload but, rather, from a persecutory internal state of mind.

For me, one of the greatest professional satisfactions stems from the fact that, as the years have progressed, and as I have become increasingly experienced in the consulting room, I can still find creative ways to unravel the invisible knots and the unspoken bombs which destroy the lives of my patients. Let me give a little example, albeit a powerful one.

Some time ago, "Mr. Creighton" and "Mrs. Creighton", a middle-aged couple, came to see me in great desperation because Mr. Creighton had slept with one of Mrs. Creighton's closest female friends. Naturally, the wife felt deeply betrayed and injured, and in response, she threw her husband out of the house. Their twenty-five-year marriage hung by a thread and Mr. Creighton had begun to drink quite heavily. They arrived at my office in a frantic state, hoping that the marriage could be repaired.

At first, I listened quietly as this belligerent and wounded couple screamed at one another non-stop. "You're a fucking piece of shit," hollered

Mrs. Creighton. "Well, not as much of a fucking piece of shit as you are," retorted Mr. Creighton. "Me? You're the one who screwed my oldest girl-friend," shouted the wife. "I wouldn't ever have screwed her if you hadn't been such a bitch," fumed the husband. And so, it continued. Amid all of this cruelty, I felt quite exhausted and secretly wished that I had never agreed to meet with these increasingly vitriolic people. As the sessions unfolded, the verbal cruelty—perhaps quite understandable—became more and more vicious, and at one point, the couple even began to make grotesque comments about the specificities of one another's genitalia, something that, I must confess, I had never encountered in clinical practice previously.

As our work progressed, I came to realise that Mrs. Creighton experienced a deep sense of psychological injury, because she simply could not understand why her husband had cheated on her after so many years of seemingly loyal marriage. The wife cried, "I just don't get it. Our kids are all doing well. We've made a good life together. I just threw you an amazing birthday party. You seemed to like it. And then I find out about this affair. I think you must be crazy."

Mr. Creighton looked deeply ashamed, and he simply retorted, "I agree with everything you're saying. We did have … *do* have … a good life. I'm not sure why I fucked your friend. Perhaps I *am* crazy."

Listening to this couple, I found myself almost overwhelmed by all of the material: powerful emotions, sadistic insults, and non-stop verbal duelling. But amid all of this brouhaha, I found myself deeply curious as to why the extramarital affair had exploded at precisely this particular point in time, rather than six months previously or, indeed, three years hence. Did the timing of the marital explosion have a secret meaning?

I also found myself quite struck that Mrs. Creighton had introduced the "amazing birthday party" into the conversation, and I became quite intrigued that a man should cheat on his spouse after she had taken so much time and trouble to organise a lavish celebration.

I enquired about the birthday party, whereupon Mr. Creighton explained, "No one has ever done something so beautiful for me. Everything about that evening was just perfect." Mrs. Creighton spewed venom, "So, is that how you treat someone who gives you a perfect night? You screw my friend as a way of saying 'thank you'? You're a goddamn fucking son of a bitch."

Clearly, Mrs. Creighton wanted to evacuate further angry and injured feelings, but I sensed that, at this point, we needed insight, rather than simple catharsis. I still wished to know about the birthday, especially *which* birthday the husband had just celebrated, and so I asked Mr. Creighton his age at the time of the party.

> "I had just turned forty-six."
> "Forty-six?" I underscored.
> "Yes, forty-six."

I soon discovered that Mrs. Creighton had never thrown a special birthday party for her husband previously, and so I wondered why she had made such a fuss over her husband's forty-*sixth* birthday, rather than his fortieth or even forty-*fifth* birthdays, which would be the more traditional decadal or half-decadal opportunities for such large celebrations. "I don't know," she confessed. "But I felt that he just needed a bit of a boost at forty-six."

My curiosity grew even more intense about the possible secret, unconscious meaning of a wife sensing that her husband needed a "boost" at forty-six years of age, as opposed to any other time. And so, I looked at Mr. Creighton with great seriousness and I asked, "Can you recall anything about your father's life when *he* turned forty-six?" Mr. Creighton stared at me as though I had gone insane and then asked me why that might be of any relevance at all. Undaunted, I repeated my question with seriousness, and then Mr. Creighton began to do the maths.

"Let's see, my father was thirty-four when I was born, so I must have been twelve when he turned forty-six. Yes, that's right. Okay, that was 1981."

At this point, Mr. Creighton's face turned ashen and his jaw dropped. Both Mrs. Creighton and I looked at him with deep concern.

"Holy Mother of God! 1981 … that was the year that my father had a nervous breakdown and had to go into a private psychiatric hospital—our local loony bin. They gave him electric shocks. And he came out pretty shredded. And shortly after that, my mother's cancer came on."

Upon hearing this, *Mrs.* Creighton went ashen and exclaimed to her husband, "You *never* told me that your father had been in a mental hospital."

"Didn't I?" shrugged Mr. Creighton. "Perhaps I thought it wasn't really important."

Although I cannot do justice to the full complexity and richness of this psychotherapy session, I can report that I then began to explore whether the psychiatric breakdown of Mr. Creighton's father (at the age of forty-six) and the subsequent cancer of Mr. Creighton's mother might have had any influence upon Mr. Creighton's marital infidelity at the time of his own forty-sixth birthday. At first, both members of the couple thought this mere coincidence, but as we considered these new biographical revelations more fully, both Mr. Creighton and Mrs. Creighton could appreciate that Mr. Creighton might have grown up fully fearful that when he turned the same dangerous age of forty-six as his father had done that he, too, would have a breakdown and that his wife might become ill with carcinoma; and so, in an effort to take some unconscious control of these fearfully antici- pated traumata, he managed to orchestrate the "breakdown" all by himself, by going "crazy", by cheating on his wife, and by nearly causing his wife's death from psychological mortification.

Although I cannot elaborate upon all the twists and turns of our very intricate conversations, I can report that my seemingly odd question about "which birthday" ultimately helped us to unmask a great deal of crucially traumatic biographical data that Mr. Creighton had dismissed, initially, as irrelevant—so much so that his wife had not known about this—but which, I propose, eventually helped us all to understand the "breakdown" in the marriage at that precise moment in the life cycle.

Through my curiosity about the seemingly insignificant detail of *which* birthday Mr. Creighton had just marked, this enervating session, which began with screams and shouts and insults, became transformed into a deeply emotionally and intellectually bracing mystery story, which helped to unravel some of the very sadistic dynamics which unfolded between this couple. Of course, in this context, I do not have the opportunity to speak about the traumas in *Mrs.* Creighton's history which gradually emerged, and which also contributed to the timing of Mr. Creighton's extramarital "break- down", but those, too, became part of an increasingly compelling, detailed and, ultimately, quite helpful set of psychotherapeutic conversations which, rather than pulverising me, kept me very engaged and very alert.

Hate in the Countertransference

As I indicated in the opening pages of this book, most of our patients treat us with dignity, respect, appreciation, and gratitude, especially as psycho- therapy progresses successfully over time. Indeed, our likeable patients become even more likeable as they work hard to process their vulnerabili- ties and their cruelties and move beyond them. But some patients will arrive at our offices in a much more ill state, and they will often relate to us in a debilitating, aggressive manner by screaming, shouting, menacing, or verbalising Nazi-style death threats. In view of this, even the most healthy, well-analysed, and loving psychotherapist can sometimes experience hatred towards his or her patients.

In his private correspondence, never intended for publication during his lifetime, Professor Sigmund Freud (1928a) revealed to his Hungarian colleague, Dr. István Hollós, that he often detested his more ill patients, noting, "Ich gestand mir endlich, es komme daher, dass ich diese Kranken nicht liebe, dass ich mich über sie ärgere, sie so fern von mir und allem Menschlichen empfinde" ["Finally I confessed to myself that I do not like these sick people, that I am angry at them to feel them so far from me and all that is human" (Freud, 1928b, p. 537)]. Although such a statement does not convey the more loving and compassionate and understanding aspects of Freud's character, it certainly reveals an honest component.

Most readers of this book will appreciate that, approximately twenty years after Sigmund Freud spoke of his hatred towards ill patients, Donald Winnicott (1949) penned a stellar paper entitled "Hate in the Counter-Transference", explaining that many patients can be objectively hateful and that, in consequence, it would be perfectly normal for the clinician to harbour angry or resentful feelings, just as even the most loving, ordinary mother will experience hateful emotions towards her newborn baby for waking her up in the middle of the night, demanding a delicious meal of milk at such an inconvenient time!

Next to Sigmund Freud's exposition of the talking cure (Breuer and Freud, 1895a; Freud, 1895c) and his path-breaking philosophy of the unconscious (Freud, 1900a), I cannot think of a more important publication in all of psychoanalytical history than Winnicott's tiny, but potent, essay on "Hate in the Counter-Transference", and I urge all psychotherapeutic workers to keep a copy of this classic text in our consulting rooms. This paper has influenced me so much that I have even written several historico-biographical articles and chapters about Winnicott's essay (Kahr, 2011b, 2015a), as well as a forthcoming book on the topic (Kahr, 2019b).

Winnicott has encouraged us to share our occasional feelings of counter-transferential hatred *not* with our patients but, rather, with our own psychotherapists or psychoanalysts and, also, with our colleagues. Only by speaking about our ill and demanding patients in a safe, adult space, can we begin to process some of the many toxic feelings that we carry as a result of undertaking such challenging, vexing clinical work.

Dr. Wilfred Bion, the great British psychoanalyst, used to tell his students that, when treating a very disturbed patient, one has only two choices: the psychotherapist can either terminate the treatment, or, alternatively, he or she can *write* about it (MacCarthy, 2002a). In many respects, both Winnicott and Bion encouraged their colleagues to find some way of verbalising (in spoken words or in written texts) the very powerful affects which patients can project onto us or into us. And by doing so, we will have the opportunity to neutralise some of the emotional weightiness and some of the burn-out potential with which we struggle.

Delightful, Honourable People

It pleases me to report that I experience the vast majority of the men and women who come to work with me as truly wonderful people.

Although these individuals will often reveal the ugliest, cruellest, and most self-destructive sides of their characters, they do so for the primary purpose of understanding and working through those areas of difficulty and vulnerability. If not, they would never have come to psychotherapy in the first place and most of them certainly would not have remained in treatment for years and years and years.

As time progresses, I find my likeable patients to be even *more* likeable because, when we develop a solid therapeutic alliance, the patients begin to improve, sometimes dramatically so, and mental health always increases one's conviviality as a human being.

At the outset, the young psychotherapist struggles to really *enjoy* his or her patients. When we first establish ourselves in practice, we worry quite considerably: Will I be any good at this difficult work? Will any of my colleagues send me patients? Will I be able to help anybody? Will I be sued by an angry patient? Will I remember the name of my patient's second cousin, or the name of his or her third puppy dog, or that of the fourth grandchild? Most newly qualified psychotherapeutic clinicians drown in a sea of quite understandable anxiety.

Our greatest fear, however, might well be that we have not yet seen a single long-term psychotherapeutic treatment through successfully, from start to finish, and so we really do not know from direct, first-hand experience whether we can actually *cure* a patient substantially. My first psychotherapy patient—a hospitalised individual suffering from a lifetime of schizophrenia—spent three years in treatment with me, during which time he made great strides and became much less hallucinated and deluded (Kahr, 2012). Although three years might seem a long time to some, it cannot be described as a full, open-ended analysis. Not long thereafter, I began to work with another patient, who remained in treatment uninterruptedly for ten years. It took a whole decade of sustained work to see this person through successfully, and thank goodness I did, both for his sake and, also, for mine, because up until that point, I had never facilitated a *truly* long-term piece of psychological work from beginning to end.

The late Dr. John Klauber, a former President of the British Psycho-Analytical Society, and the late Dr. John Sutherland, once Medical Director of the Tavistock Clinic in London, used to tell their younger colleagues that it really takes ten years after qualification to feel that one can truly call oneself a psychoanalyst (MacCarthy, 2002b), and I must admit that I tend to agree. Only after we have seen our first generation of patients through to a satisfactory completion will we feel truly, organically, authentically proud of ourselves and of our professional work. And once we have achieved this state of mind, the work becomes more and more rewarding and the potentiality to experience the best of our patients (while also tolerating the worst) becomes more highly developed than ever before.

Having now seen several generations of patients through the long process of psychoanalytical psychotherapy and intensive psychoanalysis, I can happily report that, with each passing year, I feel more and more privileged to have made an impact—often quite a large one—on the quality of life experienced by these people and their families. Sometimes, I have helped them to diminish their levels of depression and anxiety; sometimes, I have saved them from suicide and self-destruction; and sometimes, I have watched them use their newfound strength to embark upon activities which have made the world a better place. Although patients can, at times, be persecutory, they can also become the greatest source of pleasure and privilege in our professional lives and, consequently, we feel a lifelong sense of protection towards them and, also, gratitude.

For those of us who survive the training, who launch ourselves into practice with the support and friendship of warm colleagues and nourishing mentors, and who manage to create enough rich opportunities and engagements with patients and with projects during the first decade of psychological work, we now have a secure base and an experience of prospering which will allow us to flourish even more, should we have an appetite to do so.

PART III

Thriving Beyond the Consulting Room

CHAPTER ELEVEN

Nourishing Fledgling Colleagues

Enlivening the Classroom

I have never understood that hackneyed aphorism, "Those who can, do; those who can't, teach."

Perhaps in certain fields of endeavour, this observation might well apply. I suspect that Dame Judi Dench must be far too busy performing on stage or screen to teach a weekly class on dramatic technique; and it may well be the case that the person ultimately chosen to do so might not have earned a professional acting fee for quite some time. But in the mental health profession, one cannot be a good teacher, let alone a *great* teacher, unless one has also practised for a long while and unless one possesses a considerable scholarly grasp of the psychological literature. I can think of no greater honour than to be able to contribute to the training of the next generation. But, in order to do so, one must be both a solid, experienced practitioner as well as a person able to navigate the classroom with ease.

How does one become a teacher of trainee psychotherapists or of allied mental health workers? There might be many routes into a teaching career. In most instances, instructors of the next generation of students will be hand-picked, having already proved themselves to the more senior generation.

I conducted my very first teaching seminar at the ridiculously young age of nineteen years, as an undergraduate student. Having entered university with an already profound passion for the work of Sigmund Freud, I attended the third-year lectures on psychopathology, somewhat precociously, during the first term of my first year. Having done so, the instructor knew of my interest in Freud and kindly encouraged my fledgling efforts. Thus, when, during the following year, this lecturer had to leave the country for a week to attend a professional conference, he asked me whether I would substitute for him and offer a basic lecture on Freud's theories of schizophrenia. Rashly, I agreed to this preposterous suggestion—one which, I suspect, would not be permitted today.

I spent days and days and days preparing my début lecture, and although I had no clinical experience of working with psychosis at that time, I did know how to read extensively, and I presented a full and, hopefully, clear account of Freud's theories on schizophrenia, supplemented by a summary of the empirical psychological research conducted after World War II, which buttressed his prescient theories of paranoia. I must have spoken with reasonable coherence, because no one complained; and even though some of my fellow undergraduates might have muttered, "Why the hell is *this* guy lecturing us?", I did receive some kindly approbation and thus survived my first experience of teaching in a university classroom.

Although I would have described myself as a quietly spoken chap who felt far more comfortable in the library stacks than anywhere else, I did seem to come to life behind a lectern, as I felt increasingly at home with academic data; and so, teaching came rather naturally to me.

I appreciate that most people will not have begun their teaching careers at nineteen years of age, substituting for an absent lecturer; indeed, there may be other ways—*better* ways—to test the pedagogical waters. Many clinical trainings often struggle to find good people to deliver lectures, in part because most psychotherapy institutions offer teaching in the evenings, and many senior practitioners, fatigued from a long day in the consulting room, do not rush to offer their services after hours. For years and years, I taught Freud seminars—usually at 8.30 p.m.—to a number of different psychotherapy training programmes, and I always enjoyed doing so. But after a while, I simply had to stop as I realised that I wanted to preserve my evenings more and more for precious family time, and that it made absolutely no sense to work all day *and* all night as well! Thus, my "retirement" from weekly Freud seminars created a space for some newbies who have greater flexibility of time.

I recommend that those freshly qualified psychotherapists keen to develop a teaching strand should keep in close contact with their training organisations—especially the chairperson of the education committee or training committee—to enquire whether, and when, a teaching vacancy might emerge. Those who have graduated from more newly established training institutions without a large membership body may well find themselves in great demand sooner rather than later.

But we need not put ourselves in the passive position of waiting for a professor to hire us as a one-off substitute, nor must we pray for the early retirement or death of a senior colleague who has taught the Freud seminars for the last hundred years. Instead, we should use our own initiative to create new teaching opportunities which had never previously existed.

As I indicated, during my early years as a student of psychology, I established the Oxford Psycho-Analytical Forum, hosting one, sometimes two, visiting speakers per week at the university. But in view of the fact that no one taught an introductory course on psychoanalytical theory in Oxford at that time, I realised that I had an opportunity to offer a private twenty-week seminar, for which I charged a ridiculously low fee: if memory serves me correctly, I believe I requested only fifty pence per lecture from each attendee! I advertised these meetings among fellow students, simply by pinning a photocopied sheet of paper to a few noticeboards, and in no time at all I had a full classroom of eager students and, also, faculty members from the humanities departments keen to learn more about Freud, and I used the small amount of money that I earned to pay the travel expenses of the grown-up lecturers such as Dr. John Bowlby, who came from London and elsewhere to deliver their talks at the larger, university-wide events which I had arranged.

I appreciate that not everyone will enjoy teaching and not everyone will perform in a lively manner in the classroom. But if we do have an appetite to explore our pedagogical capacities, I recommend teaching highly, for a number of reasons. The classroom provides us with a real opportunity to speak from the depths of the diaphragm, projecting our voices loudly and clearly. My many years of teaching became my apprenticeship for delivering large lectures at international mental health congresses in years to come.

But teaching helps us to develop not only a full voice, it also offers us the opportunity to clarify our thoughts while educating young, impressionable minds. Virtually every paper that I have published and every book that

I have written began life as a series of more informal seminars, presented to trainees. Thus, teaching helps us to sharpen our capacity to make an argument and to substantiate it with care and conviction and evidence.

Working with young trainees not only provides us with the opportunity to hone our intellectual arguments and to develop our sense of authority. Let us not forget that our students will often become important sources of referral in due time, because these trainees know our academic and clinical worth only too well. They have a unique grasp of our reliability, our erudition, our clarity, our compassion, and our experience; hence, they often have no hesitation in recommending patients to us for psychotherapeutic consultations.

On Being a Clinical Supervisor

Although I began to teach at the age of nineteen years, it may be a relief to know that I did not begin offering formal clinical supervision until I had reached the age of thirty. In order to teach, one must have a reasonable base of knowledge, but in order to supervise, one must have many years of clinical experience under one's belt.

Supervision can be either an exhausting experience or an enhancing one, and much will depend on the quality of our supervisees. Over the years, I have worked with some very mediocre students who, I regret to say, undertook the bare minimum of work, rather than the maximum, in spite of my deep encouragement. Very few, if any, of these one-time trainees have progressed to stellar careers in mental health. I have also supervised a small number of rather narcissistic students who believed that they knew far more about psychoanalysis than even Sigmund Freud. Once again, these trainees—happily few in number—failed to make a mark in the field. Being mediocre or grandiose will generally not have favourable consequences, and future trainees might wish to take note. Certainly, I have never, ever referred a patient to a mediocre or grandiose supervisee after qualification.

Fortunately, most supervisees have proved to be great sources of professional delight. Recently, I have had the pleasure of working with one young woman, "Dahlia", who can only be described as truly impressive. She has never arrived one microsecond late for her weekly supervisory session, nor has she ever missed an appointment. Dahlia always comes fully prepared with detailed, typed copies of her session notes, which we discuss in great detail. She invariably asks interesting and thought-provoking questions, and she always listens carefully to the answers. And Dahlia seems to read every single book or article that I recommend—and I certainly recommend a lot of reading! Such a person—an ideal supervisee by anyone's reckoning—brings one great satisfaction. I feel extremely proud and pleased that by shepherding such promising young colleagues, I will have helped to shape the next generation, ensuring that once I retire and then die there will be some good people in place to keep our profession thriving on solid ground.

Practising the art of clinical supervision brings much richness to the psychotherapeutic worker. Not only do we enjoy the honorary parental status of having "sons" and "daughters" who can carry on the family tradition, but by providing supervision we also have the opportunity to learn so much more about basic psychopathology. At the moment, I have the honour of supervising five junior colleagues. One of these trainees works with a patient undergoing police investigations for having downloaded child pornography; another student treats a compulsive gambler; yet another supervisee seeks help in working with a patient suffering from a serious brain tumour; the fourth candidate visits me each week to discuss a suicidal adolescent; and the final trainee in this quintet comes to present the case of a young man who had to endure extreme sexual traumatisation during early childhood. Thus, by supervising, I not only have an opportunity to refine my own clinical theories and to review my own recommendations to students, but I also have the tremendous benefit of learning more about a wide range of interesting and challenging cases in great detail, thus supplementing and expanding my knowledge of the many manifestations of human psychopathology.

When we forge a good relationship with a talented supervisee, these young protégés will become our greatest champions, because they will often sing our praises to their contemporaries. I know that so many of my patients have come to me through the recommendation of various colleagues of my supervisees.

A talented student can often provide a fifty-minute oasis of respite during the course of a long clinical day. Although one must always comport oneself with maximal professionalism when working with supervisees, one can, if needs be, "let one's hair down" a little bit; indeed, we can allow ourselves to be somewhat more didactic or humorous or playful or self-revelatory with a supervisee than with a patient. So, if I wish to pass on a snippet of advice that I had received from Dr. Hanna Segal, I will do so happily; and if I wish to relate a story about what I learned during my tea with Dr. John Bowlby,

I do not hesitate. With a patient, however, one tries very hard to remain focused exclusively on that person and to refrain from telling stories, however relevant they might be. But with a supervisee, one can have the freedom of being a teacher, and that comes as a great relief.

In the early days of our clinical practice, each and every supervisee will be a welcome addition to our roster. And for those who have just begun to offer supervision or who may be contemplating doing so, I recommend that we should welcome all potential supervisees into our practices with gusto. But as we age, we have the right to become more discriminating. Nowadays, I will work *only* with highly motivated students who can demonstrate their passion for becoming the very best of psychotherapists. The more narcissistic, entitled trainees will often ring up a busy senior practitioner and will begin the conversation thus: "Oh, hi, Brett, I *really* want to see you for supervision, but I can only come on Thursdays at 1.30 p.m., and I cannot pay more than such-and-such an amount." By contrast, the more impressive students will ring up and will ask, "If there is *any* possibility at all that you might be able to make a space for me, I would be so grateful. I will happily readjust my schedule to suit whatever time you might have." Needless to say, if one wishes to engage a senior person as a supervisor and potential lifelong mentor, one needs the psychological finesse, if not the heartfelt charm, to help forge a relationship with a busy, overstretched person!

I know from my own experience as a supervisee how much one can learn from a very savvy, frank, long-in-the-tooth supervisor. Indeed, I stayed in regular weekly supervision with my most formidable supervisor for years and years and years, long after qualification, as this senior psychoanalytical practitioner really underpinned my capabilities in the consulting room in ways that I had never anticipated.

One should be honoured to be chosen as a supervisor for a young trainee or for a junior colleague. By working with a supervisee, one has the precious opportunity to help keep the profession safe by monitoring the development of a younger psychotherapist and by passing along one's own hard-earned "psychological D.N.A.". For those increasingly experienced psychotherapists who wish to enrich their professional lives, please do embrace the prospect of becoming a supervisor wholeheartedly.

When I began to work with trainees, my contemporaries and I became supervisors simply by virtue of being older than our students. Nowadays, many organisations have begun to offer special training courses and qualification programmes for prospective supervisors. Never having studied the art of supervision formally, I cannot speak about the quality of these courses with any degree of insider knowledge, but for those who might be some-what trepidatious about embarking upon this aspect of professional work, perhaps a diploma in clinical supervision could be of great value.

A Little Drink After Work

As an increasingly senior psychotherapist, one has the opportunity to help young students and junior colleagues not only in the classroom and during the supervision session but, also, in more informal ways, through ordinary decency. I take great delight in assisting young, aspiring practitioners when-ever I can, and this proves very satisfying.

I realised that I had begun to age when I stopped rushing to interview all the "tribal elders" in the psychological profession, and when young students and trainees started to write to me, enquiring whether I might read their newly written paper; whether I might supply them with a letter of recom-mendation; whether I might meet with them to discuss their training possi-bilities; whether I might consent to an interview as part of their dissertation, and so on. Initially, I felt very honoured that the next generation had begun to turn to me in this way, and I experienced a parental sense of privilege and strove to respond to all of these requests and queries.

Over time, however, I struggled to find space to meet with all the students who wished to have a "one-off" session with me, simply because I do not have regular protected time in which to do so. I have now reached a stage in my career where I prioritise appointments for my patients—a full-time pursuit—supplemented by a small number of vacancies for clinical supervisees. Regrettably, I no longer have *regular* gaps in which I can meet with young trainees in order to discuss their questions and projects and concerns.

So, several years ago, I began to carve out an hour-long space, only once per month, in the early evening, after work, specifically for the encourage-ment of young colleagues, and I must confess that I really enjoy meeting these students over a small glass of wine. This has now become almost a ritual and, also, a delight. If students wish to pop by for a one-off meeting, and if they might be happy to wait for that occasional space to become avail-able, I greet them with pleasure.

Last month, I had an after-work drink with a kindly young psycho-therapy trainee who wished to interview me for her doctoral dissertation, which I found very engaging, not least as this woman knew far more about that particular subject than I did. I would like to think, however, that I offered her some very helpful practical assistance as to the best way to structure her argument.

The month before that, I met up with an old student whom I had the pleasure of instructing some twenty years previously, when I taught psychology to trainee physicians at the Royal Free Hospital Medical School in the University of London. This man, who had distinguished himself as a most compassionate young medical student, eventually qualified as a psychiatrist and has since become a specialist in old age psychiatry. Although we have remained in contact from time to time across the years, this gentleman recently approached me in order to discuss his plan to train in psychoanalysis. We could not have had a more pleasurable conversation as he told me a very great deal about the current state of geriatric psychiatric service provision and its challenges and answered all my questions about the future of research into dementia. I, in turn, offered encouragement by providing my blunt estimation of all the different training programmes in London. Before we parted, my former medical student, now a senior Consultant Psychiatrist in his own right, told me that he remembered quite a lot of what I had taught him two decades previously. He even quoted some cases that I had described. Apparently, my teaching had had a lingering impact, which I certainly could not have imagined at the time.

And the month before that, I had an after-work drink and career consultation with a brilliant young woman from Iran, who has moved to London in order to undertake her psychoanalytical training, as her own country offers virtually no opportunity to do so. I learned a great deal about the nature of Iranian culture and its psychological sequelae and I listened attentively to this woman's thoughts on why Iran has remained so resistant to psychotherapeutic ideas. Before we parted, this young colleague reached into her handbag and produced a copy of a small book covered in squiggly lettering, which I certainly could not decipher. "What book is this?" I asked. "It's *your* book, Brett, *Life Lessons from Freud*, translated into Farsi." She then handed me this new Persian translation of my little book on Freud (Kahr, 2013a), already in its second printing in Iran (Kahr, 2017b), as a present. I had no idea that anyone had translated my book into Farsi as the British publishers had not mentioned this to me, and so it came as a great surprise and thrill to discover that my text on Freud for curious intellectuals had begun to penetrate a faraway land.

In view of my long, long clinical days, and my ageing body, it would be all too easy to avoid meeting up with these young people. But I find that I benefit hugely from such enlivening and, often, unpredictable encounters, which enrich me in so many ways. I also wish to repay the tremendous debt of gratitude that I have towards all the senior people who took the time to meet with me during my twenties and thirties and who offered essential encouragement and counsel.

CHAPTER TWELVE

Public Lectures and Conferences

My Very First Paper

As I indicated previously, I delivered my first classroom lecture on Sigmund Freud's theories of psychosis at the age of nineteen, owing to my instructor's absence overseas. This ridiculously premature experience both emboldened and empowered me to begin speaking publicly—no easy task for an essentially shy and quietly spoken young person who regards himself as far more of an introvert than an extravert. But this admittedly unusual opportunity certainly opened up a whole canvas of new possibilities.

Not long thereafter, I spied a poster, pinned to the noticeboard at my university, advertising a "Call for Papers" for the "Sixteenth Annual Undergraduate Psychology Conference" to be held at the State University College of New York at Plattsburgh. At that point in time, I had never before encountered the phrase "Call for Papers", nor did I know that undergraduates had their own conferences, nor had I ever heard of Plattsburgh, located in upstate New York, closer in fact, to the Canadian border than to Manhattan!

With supreme naïveté, I wrote an abstract about my fledgling undergraduate research project on the cognitive processes of adults with autism, and I posted it to the unknown conference organisers in Plattsburgh. I then thought no more about this but, some weeks later, a letter arrived, informing me that the committee had accepted my abstract and would be very happy for me to fly to Plattsburgh—at my own expense—to present a thirty-minute summary of my research.

This all happened so long ago that, in the mists of time, I cannot even recall my reaction upon having received this letter, nor, even, quite how I managed to get to Plattsburgh, but somehow, through planes and trains and buses, I arrived at this unusual location.

I can, however, visualise myself sitting in a small classroom in the Department of Psychology at Plattsburgh, waiting to deliver my little presentation. Indeed, I have a clear memory of sharing the panel with a young American lad, who presented a potentially riveting but, ultimately, disappointing paper on the psychology of musicians. This fellow undergraduate had undertaken a study of a group of classical instrumentalists, exploring what psychological factors had led some to become violinists as opposed to trombonists, and so forth. As a pianist in my own right, I found the topic fascinating, but, alas, the young psychology researcher shed little light on the deeper, biographical reasons why one aspiring musician gravitates towards the cello and another towards the oboe. Nonetheless, I found this chap's talk very lively and his topic most interesting, and I admired his willingness to expose his research in front of an audience of contemporaries and, also, some Plattsburgh professors.

After applauding this young man, I rose from my seat and then began to share my own work on autism. I believe that I spoke without notes, having already internalised my research findings reasonably well. Instead, I simply told a story about the exceptional memory abilities of an older autistic man—an "idiot savant"—knowing that I had to keep my audience members intrigued. Although this little foray into the field of experimental psychopathology and autism studies remains unpublished, the experience of presenting my research findings to colleagues in the safe setting of an undergraduate psychology conference in the northernmost region of New York State helped me to own my voice more fully.

Upon my return home, I felt sufficiently fortified, and I then applied to present papers at other undergraduate psychology conferences … and did so. In retrospect, it amazes me that I even knew about some of these conferences, because back then, we had no internet and thus, one could not google "Undergraduate Psychology Conferences". The noticeboard in my university department became one of my new best friends. Unlike most of my fellow psychology students, I scoured the posters tacked to the noticeboard carefully—virtually every day in fact—and I jotted down details of all the relevant conferences, and I made it my business to attend as many as I could.

In my free time, I would prepare my draft conference papers on a small typewriter, and then I would stand alone in my tiny room in the halls of residence and practise delivering my speech out loud. I enjoyed these experiences and I soon became sufficiently adept, and by the age of twenty-one I had already delivered quite a number of papers—an indispensable preparation for my career in teaching and public lecturing and, ultimately, in mental health broadcasting. Verbal fluency does not appear by magic!

At some point, we must all risk leaving our comfort zone and dare to speak in Plattsburgh! Certainly, I remain very pleased to have done so.

The Length of the Applause

It may be that many people will stop reading my book at this point, petrified at the prospect of having to deliver a conference paper or an invited lecture to a group of colleagues or, indeed, to the general public. Certainly, psycho-therapeutic training programmes do not require their students to talk in front of audiences. Perhaps we *should* provide our trainees with seminars on "How to Speak in Public" alongside those on "Introduction to Freud" and "Schizophrenia for Beginners".

But for colleagues with even a tiny appetite to talk in a louder voice, I strongly recommend pursuing a "sideline" by speaking to different groups of people.

Please do not forget that the practising psychotherapist will spend the vast majority of his or her professional career sitting quietly in a chair, *often in utter silence*, and only on rare occasions will we have the opportunity to express our thoughts out loud to patients, because we always ensure that they will do most of the talking! In view of this necessary restriction of our voice during consulting hours, the psychotherapist *needs* to be heard and must have multiple opportunities outside the office in which to develop ideas and theories.

For those of us who wish to conquer our neurotic inhibitionism (which we discussed in Chapter 9), lecturing in public offers many rewards to the more outward-facing clinician. Providing talks to various institutions, or accepting invitations from different organisations, permits us to clarify and sharpen our ideas quite profoundly. Nothing focuses the mind better than having a public deadline.

Moreover, sharing our work with fellow mental health practitioners offers us not only wonderful opportunities for feedback and further professional development but, also, provides us with necessary "public supervision". In other words, if we present a piece of clinical material from a session to an audience of colleagues, and if we should happen to offer something uninspiring or, indeed, downright off-base, we can rest assured that at least one member of the audience will offer us immediate supervision during the question-and-answer period and thus keep us on our toes!

In fact, simply by listening to the length of the applause after a talk, one knows precisely one's worth as a psychotherapist. As any actor or singer will tell you, the amount of applause varies considerably from performance to performance, and from audience to audience. Theatre professionals know from the duration and the intensity of the clapping precisely how much they have touched their listeners. It may be that during the final bows of the matinee performance of a play, the applause will have lasted for fifty-five seconds. But after the evening performance, the applause will have continued for as long as *sixty*-five seconds. To a thespian, that ten-second difference matters hugely. I have often heard experienced actors pontificate about what they did, or did not do, during the evening performance which made their work so much more electric.

Although the applause for most psychotherapeutic talks lasts a far shorter period of time, since most of us do not have the capacity to enrapture our audiences, we will, nevertheless, acquire a sense as to whether we actually "reached" our colleagues and "touched" them with our insights, or whether we might need to do a bit more homework. So, by exposing ourselves in public and by listening carefully to the response, we receive an immense amount of precious data which will help us to know which projects we ought to pursue and which ones we might wish to park for the time being.

But, above all, presenting in public permits us to develop our incipient ideas into full-blown papers, which can then be published, and it also enhances our reputation and, also, our referral stream. Speaking at conferences and other public gatherings affords such a multiplicity of benefits.

Assuming that one wishes to develop one's work as a presenter at conferences and at public lectures, how, then, do we nurture such a professional pathway?

I started off by reading the posters on noticeboards. But nowadays, virtually no institution maintains an old-fashioned noticeboard any more, and certainly, almost no organisations send out posters through the Royal Mail or through the United States Postal Service. Today, in the twenty-first century, psychotherapists learn about conferences either through word of mouth or by email.

For starters, one must work very hard to sign up to as many different psychological mailing lists as possible. As a graduate of a particular psychotherapy training and as a registrant of one or more of the overarching professional bodies, one will, in all likelihood, receive e-communications automatically, many of which will advertise forthcoming conferences. Our organisations invariably invite those with a sturdy "track record" to deliver the keynote addresses, but the conference organising committee will, from time to time, seek out other colleagues, perhaps less well known at the present time, who might be able to submit an abstract.

I strongly encourage younger colleagues to embrace such opportunities with zest. Often, senior members of the psychotherapy profession will be too tired from working with patients to take the time and the trouble to prepare an abstract for a conference paper, so in my experience, it will often be quite possible for neophytes to have an abstract accepted for presentation. Also, because many of us, especially in a relatively small country such as the United Kingdom, have become a little bored by the same old people presenting at every conference, we often welcome fresh ideas from newcomers with great pleasure.

While writing this chapter, I received an email from the British Psychoanalytic Council—the "B.P.C."—the United Kingdom's leading registration body for psychoanalytically trained mental health professionals. In anticipation of its conference on innovation in practice, the B.P.C. issued a "Call out": "*We are looking for examples of real innovation in our profession—whether it's working with a group in society that have not traditionally accessed psychoanalytic / psychodynamic psychotherapy or whether it is an example of using psychoanalytic theory to support the development of better public/third sector services, we want to hear from you!*" (British Psychoanalytic Council, 2018). I must confess that I find myself very struck by the friendly, welcoming tone of this "Call out", and if I had received such an email at the start of my career and believed that I had something relevant to offer, I would have embraced such an opportunity to submit a proposal for a conference presentation with enthusiasm.

Once one has given a paper here and a paper there, colleagues will start to remember one's name and areas of specialisation. I have often served on conference planning committees, and on every single occasion, my comrades and I have struggled to know whom we should invite as speakers. Inevitably, someone will begin the conversation, "Let's ask Dr. Smith," whereupon someone else will retort, "Oh, he's so overexposed, I've heard him a thousand times." Someone else will then suggest, "Well, what about Dr. Jones? I think she's terrific," whereupon another colleague will respond, "She's my analyst, and I think it would be a clash of interests to have her at this conference." Eventually, yet another member of the committee will announce, "I attended a seminar on this topic a short while ago, and I heard a very nice paper by a young chap whose name I cannot recall." Suddenly, the committee becomes very excited at the prospect of hearing from a newbie, and everyone encourages this colleague to trawl through her papers in order to find the name of that fresh prospect.

Careers in public lecturing really *do* begin to flourish in precisely this manner.

Addressing the United Nations

At the outset of a career in psychotherapy, one generally begins by delivering talks to groups of colleagues. As we know, I started out speaking to my fellow undergraduates, and from there I progressed to presenting papers at conferences for other qualified mental health workers.

Eventually, I received an invitation to address a gathering of members of the general public, albeit a very, very tiny group.

Quite early in my career, one of the administrative secretaries at the Tavistock Clinic, with whom I had developed a friendly relationship, told me, in a private moment, that she hosts a book group for women in Golders Green in North London. Apparently, she and several of her neighbours would meet on a monthly basis to discuss newly published novels. Recently, these women had held a discussion about a book which featured a psychologist, and the members wished to learn more about the nitty-gritty of daily clinical life. Consequently, the secretary asked me whether I would be prepared to give a very basic talk to this group of women one Sunday evening. Although the prospect of foregoing precious weekend time to deliver a fairly simple presentation on "Psychotherapy 101" did not thrill me, I had already developed a warm and grateful affection for this good-hearted secretary, and so I accepted her very kind invitation. In preparation for this event, I wrote up several pages of detailed notes, which formed the basis of my talk, and I then journeyed across town to meet with the North London Women's Jewish Book Club, knowing in advance that I would receive coffee and cake, but no fee whatsoever.

Upon arrival, the secretary greeted me sweetly, and then apologised that, due to the recent outbreak of influenza, several of her colleagues could not attend. As I entered the sitting room, I saw only one other person. And so, for the next hour-and-a-half, I spoke about the practice of psychotherapy to my secretary and to one of her female chums.

The two women treated me delightfully and kept plying me with refreshments. My secretary's friend even asked me whether I had a girl-friend because she thought that, if not, I might enjoy being fixed up with *her* daughter!

I very much doubt that this simple talk to an audience of two middle-aged residents of Golders Green actually sharpened my ideas on the nature of the psychotherapeutic process, nor did this opportunity necessarily foster my presenting skills. In fact, as I had a girlfriend, I could not even take up the kindly offer of a potential romantic introduction. But, in retrospect, it pleases me that I launched my career of addressing the "general public" in such a welcoming setting.

From there I progressed to larger and, perhaps, more impactful audiences. Over time, I have had the privilege of speaking before many of the United Kingdom's most interesting cultural institutions, ranging from the British Academy of Film and Television Arts (B.A.F.T.A.), Glyndebourne Opera, the Science Museum, and Tate Modern, to the Royal Academy of Dramatic Art, the Royal Academy of Music, the Royal Courts of Justice, and the Royal Opera House, not to mention the House of Commons and the House of Lords. In having done so, I have met some extremely interesting people who have wished to learn more about psychology and mental health, and I hope that, on those occasions, I comported myself as a respectable ambassador for our field. I trust, by having delivered such talks, that I have spread some good psychotherapeutic knowledge and that I have helped to de-stigmatise a profession once shrouded in mystery and secrecy, not to mention deep shame.

When I first entered this field, during the 1970s, many people regarded psychotherapy and psychoanalysis with tremendous suspicion; but nowa-days, due to the efforts of a number of outward-speaking colleagues, psy-chotherapy has become increasingly respectable, so much so that, during 2017 alone, none other than Prince William and Prince Harry, grandsons of the monarch, spoke publicly about their appreciation of psychological therapies, as did His Holiness Pope Francis, as did the Hollywood actor Brad Pitt. Psychotherapy has, at long last, become reasonably "cool". Thus, for newcomers in our profession, the future possibilities of public speaking and public outreach might well be limitless.

My dear colleague Susanna Abse, who served for many years as Chief Executive of the Tavistock Centre for Couple Relationships (later styled Tavistock Relationships), part of the Tavistock Institute of Medical Psychology, created the All-Party Parliamentary Working Group on Strengthening Couple Relationships, in which capacity she invited many mental health practitioners to address parliamentarians on psychological issues. This group continues to flourish as the All-Party Parliamentary Group for Strengthening Couple Relationships and Reducing Inter-Parental Conflict, chaired by Andrew Selous, a Member of Parliament representing South West Bedfordshire, with Tavistock Relationships serving as the group's secretariat. I regard this as a major contribution to the development of mental health achievements in the United Kingdom. Susanna Abse's visionary project has helped to educate numerous members of the British government about psychological matters (Abse, 2012, 2015, 2018; cf. Abse, 2014).

The psychoanalyst and psychotherapist Dr. Susie Orbach, a truly outstanding practitioner, has also made many blue-sky contributions (e.g., Orbach, 1999, 2016, 2018). A long-standing advocate for women's mental health and co-founder of both the Women's Therapy Centre in London and the Women's Therapy Centre Institute in Manhattan, Orbach has undertaken extensive research and public engagement over many decades, exploring the deleterious psychological consequences of the ways in which women, as well as men, harm their own bodies and minds or succumb to harm through broader cultural pressures and toxicities (e.g., Orbach, 2002, 2009). A great advocate for public well-being, she has consulted to the British government and to the World Bank on the relationship between the psyche and social development. In 2012, Orbach delivered the keynote speech to the United Nations Commission on the Status of Women at a special event in New York City on "Body Image in the Media: Using Education to Challenge Stereotypes". I only wish that I could have attended that talk in person, but I received a full report afterwards from Dr. Orbach herself and learned of the way in which she raised awareness about the dangers of a Western culture which promotes anorexia nervosa and bulimia in fashion models, as well as such perversities as the administration of Botox to five-year-old children and, also, the practice of cosmetic surgery on the breasts and genitals of females—procedures which contribute, ultimately, to women's sense of shame about their bodies (cf. Orbach, 1986).

In the wake of this talk, Orbach made links with delegates from as far afield as Indonesia, the Republic of the Sudan, and elsewhere, who shared experiences of the reality of young girls robbed of bodily safety as their cultures became increasingly infused with Western bodily hatred and consumerism. Psychoanalysts such as Susie Orbach command our deepest respect and admiration for helping to educate those in positions of international leadership about the importance of vital mental health issues.

As psychological knowledge becomes more and more impactful in the decades to come, I suspect that, before long, Buckingham Palace may host annual lectures on psychotherapy; 10 Downing Street may sponsor a Sigmund Freud Research Fellowship; and the White House might one day come to employ a team of psychoanalysts to keep its staff in good mental health. The possibilities of public lecturing for members of our profession remain limitless, and if one develops one's outreach skills now, one might well be able to enjoy a vast array of exciting opportunities in the not too distant future.

CHAPTER THIRTEEN

Daring to Research

The Humiliation of Edward Glover

Back in 1895, when Sigmund Freud wished to demonstrate that the talking cure really worked wonders in the treatment of the hysterical neuroses, he had no hesitation in writing up several case histories, which he then published in collaboration with his senior colleague, Josef Breuer, under the title *Studien über Hysterie* (Breuer and Freud, 1895a). In those days, more than one century ago, Freud knew that if he wished to excite his colleagues about this method of psychotherapy, he had only to produce a smattering of literarily engaging case studies, and, in consequence, his fellow physicians would, perhaps, be impressed.

In many respects, the single case study has always served as the veritable foundation stone of classical psychotherapy and psychoanalysis. But nowadays, in the twenty-first century, the publication of one-off case histories—though once the gold standard—has become more and more of a rarity (e.g., Kahr, 2017c). Today, if one wishes to document the efficacy of psychotherapy, one must embark upon large-scale, randomised controlled trials or follow-up studies or, indeed, upon meta-analyses of multiple empirical investigations, surveying the results of hundreds, if not thousands, of patients who have received different types of treatments (e.g., Bateman and Fonagy, 1999, 2008; Leichsenring and Rabung, 2004, 2008, 2011; Leichsenring, 2005).

Needless to say, this might be rather a daunting task for most workaday clinical psychotherapists who have enough difficulty typing up simple invoices, let alone wading through piles of complex statistics.

Back in 1992, I attended a very fancy conference in London on the role of research in psychoanalysis. Eminent speaker after eminent speaker mounted the podium and delivered impressive PowerPoint presentations—then quite a novelty—drowning us all in charts and graphs. Having trained originally as an academic psychologist, and having studied statistics for many years, I had a good familiarity with this type of approach to data, but many elderly psychoanalysts in the audience found the conference somewhat odd, if not alienating.

I shall never forget that, at one point, Dr. Anne Hayman, a very venerable London-based practitioner, who had undergone psychoanalysis from none other than Anna Freud at Maresfield Gardens, intervened during the discussion, bemused by the emphasis on large-scale statistical research. Dr. Hayman, who knew many of the members of the British psychoanalytical community from the 1930s onwards, shared an anecdote about the great Dr. Edward Glover, one of the pioneers of psychoanalysis. According to Hayman, Dr. Glover had once underscored to his younger colleagues that, "Every psychoanalytical session is a research experience." In other words, in order to conduct "research", one need only show up at one's consulting room and listen carefully to the patient. By having done so, one will have undertaken a piece of potentially valuable research.

My heart went out to Dr. Hayman because, in spite of her age and stature in the professional community and the gravitas with which she spoke, many of the hard-core empirical researchers seated in the auditorium burst out in derisory laughter. One gentleman from Germany—a leading psychoanalytical statistician—responded that Glover's recommendation, though useful in the 1940s, had no place in modern science. In order to be a proper researcher, one must undertake academic, empirical, randomised controlled trials on a large-scale basis; the so-called "research" offered by individual clinicians from the privacy of the consulting room could not be considered as reliable data.

As one of the younger participants at this imposing conference, I sat quietly and did not contribute to the discussion, much to my regret, because I do not believe that our approach to research must be quite so polarised between clinicians and statisticians. I would argue that, although we can, indeed, benefit from heaving, well-funded research projects, we can also continue to learn from the privacy of the consulting room; and these arenas of knowledge need not be mutually exclusive. A scientific study of the efficacy of long-term psychotherapy has an important role to play in public discourse, but so, too, does the first-person confession and the single case report. Thus, for those of us working in the mental health profession, we have the opportunity to communicate our research findings in a variety of styles and forms, including not only the publication of single cases but, also, the undertaking of big empirical projects; moreover, we can disseminate our work through art and literature and broadcasting as well.

Most psychotherapists, however, do not undertake formal research and do not impart their findings in any manner, and this seems quite a shame. Perhaps in view of the growing scientification of the field, practising clinicians have become increasingly inhibited at the thought of sharing even small samplings of compelling case material. But for those who lack an academic psychological background, I would urge comrades, nevertheless, to consider the multitude of ways in which we can undertake "research".

Once upon a time, I presented the case of a female patient who suffered from a profound tinnitus—ringing sounds in the ear—to a group of young psychotherapy trainees. This woman developed tinnitus in early adolescence, not long after having witnessed a very violent episode in her home in which her mother and her father—a verbally violent couple—threw plates and cups and saucers at one another in an unrestricted and frightening fashion. As most cases of tinnitus do not seem to develop in the wake of family rows, one would be foolhardy to publish a cocksure paper on the role of domestic violence in the development of this vexing audiological disorder. Nevertheless, after the patient and I "worked through" her memories of this episode, which she had not revealed to anyone previously, her long-standing tinnitus diminished in intensity and eventually began to fade into obscurity.

To my great surprise, during the discussion of this tinnitus case with my students, not one, but two of the members of the seminar interjected and informed me that they, also, had treated comparable cases of individuals who seemed to have developed tinnitus after having listened to very violent interactions between close family members.

Although most otolaryngologists would admit that they often do not know the *precise* cause of tinnitus, the vast majority would be more likely to attribute this ear disorder to organic factors such as infections, perforations of the eardrum, otosclerosis, acoustic neuromas, or hypertension, which may cause narrowing of the blood vessels. Very few, if any, physicians would rush to consider the role of fearful emotions in the genesis of what seems to be a proto-physicalistic symptom.

However, if one searches the psychoanalytical literature and the psychosomatic literature, one will find occasional references to case reports of patients whose tinnitus emerged in the immediate aftermath of an unpleasant psychological experience. For instance, back in 1939, the American researchers Dr. Jules Masserman—a psychiatrist—and Dr. Eva Balken—a psychologist—published a report of a woman who, over time, began to find the sexual advances of her husband deeply unpleasant. At one point, as soon as the husband approached her, even for just a kiss, this woman began to experience ringing in her ears, thus suggesting a sexual component to the symptom (Masserman and Balken, 1939).

Although I cannot pontificate about the psychogenesis of tinnitus in this context, I do wonder whether, in view of the references to psychological causation recorded in the literature, as well as the fact that, in my clinical seminar, we identified no fewer than *three* cases of arguably psychogenic tinnitus, Edward Glover's recommendation that, "Every psychoanalytical session is a research experience" may have more value than we often appreciate and that, in consequence, we should encourage ourselves and our colleagues and, certainly, our students, to undertake as much research as possible, in whatever shape or form.

A Search for the Traumatic Origins of Psychosis

Nowadays, those wishing to contribute to the psychotherapeutic literature have innumerable opportunities for conducting research in a multitude of styles. A sage psychotherapist can undertake not only an empirical-statistical research project, if so inclined, but, also, a clinical one, or, indeed, an historical project about the early foundations of the mental health profession and the relevance of such work to contemporary practice.

In my experience, the most interesting clinical research projects evolve quite unexpectedly and rather organically through engagement with patients.

Needless to say, if one chooses to write a definitive textbook on the psychology of depression, one could do so quite successfully, simply by reviewing the copious literature in scholarly detail, without ever having treated a depressive patient. If a colleague produced a truly comprehensive and erudite and careful study of the historical literature devoted to that form of psychopathology, I would, in all likelihood, admire the work.

But obviously, a book or paper or, indeed, an ongoing clinical research project that emerges more naturally through the daily practice of psychotherapy, may well be presented with greater authenticity and, indeed, passion.

Some of the research projects that have engaged me most profoundly have emerged from my ongoing psychotherapeutic work. For instance, my very first intensive clinical case—a long-term hospitalised patient—suffered from schizophrenia. When this gentleman and I first met on the back wards of a regional psychiatric institution, far away from London, I knew very little about the causes of schizophrenia other than what I had studied as a baby psychologist and other than what I had read in the literature. I knew that Sigmund Freud (1911) had attributed paranoid psychosis to repressed homoerotic desires and that other workers had underscored the role of sexual abuse as a potential aetiological factor (e.g., Karon and VandenBos, 1981), while the more traditional psychiatric textbooks of the period, by contrast, emphasised genetic and biochemical causation (e.g., Gelder, Gath, and Mayou, 1983). But as treatment with this man began to unfold, I learned, bit by bit, that, as a child, his mother had threatened to kill him with a knife (Kahr, 2012).

Many people endure death threats and other manifestations of death wishes throughout the course of the life cycle; but very few will end up as schizophrenic, therefore it seems foolhardy to jump to swift conclusions. But as I developed my work with other psychotic patients, and as I began to supervise cases of schizophrenia, I came to learn of many more stories of patients whose caregivers had made death threats against them or had performed symbolic acts of infanticide by killing, for instance, the family pet. One of the most severely ill patients with whom I worked told me that, during her early childhood, her mother—a severe depressive—once took a carving knife to the patient's teddy bear and slashed open its tummy (Kahr, 2012). Needless to say, an episode of this nature caused the patient very severe fright, which eventually developed into a more traditional paranoid anxiety of being tormented and tortured.

In spite of my exposure to these early cases, I certainly had never intended to pursue the topic of death threats as an area of clinical research but, over the years, I kept encountering such heart-wrenching tales of tragedy. Eventually, I had simply too much data at my disposal and I needed to turn a vast multitude of clinical vignettes into a more coherent theory. Thus, I began to systematise my clinical cases into a variety of categories of different types of death threats as potential aetiological agents in the development of psychosis (Kahr, 1993, 2007b). Gradually, I articulated a theory of what I have come to refer to as the "Infanticidal Attachment" (Kahr, 2007b, p. 119). In spite of the ugliness of this topic, my work on the infanticidal attachment and its role in the genesis of severe mental illness has become a very stimulating area of clinical research, and one which has led to numerous conference and lecture invitations and to a range of publications, including, in particular, a monograph on *The Traumatic Roots of Schizophrenia* (Kahr, 2019c).

Thus, when undertaking a piece of psychotherapeutic work, one never knows which little detail or which moment of interaction between the patient and the clinician might become sufficiently engaging and intriguing to serve as the basis of a paper, a chapter, a book, or, indeed, a lifetime of research. My schizophrenic patient's initial reference to death threats from his mother—something that many other practitioners had overlooked completely—became not only an important theme, which, I believe, contributed to the patient's eventual recovery but, also, served as the unexpected foundation for a lifetime of rich investigation.

Sexual Fantasies at the Dinner Table

I have already written quite briefly, in Chapter 4, about the research project that I undertook on the psychology of sexual fantasies. This study grew out of my early forays in the field of marital psychotherapy, during which I encountered many couples who endured spousal explosions in the wake of having discovered something often rather shocking about one another's erotic minds.

Certainly, I had never imagined that I would undertake a full-scale project on this subject, but, much to my surprise, a number of interrelated opportunities presented themselves, which permitted me to embark upon a piece of clinical and empirical research. For those keen to learn more about the methodology of the British Sexual Fantasy Research Project and its origins, I have written about this in some detail in my books, *Sex and the Psyche* (Kahr, 2007a) and *Who's Been Sleeping in Your Head?: The Secret World of Sexual Fantasies* (Kahr, 2008). In brief, the project developed after my long-standing publisher, Oliver Rathbone, then Director of Karnac Books, suggested to me that sexual fantasies would be a useful subject to explore. As an experienced psychological publisher, Oliver has always boasted a very good sense of what topics might be of interest to fellow professionals, and I responded with enthusiasm to his very direct recommendation.

Owing to the extremely sensitive nature of the subject of sexual fantasies, I knew that I could not write about my own patients and that, instead, I would have to interview voluntary research participants who would agree to speak to me candidly about their erotic minds and their childhood histories, and who would allow me to publish my findings in appropriately anonymised form. But how would I fund a large-scale investigation of this nature?

Having already worked as a mental health broadcaster for many years, I knew a large number of radio and television producers; and at one crucial supper party at the home of Dan Chambers, then Director of Programmes at Five, the British television network, I mentioned that I hoped to embark upon a research project on sexuality. My fellow dinner party guest, Georgina Chignell, a staff member at Tiger Aspect Productions, responded with enthusiasm to my plan and graciously introduced me to her colleagues who, after a period of discussion, agreed to produce a television documentary about the subject, based on my research, which they kindly offered to sponsor.

Granted, this may be an unusual way to finance a large-scale interview study, but in an increasingly technologised world, psychotherapists might benefit from exploring a range of collaborations with the media. After much planning, I received sufficient funds to pay a team of researchers to help me assemble a database of approximately 25,000 British and American adult sexual fantasies, supplemented by numerous intensive, five-hour clinical interviews, which I conducted myself, designed to establish possible interrelationships between early traumatic childhood experiences and subsequent adult fantasy constellations.

The British Sexual Fantasy Research Project, though intensive and, at times, exhausting, provided me with a unique opportunity to collaborate with television producers and crew and with mainstream publishers, not to mention the many men and women who graciously consented to share their private erotic thoughts with me as part of the clinical research. I gained quite a lot from this experience. Most especially, I enhanced my capacity to speak more fully with people about quite explicit sexual fantasies, sexual behaviours, and sexual traumata. As most of us do not address sexology as a separate subject within our trainings, I had to develop much greater comfort and frankness when engaging in conversations with research participants about such a highly sensitive topic. This extra clinical training opportunity certainly enhanced my work with patients, many of whom began to speak more fully about their sexual lives than ever before.

After the broadcast of a television documentary on this research in 2005 and after the publication of my first book on the subject in 2007, various individuals came to consult with me specifically because they wished to discuss their complex sexual anxieties, experiences, and fantasies. Virtually all those who had found their way to me through my research project began the first consultation thus: "I've never spoken to anyone about this before, but when I masturbate, I think about "X" [or "Y" or "Z"]. I'd been in therapy years ago, but I never felt comfortable to tell my therapist about these disturbing fantasies. But having read your book, I know that you've heard it all before and that you can deal with it and that you won't be shocked."

Thus, a large-scale research project can become a stepping stone to publications, to broadcasts, to psychotherapeutic referrals, and, happily, to the enhancement of one's own clinical capacity to deal with complex areas of the human psyche. Above all, I believe that my research project proved helpful to some people, whether they eventually became my patients or whether they simply read my book. After publication, one person wrote to me out of the blue: "I've been troubled by my sexual fantasies for the whole of my life. They've caused me a lot of shame. But now, I have a much better understanding of why I have those fantasies. It all makes sense now, and I feel far less tormented than ever before. Thank you so much."

Most psychotherapeutic trainings do not encourage students to engage in formal research. At best, prospective graduates will be asked to present copious clinical write-ups of sessions and might, at times, be required to produce a final paper—usually a detailed discussion of one case. This will often be a very valuable experience, and one that might prepare a candidate to engage in clinical writing in future. But, in my view, it would be helpful for psychotherapy training committees to consider how students might be exposed to different types of research or, indeed, might be encouraged to create social interventions. By helping our students to undertake their own investigations, by exposing them to the projects that we, as teachers, have already undertaken, and by encouraging trainees to explore their unique interests, we might well be able to foster the growth of a generation who can really contribute new knowledge to this vital field of inquiry.

CHAPTER FOURTEEN

Writing Articles and Books

The Agony of 300 Words and the Ease of 300,000

In my experience, most of my colleagues in the psychotherapeutic world *hate* the act of writing. Although some of them produce publications with a tremendous straightforwardness and lack of inhibition, the vast majority suffer as they struggle to find precisely the right words. One of my friends— a very successful psychological author—actually tears her hair out when writing books. Other practitioners regularly refuse invitations to contribute chapters to edited books, as they experience writing as a veritable torment.

I do understand.

At the age of twenty, I received my first writing assignment. I attended an international conference on child abuse and psychoanalysis, and I took copious notes of all the sessions, as any good student would. One of the senior participants in the conference, who edited the newsletter of the sponsoring organisation, noticed that I had become a veritable scribe, and he asked me whether I would write up a brief 100-word summary of three of the papers. Nowadays, I could undertake such a task either standing on my head or in my sleep. But at the age of twenty, the thought of writing 300 words filled me with dread. I felt very pleased and touched that this gentleman had extended such an invitation to me, but as a youngster without so much as a bachelor's degree at that point, I felt completely unprepared and unqualified to summarise even a very simple, straightforward conference presentation. I dithered and procrastinated, desperately burdened by perfectionism, and spent days and days struggling to produce these tiny summaries. In the end, I must confess, I failed to deliver anything, to my deep chagrin, as I found myself too burdened by anxiety and inexperience.

This episode might well have ended my writing career, but I knew that I wanted to put pen to paper for a whole variety of reasons, and thus I realised that I would have to find a way to overcome the fear of publication. I had no difficulty writing essays for my undergraduate courses, which I scripted solely for my benign teachers, but the thought of putting my name on a document that could be read publicly by any number of people filled me with dread. What if I made a factual error? What if I spelled Freud with a "Ph", rather than with an "F"?

I continued to struggle with writing, in part, because, as a twenty year old, I had little to say.

Not long thereafter, I received a further invitation to pen a short essay about madness for the theatre programme of a student production of the play *Equus*, directed by a fellow university student—one of my close chums at the time. This young man, Simon, who subsequently became a producer at the British Broadcasting Corporation, knew of my budding interest in psychoanalysis and he urged me to write 300 words which could be inserted into the hand-produced programme distributed to ticket buyers upon entering the tiny local theatre. Virtually all the punters would be fellow undergraduates, and few if any of them would have known anything technical about madness. Once again, I laboured and laboured for days, agonising over exactly what I might say and how I might phrase my thoughts. Eventually, I produced something. Simon arrived at my college room and told me that he needed the copy at once, so that it could be photocopied and included in the theatre programmes. I pleaded for more time in order to make further revisions. He looked at me and snarled, "You haven't got more time. I need the piece *right now*." I balked, but Simon pulled the page out of my trembling hands and read what I had written. "It's absolutely perfect," he pronounced and then walked out of the room with my typescript before I could raise any further objections. Had Simon not taken executive responsibility, I rather suspect that I might still be working on that 300-word introduction about the psychology of madness to this very day. That experience certainly helped me to overcome my fear of writing and, happily, I managed to put pen to paper rather smoothly from that point onwards.

I have come to regard writing—whether books or articles—as a skill akin to riding a bicycle in childhood. At the very outset, before one has acquired any mastery, most youngsters suffer from marked anxiety. Certainly, I found my first attempt to ride a two-wheel bicycle rather terrifying, but with my father standing protectively by my side, I gradually mastered the sense of dread. In many respects, my old friend Simon helped me to ride my "writing bicycle" without falling down. He stood by my side and, albeit a bit brusquely, acknowledged my competency. Once I saw my first 300-word essay printed in a theatre programme, I never looked back.

Writing might well be considered a muscle. Just as constant weightlifting at the gym will pump up one's biceps, so, too, will regular writing improve one's "scriptive" muscles.

Last year, I completed not one ... not two ... but *three* books, each approximately 100,000 words in length. And although I worked extremely hard, I also worked steadily, without interruption and without too much inhibition. I can honestly claim that, after several decades of writing, I now find it much, much easier to write 300,000 words than 300 words, and I have no doubt that others who wish to develop such musculature may well come to have a similar experience with application and perseverance.

Since those halcyon student days, I have gone on to write book reviews, obituaries, forewords, conference reports, abstracts of published literature, tributes, news items, clinical essays, historical essays, book chapters, edited books, and single-authored books. In more recent years, I have even written for the internet, having produced blogs and website articles, which I consider rather modern!

In retrospect, I quite understand why I felt so inhibited as a twenty year old. I knew virtually nothing at that time, and I had no claim to expertise; hence, I felt sheepish, even about summarising the work of someone else, at least in print. Moreover, I had not yet survived the first anticipated attacks from critics. Every writer absolutely dreads being assassinated in public. When I "published" my theatre programme notes for the student production of *Equus*, no one savaged me afterwards. Perhaps none of the punters had even read my little contribution, but in any case, I survived. Thus, to be a writer, one needs experience, muscles, and the capacity to withstand potential murder!

Publishing as a Relational Experience

I have a very dear friend—a kindly, compassionate, warm-hearted woman—who has facilitated some quite remarkable clinical work with adolescent patients over the years. An experienced social worker, she later trained as a psychoanalyst and became increasingly adept in her professional activities. However, although she had finished her coursework in record time, it took her eight years thereafter to qualify as an analyst, because she simply could not complete her final clinical paper. Her tutors nudged her, cajoled her, even threatened her, but this lovely lady remained completely inhibited. She had never written anything much before, and the thought of having to commit herself to paper proved too terrifying. Finally, a rather straight-shooting senior colleague upbraided my friend and told her that if she did not submit her paper within four weeks, the training committee would have to consider termination of her candidacy. The older colleague looked my friend in the eye and exclaimed, "You're making such a meal out of this. Just write the fucking paper!"

Happily, my friend responded well to this "intervention", and she finally completed her paper and then qualified, much to everyone's relief and delight. In discussing this situation afterwards, I asked my friend how she had, at long last, mobilised herself to finish this much overdue essay. Certainly, I wondered whether the threat to terminate her candidacy had proved persecutory or, rather, helpful. She replied, "The real awakening came when that tutor told me to stop making a *meal* out of it. You know that my mother was a professional cook, who spent her whole life making meals out of everything. And she took ages—that is why she was such a good cook. But my Mum died when I was very young. And I only just realised that I, too, have been making a meal out of everything, perhaps as an unconscious way of keeping my mother alive."

I found this conversation deeply moving and revealing because my friend, through a useful piece of self-analysis (and a bit of cajoling), had discovered one of the deeper reasons for her writing inhibition. She processed and digested the insight, and this helped her to finish the final paper in record time.

These tales of creative blocks underscore that writing, like any skill, has its own developmental trajectory. And although the ability to write depends in large measure upon craft, one often unearths a psychodynamic underbelly to the writing process, and through sustained analysis, one will usually be able to uncover the roots of any neurotic inhibition.

Over the years I have treated many professional writers, all of whom entered analysis with profound blockages, but, happily, each one eventually left analysis, able to generate new work in a much more unfettered, unrestricted manner. Psychotherapists, I believe, can fall prey to the very same traps.

Thus, in order to become a good writer, one needs to undertake a thorough course of personal psychotherapy or psychoanalysis in order to unravel any inhibitions or blocks which might stem from intra-familial fears and terrors. In my experience, the best psychoanalytical writers have all undergone a lengthy period of psychoanalysis. Donald Winnicott, for instance, spent approximately fifteen years on the couch (Kahr, 1996), and having done so, he really found his voice, which he could then translate from the consulting room to the writing pad. Sigmund Freud may well be the great exception, as he had no one to psychoanalyse him, and yet he became a magnificent writer, perhaps, in part, because although he lacked an analyst, he had, over many years, poured out his heart to his long-standing intimate colleague, Dr. Wilhelm Fliess, the Berlin otorhinolaryngologist, who read Freud's (1950, 1986) letters and early drafts about psychoanalysis and psychopathology in minute detail.

In many respects, Freud's eager missives to Fliess, and Fliess's exquisitely attentive responses to Freud, help us to appreciate that writing must be understood as a *relational* experience. It can be extremely difficult to write in *isolation*. We need to know, in advance, that someone else will be keen to read what we have written.

So, writing and publishing must be conceptualised as developmental and relational processes, which improve over time and which require good people who will attune to our work. Reading the drafts of our colleagues' scribblings and, also, sending our own drafts to these same colleagues in return becomes a truly vital part of the process.

Over the years, I have met many mental health practitioners who have confessed, "When I retire, I shall have all the time in the world to write." Most of them, in fact, never do, unless, of course, they had *already* established themselves as authors. So, if you do have an aspiration to enshrine your thoughts into words, please work hard to assemble a team of close comrades who will read your fledgling efforts with willingness and helpfulness.

Back in 1981, the American composer and lyricist Stephen Sondheim wrote a musical for the Broadway stage entitled *Merrily We Roll Along*, about a team of songwriters. At one point, during the first act, an interviewer asks one of the lead characters—a lyricist called "Charley Kringas"—about his collaboration with composer "Franklin Shephard", wondering which comes first, the music or the words. Kringas replies sardonically,

"Generally, the contract" (Sondheim, 1981, p. 391). The wit of Sondheim's banter actually underscores quite profoundly that in order for a creative project to materialise, we will always benefit from having an *other* who has issued a contract beforehand: someone who cries out, "I want to read your work!"

Thus, I strongly urge any prospective writers to seek a commission from the editor of a tiny in-house newsletter or from the book review editor of a journal who will function as an honorary, receptive parental figure. With such an ally on board, one will have a much better chance of completing one's writing tasks.

"Not Another Book on Projective Identification"

When scouring the shelves at Karnac Books on London's Finchley Road, or when browsing through any good psychotherapeutic library, my heart often sinks as I find myself overwhelmed by a host of relatively mediocre titles, all written about the same topic. Today, alone, I received no fewer than two separate emails advertising different books on countertransference. On the previous day, I received notification of three new books on the work of Donald Winnicott. And the day before that, I found myself bombarded by a welter of new titles of the "Introduction-to-the-Art-of-Psychotherapy" variety! I shall never forget when, one day, I popped into the offices of Karnac Books to speak to my publisher, and I found the staff team sifting through a pile of new book proposals from prospective authors. It hardly surprised me when one of them cried out, "Good Lord, not another book on projective identification."

Alas, we, as authors, repeat ourselves all too frequently, and publishers have sometimes colluded, commissioning too many books on hackneyed subjects and not nearly enough on blazing new topics. However well written and however virtuous one's latest book on projective identification might be, I very much doubt that we need yet another one at this point in time. Instead, we need books which tackle complex, "blue-sky" projects, such as *What Psychotherapists Can Do to Stop Climate Change*, or *How Psychotherapists Can Help Perform Mental Health Evaluations on Politicians and, Also, on Voters*! I do not pretend that such titles can be produced easily, but I hope that prospective writers will endeavour to broaden their canvases of possibility.

Once we have cut our teeth by writing the odd conference report or book review, it might be worthwhile to attempt a full-scale journal article. Most contributions to academic periodicals tend to be approximately 5,000 to 7,000 words in length—enough space in which to provide a detailed study of a particular topic of interest. Nowadays, the majority of journals operate a process of peer review: after one has submitted the potential article, the editor of the periodical will then send the typescript to one or two (or sometimes three) peers who will write anonymous reports as to the suitability of the paper. Sometimes this can be an irritating process, especially if the author happens to inflame the envy of one of the reviewers. But in most instances, the anonymous readers will offer useful feedback. Surviving the peer review process can be a helpful experience, as this often provides the author with a taste of how the broader professional community will ultimately respond after publication.

Those with a greater need or hunger for writing should begin by penning a few peer-reviewed articles before progressing to the writing of books. As we become better known for our expertise in a particular branch of psychotherapeutic work, colleagues will begin to offer invitations to write chapters for edited books; and this will often be a very good way of progressing from the world of articles to that of full-length tomes.

Although the psychotherapeutic publishing landscape changes all the time, with old publishers going bankrupt or retiring and with new publishers arriving full of vigour, members of our profession will always have the luxury of several potential options. Having an older mentor with a publishing track record can be very useful, as such a person can readily facilitate an introduction to an editor or publisher with a certain amount of ease, providing that the young writer has a worthwhile project in the making which the mentor will champion fervently.

Prospective authors must, however, be mindful of their own narcissism. Just as every pregnant mother hopes that her baby will be the most beautiful, healthy, and talented newborn in history, so, too, does every book writer hope that his or her work will attract limitless attention and will take the mental health community by storm. I cannot tell you how many times newly published writers have lamented to me, "I went into Waterstones and I could not find a single copy of my book on *Post-Kleinianism and its Vicissitudes: Contemporary Insights into the Theory of Psychotic Anxieties*". Authors must appreciate that such a book will sell no more than 100 copies at best, and most of these will be purchased by the author as gifts for family and friends! So please do not fume at your publisher because your latest book does not appear on the front table at Foyles or at Barnes & Noble next to the autobiography of Barack Obama.

Specialist psychoanalytical theoretical books simply do not sell in large quantities, and we should not blame our publisher; rather, we can only upbraid ourselves for having tackled such a niche topic, written in such an arcane style. Authors who wish to make an impact must write in a warm, accessible, literarily pleasing manner and must choose subjects of broader relevance if they wish to make an impact beyond their immediate circle of clinical colleagues.

In the olden days, one could happily publish a new textbook on projective identification and few, if any patients, would ever come to know about this volume. But in our technologised world, most prospective patients will google our name before arranging for a consultation, and if we have written one or more books, those titles will feature quite prominently in any web search. Thus, in the twenty-first century, we must assume that not only might some colleagues read our writings, but that future patients will do so as well; and if we should write really obscure books, many prospective clients will shun such author-practitioners like the plague.

Despite the challenges of being a psychotherapeutic writer, which include lack of time, anxieties about disguising confidential material, and fear that no one will read our books, the experience of penning papers and preparing full-length texts has the potential to offer much joy. Transforming our many thoughts and experiences into sentences and paragraphs certainly helps us to digest our complex clinical encounters and might, from time to time, provide our colleagues and our students with useful, educational, even inspirational, material. I recommend writing highly as a marvellous way to develop our voice. And if we apply ourselves with care, writing can not only enhance our reputation among others but, above all, our own personal sense of achievement and usefulness.

CHAPTER FIFTEEN

Blue-Sky Projects

Freud Thinks Big

No one in the history of mental health had greater vision and ambition than the young Sigismund Freud. For a poor Jewish boy, son of a wool merchant, to have trained in medicine and to have risen to become one of the most prominent physicians in anti-Semitic Vienna, represents quite an achievement.

With unusual bravery, Freud challenged the regnant treatment methods so prevalent among nineteenth-century Continental neurologists and psychiatrists. Strikingly, while other physicians prescribed rest cures, hypnotism, hydrotherapy, electrotherapy and, in certain circumstances, hysterectomy and genital surgery (e.g., Brown, 1866; Flechsig, 1884; Coe, 1890), Freud offered his patients the simple but profound opportunity to relax upon his divan, and encouraged them to speak to him in a setting of complete privacy. Freud created, in many respects, the first *hands-off* treatment, prioritising conversation and understanding over bodily interventions which often caused more harm than good (e.g., Kahr, 2018c).

Not only did Freud devote the bulk of his professional life to the creation of a profound method for treating the neuroses, namely, psychoanalysis, but, moreover, he sculpted an entire corpus of theory to underpin his model of talking therapy, and he found exciting ways in which to apply his lens to the study not only of medicine but, also, to an understanding of art, litera-ture, sociology, history, and politics.

If Freud had done nothing else than create the technique and theory of psychoanalysis, he would, of course, have earned himself a place in the galaxy of great thinkers. But Freud did much more. He also forged an entirely new profession, replete with trainings, qualifications, and institutions, as well as clinics, publications, conferences, and a whole host of other specially branded Freudian products. As a result of a lifetime of heaving work, Freud engaged in profound blue-sky thinking to create an entirely new paradigm and a whole new industry: the very birth of modern psychotherapy.

Of course, others had anticipated notions of the unconscious mind in previous centuries (e.g., Ellenberger, 1970; ffytche, 2012). But no one sculpted an entire mental health empire quite like Sigmund Freud. While some might regard Freud's (1900d) conquistadorial temperament as a sign of grandiosity and greediness, we must acknowledge that this man, however full of himself, could certainly think in an unusually visionary manner. And without his gargantuan achievements, none of us would have a job today.

Although Sigmund Freud led the way, he did not have a monopoly on the creation of great ideas and innovative projects within the history of psychotherapy and psychoanalysis. The field has glistened with fine minds who have, over many decades, worked hard to expand the initial parame-ters of those early Freudian discoveries. Inspired by Sigmund Freud's (1909) case history about the little boy who suffered from a phobia of horses, a number of early female progenitors of psychoanalysis, such as Dr. Hermine von Hug-Hellmuth (1921), Anna Freud (1927), and Melanie Klein (1932), helped to create, for instance, the new field of child analysis, not only by providing treatment for neurotic youngsters but, also, by creating a strategy of early intervention to protect troubled children from becoming even more severely ill in later life.

Other Viennese pioneers, such as Dr. Josef Friedjung (1931), introduced psychological concepts into the study of paediatrics, while those such as August Aichhorn (1925, 1932) developed psychological treatment methods for delinquent adolescents. Perhaps most impressively of all, Dr. Wilhelm Reich, one of the more controversial and outspoken members of the Viennese psychoanalytical community during the 1920s, endeavoured to create a sub-stantial programme of social reform by introducing post-pubescent young-sters to the basics of human sexuality in an era of tremendous repression and shame. Reich (1932) mounted a large-scale community intervention project to help de-stigmatise sexuality and to encourage young people to enjoy a healthy engagement with the human body. This included the provision of sexual education pamphlets, contraceptive devices, as well as private spaces in which consenting young people could make love and could, if necessary, be helped to obtain abortions (cf. Sharaf, 1983; Danto, 2005).

In Berlin, during the 1930s, other psychoanalysts forged equally new pathways. For instance, Dr. Franz Alexander and Dr. Hugo Staub (1929) founded the field of forensic psychotherapy by participating in legal proceedings, offering expert testimony on the unconscious motivations of criminals. Alexander not only made huge contributions to the psychoanalytical study of criminology but, also, after his emigration to the United States of America, he helped to mastermind the field of psychosomatic medicine, investigating the ways in which early conflictual psychological adversities could result in diseases such as bronchial asthma, ulcerative colitis, and much more besides (Alexander, 1939a, 1939b, 1939c, 1941, 1957).

Although one cannot do justice to the range of blue-sky thinking undertaken by the early founders of the psychoanalytical movement, as so very many of these men and women helped to open up entirely new canvases of investigation, no list would be complete without an appreciation of the contributions of some of the truly inspirational English clinicians, in particular, Dr. Donald Winnicott (1930a, 1930b, 1931a, 1931b, 1932, 1933a, 1933b), who introduced psychological concepts into the study of children's medicine in Great Britain, and Dr. John Bowlby (1940, 1944a, 1944b, 1946), who explored the impact of separation upon the development of delinquency and, also, depression. At the outbreak of the Second World War, these two prescient child psychiatrists collaborated with a third child mental health colleague, Dr. Emanuel Miller—somewhat less well known nowadays—and, in 1939, this trio wrote a strong letter of protest against the evacuation of London's youngsters. Although Bowlby, Miller, and Winnicott (1939) could, of course, appreciate the dangers of remaining in wartime London, they dared to suggest that by separating children from their caregivers, these boys and girls might suffer even more profound harm in the long run. Having had the privilege of working psychotherapeutically with many adults who, decades previously, had to endure evacuation to the British countryside during the war, I can confirm that these individuals all suffered from severe, lifelong depressive episodes.

The extremely impressive forefathers and foremothers of contemporary psychotherapy deserve our thanks for thinking big, in the tradition of

Sigmund Freud himself. Most of them—indeed, all of them—had exposed themselves to slander and ridicule and marginalisation for having championed a rather odd new theory of sexual psychology, which many reviled as a Jewish plague (e.g., Jones, 1955). But in having done so, each of them ultimately created an important new arena for thought and application, and each has, in fact, withstood the test of time in quite a robust fashion.

How can twenty-first-century psychotherapists engage in pioneering, blue-sky projects, especially when we have so much training to undertake, so much literature to read, so many patients to treat, and so many emails to which we must respond in the course of our increasingly long and exhausting working days?

Although I have no simple solution as to how we can create spaces in our minds and in our diaries to engage in big paradigm-shifting projects, I can draw upon my *bibliophilia psychotherapeutica* and provide a brief account of some encouraging role models who can provide us all with tremendous inspiration.

A Bestseller and a Serial Killer

Back in 1984, I had the great privilege of embarking upon a friendship with two remarkable women, each of whom became an honorary professional grandmother to me.

I had long admired Professor Flora Rheta Schreiber, a venerable academic and author, and I invited her to speak at the University of Oxford. A woman of great charisma and panache, Flora had, years previously, made a pioneering contribution to the study of multiple personality disorder (now restyled as dissociative identity disorder) through the publication of her extremely popular book, *Sybil*, the tale of a young woman with sixteen separate sub-personalities who underwent a comprehensive and successful psychoanalysis (Schreiber, 1973). This book made a huge contribution to the study of child abuse as well as multiple personality disorder, then both highly neglected topics. Subsequently, Schreiber (1983) published an even more extraordinary book, *The Shoemaker: The Anatomy of a Psychotic*, exposing the early childhood traumata experienced by Joseph Kallinger, a notorious, real-life multiple murderer who, having killed three people (including one of his own children) ended his days in a forensic psychiatric institution.

In her book on Kallinger, Schreiber demonstrated quite powerfully that one does not become a murderer by accident; rather, Kallinger, as a young boy, had endured numerous attacks and assaults of both a physical and a sexual nature. With the consummate skill of a psychoanalytical crimino-logical investigator, Schreiber explored in precise detail how Kallinger, as a youngster, had often suffered threats at knifepoint, and would then repeat these traumas in adult life, always killing his victims with knives, rather than with guns.

Although many psychoanalytical practitioners have studied the nature of murder, no one, in my estimation, has ever undertaken as comprehensive a study of the childhood of a single murderer as deeply as Flora Schreiber had done. She spent years interviewing Kallinger as well as many people who knew him directly; hence, she drew her portrait not from idle armchair speculation but, rather, from a detailed oral historical reconstruction of his traumatic early years. I cannot recommend Flora's book on Joseph Kallinger to the faint of heart; she wrote about the abuse that he experienced and, sub-sequently, the murders that he committed, in chilling, graphic detail. But for those who can manage to digest this regrettably neglected work, I know of no better study of the psychology of the murderer than this one. Flora Schreiber's profound examination of this vicious, traumatised killer con-stitutes a truly seminal contribution to modern mental health and, also, to criminology as well. Moreover, it has profound implications for our under-standing of the origins of terrorism. Flora's book really demonstrates that if we can prevent child abuse, we might have a chance of forestalling murder and, indeed, warfare.

In due course, Flora introduced me to her great friend, a fellow psy-choanalytical writer and journalist, Lucy Freeman, who had once served as the mental health correspondent for *The New York Times*. Back in the 1940s, Lucy underwent psychoanalytical treatment in New York City, and it proved to be a miraculous experience and cured her of some of her many long-standing psychosomatic symptoms which had not responded to any previous medical interventions. An adept author, Freeman (1951) actually wrote an entire memoir about her very helpful experience on the couch, *Fight Against Fears*, first published in 1951, which became a stonking bestseller, and which generated an immense amount of interest in psychoanalysis across the United States. Not long thereafter, the American Psychoanalytic Association co-opted Lucy to advise on its public relations strategy, and she helped this national organisation hugely to popularise the virtues of the talking cure.

Lucy wrote literally dozens and dozens of books about various aspects of psychoanalysis—sometimes solo books (e.g., Freeman, 1969, 1970, 1972, 1980, 1992), and sometimes books which she co-authored with eminent clinical practitioners (e.g., Freeman and Greenwald, 1961; Freeman and Strean, 1981). In many ways, she became the veritable pioneer of contemporary media psychology, having devoted a lifetime to the public dissemination of psychotherapeutic ideas to a wide audience.

Both Flora Rheta Schreiber and Lucy Freeman deserve infinite credit as very inspiring thinkers who did a great deal of original work as visionary public intellectuals, each of whom enhanced both the professional and the public understanding psychotherapeutic ideas during the 1940s, 1950s, 1960s, 1970s, 1980s, and in Lucy's case, even into the 1990s. I rate these two women as true innovators, and I hope that many will read their now neglected writings which, at the time of publication, had become bestselling works. I truly believe that, collectively, these two great authors (who also enjoyed a warm friendship with one another over many years) made a hugely significant contribution to the understanding of how psychological concepts might contribute to a cure for numerous ills (Kahr, 1999a, 1999b, 2002, 2011a).

Psychotherapists in Prison and in the Middle East

In more recent years, large numbers of clinical colleagues on both sides of the Atlantic Ocean have undertaken some truly magnificent projects which, I suspect, have the potential to change innumerable lives outside the consulting room, and which deserve the designation of blue-sky works.

So many worthy projects leap to mind, and I cannot do justice to any of them in such a concise study as this, but I can, at the very least, highlight some of the work that I have found quite impressive. Dr. Stella Acquarone (2002, 2004), the Director of the School of Infant Mental Health in London, and a specialist in parent–infant psychotherapy, has, for instance, improved our ability to diagnose autism and other forms of infant and child psychopathology at an earlier stage than ever before, and as a result, she and her colleagues have intervened sooner rather than later, thus facilitating the cures of many young people in great distress.

Dr. Carine Minne, a forensic psychiatrist and psychoanalyst, along with her colleague Paul Kassman, has created a remarkable project, "Changing the Game", which provides psychotherapeutic interventions to members of violent ethnic minority street gangs who had committed horrific murders. Minne and Kassman (2018) became deeply engaged with these perpetrators in prison and helped these men to transform their violent affects and painful traumata into words. At the end of this clinical intervention, many of the prisoners became thoughtful, reflective citizens who enriched their lives by undertaking online university degrees, in spite of their institutional confinement. "Changing the Game" serves as a potential model for how one might reduce violence within impoverished, marginalised communities.

Professor Sheila Hollins (1997), a psychiatrist and psychoanalytically orientated psychotherapist who has specialised in the treatment of the disabled, became, in 2010, a baroness in the House of Lords. She, along with fellow psychiatrist Dr. John Alderdice—subsequently Lord Alderdice—represents our profession heroically at the forefront of government. Baroness Hollins has made a particularly impactful contribution with the creation of the annual Mental Wealth Festival. Thus, the intersection between mental health professionals and politics has become increasingly potent (cf. Samuels, 2015).

Many other colleagues deserve blue-sky status as well. For instance, Andrew Balfour (2007, 2014), the Chief Executive of Tavistock Relationships at the Tavistock Institute of Medical Psychology in London, has undertaken groundbreaking work on the application of psychotherapeutic concepts in work with individuals and couples who struggle with dementia, as has Kate White (2019), one of the founders of The Bowlby Centre in London. Professor Caroline Bainbridge and Professor Candida Yates, two first-class contributors, founded an organisation called "Media and the Inner World", devoted to the application of psychoanalytical concepts to an in-depth study of popular culture and political culture and have produced numerous books and papers about their work (e.g., Bainbridge and Yates, 2007, 2014; Yates, 2014, 2015, 2018).

Dr. Oliver James (2002), a clinical psychologist and psychotherapist of long standing, dared to challenge the bombast of many of the genetic theories of mental illness in his deservedly best-selling text, *They F*** You Up: How to Survive Family Life* (cf. James, 2016). And Dr. Valerie Sinason (1992, 2010), the noted child psychotherapist and adult psychoanalyst and, also, a pioneer of disability psychotherapy, has assumed huge responsibility— alongside colleague Dehra Mitchell—for working with the survivors of the ghastly Grenfell Tower fire, which claimed many London lives in 2017.

Gabrielle Rifkind, a group analyst and adult psychotherapist based in London, has contributed in stellar fashion to our field through her extraordinary work in the Middle East. Over the course of many years, Rifkind has made numerous trips to Egypt, Iran, Israel, Jordan, Lebanon, Saudi Arabia,

Syria, and other countries steeped in political conflict and, quite extraordinarily, she has succeeded in facilitating dialogue among leaders from different countries and different factions in an effort to invite these traditionally warring people to sit down at the very same table and *talk*. As founder of the Middle East programme sponsored by the Oxford Research Group, Rifkind has created high-level political dialogue for those involved in conflict, deploying her psychotherapeutic knowledge to create a safe space in which warring parties in the Israeli–Palestinian conflict, and beyond, might engage in conversation and, also, examine opportunities for ending conflict. More recently, she has established Oxford Process, a preventative diplomacy initiative for peace-making.

A compassionate public speaker, Rifkind has addressed a wide range of audiences about her psychological interventions. She speaks in a voice which I would describe as both strong and quiet at the same time. Unlike many political activists, she does not bellow; rather, she utilises her consulting room tone and manages to engage people with her sincerity and her empathy. She has addressed a wide range of public institutions, including the Royal Institute of International Affairs in London, as well as the Woodrow Wilson School of Public and International Affairs at Princeton University in Princeton, New Jersey, not to mention the Oxford Union and the House of Commons. Back in 2009, I had the pleasure of hosting an "in conversation" with Rifkind (2009) in the Library at the Anna Freud Centre in London, as part of the public programme sponsored by the Freud Museum, during the course of which she spoke about opportunities for psychotherapists to work in the field of international conflict resolution.

Rifkind has also produced a series of publications in which she discusses various aspects of her work (e.g., Rifkind, 2007, 2008; Rifkind and Picco, 2014); and more recently, she has produced a short book entitled *The Psychology of Political Extremism: What Would Sigmund Freud Have Thought About Islamic State?* (Rifkind, 2018), which provides a useful summary of her thoughts on the ways in which one can intervene judiciously in the political sphere, behind the scenes, much as the psychotherapist will do in the consulting room.

Other mental health professionals have also made landmark strides in the field of international relations, most notably the American psychoanalyst of distinction, Professor Vamik Volkan (1988, 1997, 2013, 2014a, 2014b), a Nobel Prize nominee who founded the International Dialogue Initiative and who has provided a unique platform from which psychological

practitioners of all different backgrounds can contribute to public awareness about political conflict. I can most happily recommend this work to
newcomers in our field, in the hope that such blue-sky thinking will help us
all to raise the bar.

And one need not be an "old-timer" with half a century of experience under one's belt in order to make an extraordinary contribution. For
instance, Dr. Sheri Jacobson, a young practitioner, has mounted a national
campaign through her consultancy Harley Therapy to make psychological
treatment more accessible to a wider variety of potential clients across the
United Kingdom. During the last year, she and her colleagues have worked
hard to destigmatise psychotherapy and have provided approximately one
quarter of a million sessions to patients!

Needless to say, in spite of my extreme admiration for all these aforementioned psychotherapeutic workers (as well as those cited in previous
chapters), and in spite of my tendency to nudge young colleagues to undertake the *maximum* rather than the *minimum* amount of work in order
to make an impact in our field, such amazingly creative and potentially
transformative projects cannot be undertaken in the short ten-minute
gaps between our 7.00 a.m. patient and our 8.00 a.m. patient. For those
with full-time clinical practices, the launching of such undertakings will
be challenging, if not impossible. But those who have the courage and the
cunning to collaborate with some of these aforementioned workers or who
wish to forge entirely new organisations must preserve some sacrosanct
space in which creativity of this sort can grow and develop.

PART IV

Surviving Success

CHAPTER SIXTEEN

Avoiding Isolation

The Need for Solitude

Having now built a secure base for a clinical career, having begun to prosper in daily practice, and having developed the courage to thrive outside the consulting room with wonderful projects and plans, how, then, do aspirational psychotherapists negotiate these newfound successes and pleasures? Certainly, we need a very strong mind to help us bear the fact that we might, by this point, have done reasonably well.

Years ago, Sigmund Freud (1911, 1916) observed that many of us will be more likely to suffer a breakdown not after we have experienced *failure*, but, paradoxically, after we have had a *success*. Freud hypothesised that the unconscious guilt of doing well, perhaps even outstripping our parents or siblings, can be crippling. I must note that, over the course of forty years of clinical practice, I have encountered this phenomenon on innumerable occasions. Often people will present for psychotherapy in the wake of an outstanding achievement which has rendered them almost catatonic, rather than celebratory.

The flourishing psychotherapist must find a variety of ways to *enjoy* his or her accomplishments, rather than succumb to misery and guilt.

Should we, as psychotherapists, ever become paralysed by our achievements—due to guilt at having succeeded, or due to fear of being attacked—we always have the option to return to the couch for another *tranche* of personal psychotherapy or psychoanalysis. Many of our colleagues have undergone more than one course of therapy; and Freud (1937) had firmly recommended that we should consider this option. But there may, of course, be many other ways of feeling enriched, short of having to undergo a full re-analysis.

Although I have entitled this chapter "Avoiding Isolation", as the dangers of being lonely can be very perilous for the hard-working, original-thinking psychotherapist, there may be times when we absolutely *must* embrace a creative solitude.

At the end of a very long clinical day, I remove my patent leather work shoes and substitute them with a pair of comfortable trainers (i.e., sneakers). I then don my coat and exit my office building and begin the long walk home when the weather permits. This journey by foot has become a joyful period of solitude.

I never use a mobile telephone in my professional work. As I have indicated, I prefer the indoor calm and quiet and groundedness of the old-fashioned landline telephone, which I have found to be very containing. But I do own a mobile telephone which I use when speaking to family and friends. I resisted purchasing a cell phone for many years, but eventually I relented, and I can now most certainly appreciate its benefits.

In the early days, I would chat constantly on my mobile phone during the long walk home. It seemed the most wonderfully convenient and efficient means of catching up with old chums, of discussing ongoing projects with colleagues, and so on. But over time, I have come to use the iPhone less and less while walking, as I find that I need some absolutely solo time— *private* time—in which I do not have to listen, do not have to engage, do not have to relate, except to my own self and to my own thoughts. Occasionally, I feel that my internal archive has already absorbed such a huge amount of raw data during the course of my working day that I have very little free space remaining, so I treasure this rare canvas of solitude as I pound the London pavements.

Sometimes, while enjoying my walk from the office, I will review the day's clinical sessions, so that I can really absorb and underpin certain key pieces of biographical information or can engage in some self-supervision, rethinking what I had interpreted, or could have interpreted, or *should* have interpreted to patients at particular moments. I find that this helps me to process the intensity of the psychotherapeutic day. But when I have finished doing so, I then like to let my mind roam freely. At times, I will put on my headphones and listen to a podcast or to some music, which I experience as both pleasant and liberating. At other times, I will simply stare at all the interesting visual sights before me: lovely homes and gardens, people with compelling faces, cats and dogs and birds, as well as heaps of rubbish on the London streets!

Needless to say, although I try to preserve this walk for some solitude, I do, still, talk to friends and colleagues on my cell phone, simply because I have no other space in which to do so. I find that as I have begun to age more and more, my friends and acquaintances have become increasingly burdened by the ravages of the life cycle. Everyone has at least one, or two, or three, or four, or five relatives or comrades recently diagnosed with cancer, and naturally, we all want to rally round. Sometimes, I undertake my most stressful and challenging "clinical" work on the way home from the office, aware that my patients, by contrast, often seem a blessed relief!

But when I can, I do preserve my quietude, and I find this refreshing.

Committed psychotherapists with large caseloads have very little privacy during the daytime. Perhaps we should have more. But most of us, in our zest to fill our time as efficiently as possible, and to help as many people as possible, leave a mere ten-minute gap between our clinical appointments (Kahr, 2007d). Perhaps we ought to revisit this long-standing historical tradition. The ten-minute gap, though restorative and essential, may not give us enough time in which to recharge our emotional batteries.

In the olden days, when many people smoked unthinkingly, it would be common practice for office workers to pop out for a cigarette break. Although I have never smoked, I do remember that period of history only too well. One of my old colleagues at the Tavistock Clinic, "Dr. D.", smoked incessantly; and everybody knew that if one needed to speak to this man, one would never find him in his office on the fourth floor but, rather, just outside the entrance to the building, adjacent to the car park ... surrounded by a cloud of fumes! I must have passed Dr. D. in full puffing mode on thousands of occasions—deeply absorbed in thought—and though I did not envy his lungs, I did appreciate the way in which he kept refreshing his mind, for he ended up writing a stream of papers and books which won international acclaim, and I suspect that he used his cigarette break to organise his thoughts in a creative manner.

Thus, we non-smokers must find ways of taking honorary smoking breaks for ourselves, so that we may enjoy the creative and restorative opportunities afforded by some special moments of solitude during our taxing and highly responsible working lives.

Beware the Ethics Committee

Having thus extolled the delights of solitude, I will now express a very strong warning. Solitude must be enjoyed with great caution, and we should be wary of becoming too isolated within the psychotherapy profession— something which happens all too frequently and, I regret to say, all too easily.

Many years ago, I had a very interesting conversation with Dr. Brendan MacCarthy (2002b), a former Chair of the Ethics Committee of the British Psycho-Analytical Society, about psychotherapists and psychoanalysts who engage in unethical behaviour, whether by being unreliable or exploitative in some way, or, more shockingly, by embarking upon a sexual liaison with a patient. Fortunately, such transgressions occur very infrequently indeed in the psychotherapeutic world, but they do occur from time to time; consequently, ethics committees exist so that patients have the opportunity to lodge formal complaints if they have experienced professional abuse. Dr. MacCarthy, my senior by many years, told me that, in his experience, those most likely to be hauled before an ethics committee will be those members of the community who had completed their trainings honourably but who then disappeared from view, either by moving to some obscure part of the country or by shielding themselves from professional gatherings, never attending lectures or conferences or committee meetings.

This observation, rendered by an astute clinician, must be taken very seriously indeed. My own experience of colleagues who act unethically certainly confirms the observation of Brendan MacCarthy. Isolation from one's professional community represents, therefore, a major risk factor in the perpetration of unethical behaviour. Although sometimes the sociable, well-integrated mental health practitioner will commit an offence, the much more isolated psychotherapist or psychoanalyst or psychologist or psychiatrist will be at even greater risk of doing so.

Colleagues become our best source of protection because they have the potential to see us, to monitor us, to interact with us, to listen to our lectures, to read our works, and to hear stories about us in the consulting room. I believe that having a large collegial network serves as a containing structure for overworked, overstretched, overburdened clinicians, and hence, our colleagues can become a protective cordon. Colleagues can also intervene at an early stage if they sense that we have begun to struggle with a certain difficulty in either our personal or professional lives.

Of course, not only will lonely, retreated psychotherapists be at risk of acting unhelpfully or unethically but, so, too, will every human being who lives in isolation. We now have access to a very large scientific literature about the dangers of loneliness, and we know, only too well, that solitude can exert a very heavy toll.

I recently read a remarkable study undertaken by Professor Robert Wilson—a neuroscientist—and his colleagues at the Rush Alzheimer's Disease Center, part of the Rush University Medical Center in Chicago, Illinois, who monitored a sample of some 823 physically healthy older men and women over time. At the outset of this innovative research project, the investigators administered the de Jong-Gierveld Loneliness Scale to the participants, and hence obtained a good sense of how isolated each person felt. The researchers then followed up these 823 elderly people until their deaths, and they discovered that fully seventy-six of them had developed clinical Alzheimer's disease. Extraordinarily, those who had scored more highly on the de Jong-Gierveld Loneliness Scale at the outset of the study became more than twice as likely to develop dementia than those who did not, leading Professor Wilson and his team to hypothesise that loneliness might be a contributory factor in the development of memory loss (Wilson, Krueger, Arnold, Schneider, Kelly, Barnes, Tang, and Bennett, 2007).

Thus, too much isolation must be avoided at all costs.

As a matter of related interest, having published this groundbreaking study on the role of loneliness in the development of Alzheimer's disease, Robert Wilson and his co-workers produced a further piece of seminal research on the prevention or slowing of dementia. These neuroscientists discovered that those who exercise their minds with activities as diverse as studying for tests, deciphering Morse code, performing cognitive exercises and, even, training to become London taxi drivers, will enhance their memory abilities over a longer period of time (Wilson, Boyle, Yu, Barnes, Schneider, and Bennett, 2013). In fact, on the day of the online publication of this study in the prestigious journal *Neurology*, the American Academy of Neurology (2013) issued a press release entitled "Does Being a Bookworm Boost Your Brainpower in Old Age?", inspired by the research of Wilson and his team. Apparently, the American Academy of Neurology strongly endorsed the recommendation that reading books will help to preserve memory across the life cycle.

Having written an earlier chapter in this book entitled "On Marrying a Library", I feel quite vindicated in having recommended such extensive reading to up-and-coming psychotherapy colleagues.

So, let us heed Brendan MacCarthy's cautionary words about the ethical dangers of isolating ourselves from clinical colleagues, and likewise, let us embrace Robert Wilson's research on the neurobiological dangers of loneliness.

Naturally, every psychotherapist must find creative ways of navigating the essential need for solitude and the biomedical hazards of isolation—an ongoing tension, but one that must be embraced. As in all matters, Donald Winnicott had, perhaps, anticipated such a discussion when, in his wonderful essay on "Communicating and Not Communicating Leading to a Study of Certain Opposites", he wrote that, in healthy development, we need to have the capacity to be alone without being isolated, as well as the ability to be alone in the presence of another. Famously, Winnicott (1963, p. 186) opined that, "*it is joy to be hidden but disaster not to be found*".

To be a truly flourishing psychotherapist, one certainly needs to be found.

Choosing the Best Dinner Parties

Although it helps to have a wide circle of friends, psychotherapists often complain that when they attend dinner parties, they often feel "on duty" and not fully able to relax. Sometimes, merely the idea of receiving an invitation to a dinner can fill the psychotherapist with dread, in part because of the possibility that we might meet one of our patients, quite unexpectedly, in an intimate social situation, which might feel awkward for both parties.

Whenever friends extend a kind invitation to me for a supper gathering, I always ask, in advance, who will be in attendance. With good friends, one can readily enquire in a thoughtful and non-intrusive manner, and our chums will certainly understand the reasons for the question. In most circumstances, the guest list will be entirely unproblematic, but, on two occasions, I asked the host who else would be invited to the dinner, and in each instance, the guest list contained the name of a current patient. Upon learning of this news, I maintained my professional discretion and certainly did not reveal that I could not come because "Mr. A." or "Mrs. B." happens to be in treatment with me; rather, I simply thanked the host for the kind invitation but excused myself, having suddenly realised that I could not attend on the night in question.

We must, therefore, select our dinner parties wisely.

As I mentioned, sometimes a supper with lots of narcissistic people can be exhausting, because one becomes the professional listener to the plights of others; but often, a dinner party full of actors can be joyful because such men and women speak with so much zest and *joie de vivre* that one feels very well fed emotionally, irrespective of the quality of food on the table.

Often, however, narcissistic guests, or those who work in what we might refer to as the "non-helping professions", can become very absorbed in the minutiae of their own lives. I shall never forget an evening with five actors— all adorable, attractive people, but somewhat self-obsessed. At a certain point, one of the guests began to moan that her microwave oven had stopped working and that this disaster practically ruined her week as she had to spend an enormous amount of time researching replacements. The other four actors all jumped in and offered extensive, concrete recommendations, suggesting particular shops or websites which offered deals on new micro-waves. I must confess that, having spent the day in my consulting room listening to narratives of child sexual abuse, recent diagnoses of carcinoma, stories of marital violence, and such like, I found it rather hard to become engaged in this banter about microwaves, which, I concluded, served as a defence among the actors against talking about anything real and meaningful. In fact, I even wondered whether that actress who spent ages lamenting the broken microwave had wished to speak to me professionally about feeling "broken" in some way herself and thus, in need of help; but I did not feel authorised to verbalise such an interpretation in a semi-public social setting.

Fortunately, dinner parties centred on kitchen appliances tend to be a rarity.

If a psychotherapist should find himself or herself trapped in an uncomfortable social gathering, he or she also has the luxury of using a considerable storehouse of conversational capacities to shift the discussion to something more interesting or more relevant. On that occasion, however, I felt overwhelmed by too many microwave enthusiasts.

Certainly, I would avoid the strategy deployed by the venerable Viennese psychoanalyst, Dr. Hermann Nunberg, one of Sigmund Freud's most respected disciples. After emigrating from Austria to the United States of America, Nunberg became one of the most eminent members of the New York Psychoanalytic Society and treated patients over many decades. Years ago, I had the privilege of interviewing one of Nunberg's former analysands who spoke to me at length about his experiences, during the 1940s, on Nunberg's couch. This patient admitted that, on one occasion, he and Nunberg each found themselves at the same social gathering. But they had very different experiences. While the patient enjoyed chatting with the other guests, Nunberg sat sulking, all by himself, on a settee in the host's drawing room. The next day, in session, the patient—somewhat distressed at having seen his psychoanalyst behave in such a cut-off, forlorn manner—asked Nunberg why he had not talked to any of the other guests at the party. Nunberg shrugged and grumbled, "So, what should I say to those people?" I cannot reproduce the vocal tone with which the patient relayed Nunberg's response, but one could only regard the timbre as quite dismissive, as if Nunberg regarded his fellow guests as idiots. We must remember that, even in social gatherings, we remain representatives of our profession, and our behaviours will be noted.

I do not recommend suppers composed entirely of psychotherapists, as these can be quite boring, but, although many clinicians marry other clinicians, many do not. Often, one will have a dear friend in the psychotherapy field who has partnered with a lawyer or a doctor or a dancer or a singer or an academic or a full-time parent, and so forth, and these people can be delightful, providing opportunities for discussion of serious psychological topics when needed, interlaced with more ordinary conversational matters.

Friday nights and Saturday nights tend to be best for socialising. Because most psychotherapists work the "evening shift", seeing patients after the end of the traditional working day, many of us do not finish until 6.00 p.m., or 7.00 p.m., or, indeed, 8.00 p.m., or even later (which I certainly do not recommend). Thus, by the time one travels home or to a friend's house, it will already be quite late. And as we might have early-morning patients, we do need a good night's sleep more than a dinner party. Thus, I recommend an early bedtime on a "school night".

Fine dinner parties and other social gatherings will become increasingly important to psychotherapists who, through application and drive, forge successful careers. In part, such occasions provide us with warmth and fun and friendship, and they also help us to avoid the nastiness of isolation; moreover, such occasions help us to deal with the envy that inevitably results from one's growing body of achievements. Although one might be envied by an actor for having a steady job, or one might be envied by an accountant for having rich emotional conversations rather than innumerable spreadsheets, no one envies the successful psychotherapist more than the *unsuccessful* psychotherapist—the subject of our next chapter. Thus, dinner parties need to be chosen judiciously, as they will serve as an important forum, providing shelter from some of the attacks that creative psychotherapists must inevitably endure from highly competitive colleagues.

CHAPTER SEVENTEEN

Navigating Envy

Winnicott's Mutterings in Geneva

Gluttony, greed, lust, pride, sloth, wrath and, of course, envy: our forefathers and foremothers in the ancient world referred to this constellation of personality characteristics as the seven deadly sins.

Interestingly, although psychotherapists work with gluttonous, greedy, lustful, prideful, slothful, wrathful, and envious people all day long, and although we encounter evidence of such characteristics in virtually every clinical report, only envy has become enshrined as a specialist concept within the psychotherapeutic literature, in large measure due to its very profound, fundamental presence at the heart of every human being.

Sigmund Freud referred to enviousness as early as 1875 (p. 99), when, at eighteen years of age, he confessed to his young friend, Eduard Silberstein, that, during childhood, he feared "den Neid"—the envy—of the gods who might attack him for his successes. But, although the concept of envy appears throughout Freud's later writings (e.g., Freud, 1900a, 1914a, 1927, 1931), it did not become a crucial part of global psychoanalytical theorisation until Melanie Klein presented her landmark paper on the subject at the congress of the International Psycho-Analytical Association held in Geneva, Switzerland, in 1955.

On that occasion, Klein spoke frankly about her views on envy, which she regarded as the innate, inescapable underbelly of the human personality, and as a manifestation of Freud's concept of the death drive, which propels us to enact our most destructive urges. Although many psychoanalytical colleagues at the Geneva conference embraced Klein's engagement with envy in an enthusiastic manner, Donald Winnicott became extremely distraught. His wife, Clare Winnicott, recalled that, as Klein delivered her paper, the great Winnicott clutched his head in his hands, quite stunned, and muttered aloud, "Oh no, she *can't* do this!" (quoted in Grosskurth, 1981, p. 414). Some years later, Klein's disciple, Dr. Herbert Rosenfeld, recalled that the theory of envy made Winnicott "completely furious" (quoted in Grosskurth, 1987, p. 30).

Klein (1957) subsequently elaborated her work on envy in a full-length monograph, the now famous *Envy and Gratitude: A Study of Unconscious Sources*, and ever since that time the concept has become a mainstay of psychoanalytical theory. Nevertheless, envy still evokes much controversy among psychotherapeutic practitioners. Although fervent Kleinians have embraced this notion as a very straightforward and necessary one, convinced that envy does represent an essential primitive underpinning to our psychological make-up, the non-Kleinians, by contrast—especially modern relational psychoanalysts—have questioned the inborn nature of envy, as they regard the human being as a much more loving creature. Whatever one's views, few would deny that envy does exist, and we, as psychotherapists, cannot claim to be exempt from the capacity to be envious.

I do not propose to elucidate the theory of envy, as Klein has already examined its ingredients quite well in her classic text, but I do wish to call attention to the fact that one cannot practise psychotherapy, especially as one becomes increasingly successful, without having to manage the envy of one's patients.

Certainly, our analysands have every reason to envy us. After all, we sit quietly and calmly in our chairs and we respond in thoughtful, dulcet tones, and appear quite sturdy and sane. Consequently, we will often find ourselves on the receiving end of an envious attack.

Years ago, I published a book which received much attention in the press. Although I had garnered some very favourable reviews, a certain newspaper wrote quite a dismissive account. At that time, one of my patients had a habit of googling me compulsively, and this person managed to locate every single review of the book that had appeared in print, including some that I had not even clocked. While a patient in a more generous state of mind might have complimented me on the encouraging reviews or might have expressed pleasure at being in psychotherapy with me, this particular individual—a frustrated person with a writer's block—seized on that one negative review and used it as a verbal axe. The patient fumed, "I saw that nasty review and it made me very happy. I am really glad that somebody thinks that your book sucks."

Naturally, I experienced the patient's remarks as hurtful, but, by no means unexpected. This patient had grown up in an overcrowded household in which no one ever took time to cherish the children's achievements. Unsurprisingly, this person grew to become a very angry adult who could never bring a project to completion. Thus, the envious attack on my creativity in having published a book discussed and dissected in newspapers around the world proved too much for this individual, who had no choice but to hurl venom in my direction.

Some of the men and women who come to consult with us will, thankfully, manage their enviousness in a more considered manner. I recently worked with a patient who drank eighty units of alcohol per week—a huge amount—which endangered this person's health. Naturally, we spent a great deal of time psychoanalysing the unconscious destructive forces which contributed to such long-standing, self-attacking behaviour. At one point, the patient turned to me and expressed a very envious comment: "I really hate you, Brett, because I know that you are too stable ever to have drunk eighty units per week. You seem to have everything in your life sorted and under control. I know you would never do what I do. I wish I could be more like you."

I derived considerable hope from the fact that this person could transform envious feelings into words and could, also, turn to me as an object of identification. At one point, the patient even succeeded in proclaiming, "Since you, Brett, can manage without eighty units of alcohol, then perhaps I can as well."

For many years, I worked with a wonderful clinical supervisor who, upon hearing that a particular analysand might be envious or neurotic or self-destructive or attacking, would often remark, "Well ... patients are patients." After all, just as a physician in respiratory medicine would expect his or her patients to cough or to wheeze on a regular basis, so, too, do we in the field of psychotherapy anticipate that we will encounter a great deal of envy.

But what happens when the expressions of envy, including full-scale envious attacks, stem *not* from our clinical patients but, rather, from fellow colleagues within the mental health profession?

"Thank God I'm Overweight"

Envy among psychotherapists can emerge at any point in time and for any reason at all. One need not be a venerable old sage to be envied; sometimes we might envy a younger colleague whom we regard as more attractive, or as sexier, funnier, taller, slimmer, richer, smarter, better read, or more widely published. Every psychotherapist began life as an infant who looked towards a parent with envy for being more capable and more resourced, so it would be most unusual if psychotherapists—however well analysed—did not retain some of those archaic sentiments.

During my training, I had the good fortune to undertake clinical supervision with the engaging and witty Dr. Susanna Isaacs Elmhirst, a venerable Kleinian psychoanalyst and a sometime protégé of both Dr. Wilfred Bion and Dr. Donald Winnicott. Back in the 1990s, Dr. Elmhirst served as Vice President of the British Psycho-Analytical Society—a role which she found predominantly administrative and, hence, rather tiresome. After she completed her term of office, she and I had a very interesting conversation about envy. I shall never forget that, in a humorous, but serious, moment, Dr. Elmhirst remarked, "People can envy you for any reason at all. Even *not* being Vice President anymore can be a source of envy." I must have looked perplexed, not entirely certain that I understood precisely what she meant, whereupon she clarified, "Well, I'm sure that my successor as Vice President—a role which requires a lot of tedious committee work for very little reward—must envy me for no longer being in that position!"

Dr. Elmhirst's observation struck me as both astute and profound and helped me to appreciate that mental health professionals have the capacity to suffer from envy as much as our patients do. But hopefully, those of us who have undergone a long analysis will be more adept at containing our envy, and processing our envy and, also, verbalising our envy. But this may not always be the case.

I shall never forget another memorable conversation with an esteemed female psychoanalyst of great brilliance who had published extensively and who had made numerous original contributions. As a young woman, this colleague had boasted a very slender, almost model-like physique, but having given birth to four children in a row, her shape changed dramatically and, as the years progressed, she became extremely plump. On one occasion, this smart clinician delivered an outstanding paper at a conference, and quite rightly so, she received copious applause. During a private conversation afterwards, my colleague giggled and confessed to me, "Do you know, nowadays, I receive more and more compliments than ever before." I retorted, "Surely you must have had great comments all along the way. Your papers are always so wonderful." "Oh, no," she replied. "When I was thin, all the women in the clinic hated me for being clever. But now that I've gained all these pounds, they manage their envy so much better. Thank God I'm overweight. It's really helped my career!"

Both Susanna Isaacs Elmhirst's observation about being envied for no longer serving as Vice President, and this overweight woman's comment about not being envied for her chubbiness had impacted upon me hugely. And I have mulled upon these thoughts more and more as I have aged and have had to navigate my own exchanges with envious colleagues. As one becomes more and more successful, in whatever way, shape, or form, one will receive greater amounts of gratitude and appreciation but, also, an increasing degree of envy as well.

Generally, envious attacks tend to be rendered in quite an unconscious way.

Once, I had the pleasant opportunity to deliver a prestigious eponymous lecture before a large group of colleagues. The organisers had invited a much older colleague to chair the talk; and although I had heard of this woman before, she and I had never met. She wrote to me before the lecture, gushing about how much she looked forward to introducing me, and asked me to send her a detailed biography so that she had the most up-to-date information to hand. I then obliged. On the day of the lecture, many fellow clinicians and, also, many members of the general public, packed into the auditorium and sat in wooden chairs on the floor while this woman and I took our seats on the raised podium. The chairwoman welcomed all the guests to this very special event—a lecture in honour of a famous mental health professional, now deceased—and began by saying, "Good morning everyone. Our speaker today is Brett Kahr. Well, you all know him, so there's really no point in my saying anything about him. He will now give his paper."

Over the years, I have delivered more than 1,000 public lectures, perhaps close to 2,000, and I have become quite used to the fact that some chairpersons will introduce me with fulsome praise while others will do so more clumsily. But I must confess that I experienced this particular chair-woman's style as deeply anti-collegial and as extremely lacking in profes-sionalism, let alone grace. Nevertheless, I proceeded to read my paper, and I enjoyed the experience, not least the creative discussion which fol-lowed with members of the audience. Over lunch, a very intimate colleague asked, "What's the deal with that woman who introduced you? I've never heard such an *envious* introduction in my life. Did you do something to offend her? She didn't mention any of your publications or institutional positions or *anything*." I explained that, until this morning, I had never met her at all, whereupon my friend simply winked, "Well, she must hate you for having written so many books when she has written so few. She just killed off all of your honorary 'babies' in public."

This sort of experience helped me to appreciate that, as one flourishes more and more, and as one becomes better known and even better regarded, one will evoke all sorts of enviousness in certain fellow profes-sionals. Happily, I survived that particular chairwoman's rather withholding introduction, especially as she had asked me specifically for a copy of my biographical notes in advance. In the grand scheme of life, this tiny interac-tion could undoubtedly be managed. But this experience made me aware that, as one becomes a success, one also becomes, potentially, a target.

As a younger man, I expected, quite naïvely, that all my colleagues would relate to me in the way that my parents, my teachers, my mentors, and other protectors had always done, with a sense of kindly encouragement. But now, having spent many more years in the trenches, I assume that, no matter how much praise I might receive for a piece of work—whether hosting a conference, writing a paper, teaching a seminar, or chairing a committee—somebody will experience a certain degree of destructive enviousness.

Occasionally, the envy will manifest itself not in the begrudging, with-holding way in which the aforementioned chairwoman introduced me as a speaker, but in a more overt attack. Shortly after my appointment as the Resident Psychotherapist on B.B.C. Radio 2—a position which received a great deal of coverage in the national press and which afforded me a weekly listenership of millions of Britons—a certain colleague made some very hostile remarks about me at a social gathering, which I came to hear about through a trusted comrade. Like anyone who has become a public figure, even for a brief time, I took this experience in my stride. I knew very little about the man who had lambasted me at that party, but not long thereafter, a very elderly psychiatrist happened to mention that she, too, had attended that social event, and wondered why that person held such a grudge against me. Once again, I replied, "I don't know. I met the man only once or twice." This older person then explained, "You're very naïve Brett. Don't you know that this chap has been trying to get a foot in the door at the B.B.C. *forever*. He once told me that *all* he wants to do is to appear as a psychoanalyst on radio and television. He must feel that you've stolen his dreams."

Every psychotherapist has the capacity to experience envy, myself included. But as mental health professionals, we have an obligation to deal with our shadowy sides and to transcend the primitivity of our personalities. I have written this very book on how to flourish as a means of offering some small assistance to younger colleagues in the hope that by encouraging us to speak in a louder voice and to develop our capacities, each of us will feel more nourished and thus, less likely to commit envious attacks. But as we flourish, we must be under no illusion that everyone will respond with generosity and benignity.

As a rule of thumb, I have come to appreciate that those who can best tolerate the success of another person will be those who already possess a great deal of internal richness. Those least able to bear the success of another tend to be colleagues who live in a state of frustration and impoverishment and who, in spite of their copious qualifications, feel that they have never found their voice.

On Being Provocative

Thus far, I have considered the ways in which envy can emerge not only in the nursery and, then later, in the consulting room, but also, at collegial conferences. Any psychotherapist can be envied at any time and for any reason, and as we become better at flourishing, we will experience the envy of others more and more.

But my comments on this subject would not be complete without alerting readers to the fact that not only might one *be* envied, one might also *provoke* envy, perhaps unconsciously, in others.

Back in 1308, at the coronation ceremony of Edward II, the courtier Piers Gaveston, earl of Cornwall—the king's favourite—dressed himself in purple robes. During the medieval era, only monarchs wore the colour purple; hence, for Gaveston to have donned such a costume stirred tremendous envy among members of the nobility. Unsurprisingly, hatred towards Edward II's protégé grew over time and, eventually, in 1312, several rivals murdered Gaveston (Murimuth, n.d.; cf. Davies, 1918; Phillips, 2010; Warner, 2016).

Although most psychotherapists do not stab and behead one another with swords, as Gaveston's killers had done, many of us still have the capacity to be enviously cruel. Thus, as members of a collegial network, each of us must, over time, find a way to position ourselves so that we receive appropriate recognition or responsiveness from one another without secretly stimulating an attack.

Let me offer an example. One member of our field—an outstandingly creative thinker and, I believe, a kindly soul with a good heart—has created a new theory about a certain aspect of psychoanalytical work. This person— let us call him "Dr. C."—has become so narcissistically invested in this particular theoretical contribution that he talks about it *incessantly*. Moreover, he sends emails to colleagues about his latest work *incessantly*. And he makes blog entries about his achievements *incessantly*. I recently read an announcement, which Dr. C. had posted, informing us that someone in China had just delivered a lecture about Dr. C.'s wonderful work. I happen to know a number of psychoanalytical colleagues who have made an impact in China, but most of them have never bombarded the rest of us *incessantly* with press releases and emails about their various world conquests.

I think everyone would agree that Dr. C. has, indeed, made a big contribution, and that his new theory has much merit. But Dr. C. has also provoked concern among the wider collegial network because of his need to tell everybody about every citation that he has received in the psychoanalytical literature. Some have become envious of Dr. C.'s achievements as a result; some have even expressed an envy of Dr. C.'s remarkable capacity to promote himself far and wide; but some have experienced concern about a sense of emptiness within Dr. C. for his seemingly endless need to be lionised and fêted.

Recognition is a human need; thus, no one should ever be ashamed about that. In fact, I would describe recognition as a huge *necessity*. Unrecognised infants, as we know, become deeply depressed.

But the psychotherapist who provokes *unnecessary* envy in others must become more mindful about his or her potential impact. Of course, we all have the right to share our private achievements with our most intimate family and friends, but we must also find a way to wear our success and authority very lightly.

CHAPTER EIGHTEEN

Nurturing the Ageing Spine

The Ultimate Narcissistic Injury

Some professions can be very endangering to the body. Athletes and dancers risk serious injury to their limbs on a daily basis, while pilots and soldiers actually risk their very lives. Comparatively speaking, the daily world of the psychotherapist—however emotionally exhausting at times—seems rather safe by comparison. After all, by sitting calmly and silently in a chair, we never do anything which would jeopardise our bodies. In over forty years, I have never, *ever* encountered a psychotherapist who tripped over the analytical couch and broke a leg.

But in spite of the relatively quiescent nature of our work, we, too, no matter how successful, no matter how experienced, and no matter how flourishing we may be, will have to accustom ourselves to the inevitability of the ageing process.

One of my friends—a fellow psychotherapist—joked, "Gosh, just as I have finally developed a full practice and just as I have figured out how to do this job well, my body starts falling apart." I suspect that every clinician of a certain age will recognise the paradoxical perversity of growing older and will appreciate both the irony of the crumbling body and the narcissistic injury to our sense of self.

Ageing can, indeed, be a narcissistic assault, because most of us will have had the good fortune to grow up in reasonably, if not very, healthy bodies throughout our youth. In fact, many of us did not have to think about our bodies at all. I remember that, as a young practitioner, having a cold or, occasionally, the 'flu constituted a calamity, as I hated having to cancel any sessions with patients. But nowadays, I look back on the good old days of a nasty sore throat with nostalgic longing, for as one ages and develops new symptoms, one must entertain the serious possibility of something far more sinister.

My own training analyst lived until a ripe old age. From time to time he used to tell me that having a full, long-term psychoanalytical practice might be the best way to stay alive, because the responsibility becomes so profound, and one wants to be available and *needs* to be available to one's patients, just as a parent wishes to be present across as much of a child's life as possible.

We do have some good news: whereas football players and ballet dancers have to retire by their thirties or forties, psychotherapists can continue to work well into our nineties, if needs be, as we do not have to run across a pitch or do pirouettes on point in order to facilitate a curative session with a patient.

But we also have some bad news: even if we have committed to a physically low-impact profession, the ageing process always catches up with us, and even mentally healthy psychotherapists will have to bear the terror of illness and disability. One of my colleagues—a man in his early fifties who kept quite fit by cycling to the clinic each morning—fell off his bicycle and suffered some brain damage in consequence. Another one of my colleagues—a trainee psychotherapist in her thirties who also cycled compulsively—died shortly before qualification, after a lorry crashed into her on a busy road. Yet another co-worker developed a serious cancer and died at the age of forty-two years; and still another became quadriplegic after a fall while mountain-climbing during a much-anticipated summer holiday. In spite of being well analysed, and in spite of working in a physically protected environment, psychotherapists can endure devastating injuries and deaths.

Although clinical psychotherapists can succumb to horrific life events just like anyone else, we also suffer from a bodily illness that does not afflict members of other professions to quite the same degree. *Our spines age quite rapidly from decade after decade after decade of enforced sitting.*

Recently, a health care colleague of mine who practises physiotherapy in North London told me that two-thirds of his regular patients work as psychotherapists! I found this an extraordinary statistic indeed. One would expect that a physiotherapist would be overwhelmed with racing-car drivers, acrobats, gymnasts, ski champions, bungee-jumpers, and alcoholics who have fallen off ledges. I certainly would never have imagined a clinic full of psychotherapist-patients. But, if one thinks about the matter more carefully, it begins to make sense.

Nowadays, we often hear physicians bandying about the phrase, "Sitting is the new smoking." As we age, so, too, do our spines, and every human being will be prone to increased spinal curvature, sometimes resulting in a loss of height, as well as degeneration of the discs which cushion the spine. Many of us will develop osteoporosis, spondylosis, or vertebral compression. And for those of us who sit for a living, the risks may be even greater. Thus, the idea of a physiotherapist in Hampstead or on Park Avenue with an overflow of psychotherapists as patients may not be quite so unusual.

Indeed, as we become older, the seeming physical comfort of the leather chair in the consulting room may become less joyful, and if one ever has the opportunity to listen in on a conversation among psychotherapists in their fifties, sixties, or seventies, it will not be long before somebody asks, "What type of chair do you use?" or "Which physiotherapist do you see?"

Thus, if one wishes to succeed as a psychotherapist and enjoy the possibility of practising into old age, one really needs to become increasingly aware of the inevitable physical deterioration of the body and of the accompanying narcissistic assault. Happily, if we do find ourselves suffering from an ageing spine, we can do much to remedy the situation. Moreover, younger colleagues can begin to train themselves at an earlier stage in the hope of enhancing lifelong spinal fitness.

The Ten-Minute Gymnasium

It saddens me deeply that, in spite of all the zillions of books and chapters and essays and *pièces d'occasion* written by psychotherapists across the last century, virtually no one has ever scripted a proper contribution about the physical well-being of the hard-working mental health clinician.

Almost a century ago, the pioneering British psychoanalyst, Dr. David Forsyth (1922, p. 30), wrote an engaging textbook on *The Technique of Psycho-Analysis*, now much forgotten, in which he did make brief mention of the possibility that clinicians might experience a "cramped feeling after sitting so long at work". Forsyth did not prescribe any particular stretching exercises; instead, he recommended a simple five-minute-break in between sessions—then a rarity, at a time when psychoanalysts literally treated their patients back to back. Apart from Forsyth's use of the word "cramped", one would be hard-pressed to find any other references in the literature to the psychoanalytical spine.

Fortunately, the distinguished contemporary psychoanalyst, Professor Joan Raphael-Leff (2002), a woman whom I admire greatly, did write a short essay entitled "Presence of Mind and Body", which contains helpful, practical exercises for the cramped psychotherapeutic practitioner. I cannot champion this lovely piece of writing highly enough. In clear prose, she has provided the busy, workaday psychotherapist with a host of simple and useful exercises which we might undertake quite easily in between appointments. Some of these recommendations can be completed while sitting in our chair, whereas other exercises must be practised while standing or while lying on the floor. For instance, Raphael-Leff has suggested a whole host of leg stretches, ankle rotations, waist bending, and so much more. Helpfully divided into categories, including warm-ups, quickies, chair exercises, standing exercises, and lying-down exercises, this chapter should become standard reading for all mental health practitioners. Raphael-Leff has also included useful tips on the best chairs for the consulting room.

Of course, for those colleagues with more severe pains in the neck or back or hips or joints, one should consult a physician or a physiotherapist in order to ensure that one exercises in the proper manner. Certain physiotherapists may recommend particularly targeted routines for each individual spine.

When I first opened my private practice, I always left a ten-minute gap between clinical appointments, but I would invariably use that time to return a telephone call, to write up notes, to read a page or two of a book, or to enjoy a few sips of tea or coffee (Kahr, 2007d). But nowadays, as an increasingly older person, I much prefer to stand and flex my muscles or to stretch out on the floor in order to straighten my back! In this way, I have tried to turn the consulting room into an honorary gymnasium, at least for the brief interval between patients.

Simple ten-minute exercises can, in fact, be very helpful, but in my experience, as one ages, each of us needs to invest much more time and energy into bodily care than ever before. A bit of stretching simply will not suffice. So, round about the time of my fiftieth birthday, I began to walk to work in the early morning and, once again, back home at the end of the day, whereas in previous years, I would ride on the underground or even take a taxi. Since I have begun this process (to which I have already referred in Chapter 16, in reference to solitude), I have become increasingly addicted to walking, and if I cannot do so for whatever reason (e.g., an after-work meeting in an odd location which requires travel by tube or by car), then I feel rather cheated! I now pride myself on accumulating 10,000 steps per day at the very least, which I monitor with a little pedometer, and sometimes I manage as many as 20,000 steps—a source of great pleasure and pride. My physiotherapy colleague has told me that most of his psychotherapist-patients manage little more than 2,000 steps per day.

In addition to a stretching routine in the ten-minute pauses, and in addition to my regular walks, I also visit a gymnasium as often as I can manage in order to undertake more intensive exercises. And once per week, I always play a game of squash with a very dear old chum, which remains a much-cherished highlight of my week.

It may be that those of us who gravitated towards academia and towards the health care professions did so, in part, because of our love of learning. Although I played some sport as a child, I spent far more time in the library, as I have already revealed; therefore, I always prioritised the mind over the body. I dare say that many of my fellow psychotherapy colleagues had done likewise. But as we age, we must begin to redress this imbalance. I still adore libraries, but now I enjoy exercise far more than ever before.

By the way, as I have already championed the use of libraries, I must give a further plug to the London Library, which I mentioned earlier, in Chapter 3. A private library which requires payment of a fee, the London Library contains a wealth of great books which one can borrow. But even better, one can also use the library as an aerobic workout space, because, unlike other libraries, this one requires an *enormous* amount of climbing up and down innumerable staircases. When I have the privilege of spending a day there, conducting historical research, as I often do, I find myself dashing up to the seventh floor, then down to the basement, then up to the third floor, and so forth, in search of a wide range of texts secreted across different parts of the library. Before long, I will have chalked up 15,000 steps with little difficulty while also having exercised my mind at the very same time.

Lounging on the Beach

Recently, a gentleman telephoned me in order to arrange a consultation. I offered to see him the following week on a Tuesday at 3.45 p.m. "I can't possibly come at that time," he complained, underscoring, "I have a crucial meeting on Tuesday." I then suggested a Friday at 12.30 p.m.—my only other available slot that week—whereupon this prospective patient moaned, "Damn, I have another meeting then, so, no, I can't do Friday. How about at 8.30 p.m. any night of the week?" I explained that I could not accommodate him at that rather late time. He then suggested, quite feverishly, "Well, what about Saturdays? I am always free on Saturdays. Let's fix up a time for a Saturday. Or a Sunday." I explained that this would also not be a possibility. Eventually, with grumpy reluctance, he agreed to rearrange one of his meetings in order to manage the initial time that I had proposed.

As an older practitioner with little availability in my diary, I have an extremely clear sense of when I can offer appointments and when I cannot. Of course, if a regular, ongoing patient or a former patient should happen to be in a state of emergency, I would meet them at any time and on any day of the week if necessary. Once, during the Christmas holidays in 2004, I received an emergency telephone message on my answering machine from a patient who had gone on holiday to India with family members, two of whom died most unexpectedly in the dreadful tsunami which made world news at that time. I listened to the message quite late on a Sunday evening, but, naturally, I returned the call at once and I spent a lengthy time on the telephone, desperate to offer some comfort to this tragically distressed and bereaved person.

But in non-emergency situations, I restrict my working hours to the traditional five-day week. In doing so, I endeavour to keep my mind and my spine much healthier in consequence.

Younger practitioners, eager to launch their careers, do, in my experience, offer late-evening appointments, Saturday appointments, even Sunday appointments all too readily. I certainly cannot tell another man or woman how he or she should handle the timetable, but I would beg newly qualified psychotherapists to think very carefully before committing themselves to such extreme, non-traditional hours, as the toll can be immense.

Not only must we be vigilant about how we structure our working week but, likewise, we must become increasingly thoughtful about how we arrange our working *year* in terms of holiday periods and other pauses.

In my experience, young, up-and-coming psychotherapists do not treat themselves to sufficiently lengthy holidays.

I appreciate only too well that the planning of a calendar requires much careful consideration, based on the clinical needs of one's patients, based on one's own financial requirements, and based, also, on the timetables of one's spouse and children. We cannot always operate as lone rangers when finalising our diaries.

First and foremost, I recommend that, if at all possible, one should attempt to sculpt a template diary during the first year of practice and decide with one's partner—if one has a partner—when the summer holidays might be. Traditionally, most British psychotherapists and, indeed, most American practitioners as well, take off the entire calendar month of August, for obvious reasons. No month could be better than August, because one's children will not be at school, one's patients will likely be away (due to the lovely weather), and so on. Obviously, if the psychotherapist's husband or wife might be required to work during the month of August, then this presents a challenge. But by and large, I recommend August heartily.

Sometimes, young psychotherapists will hold institutional posts, and many will also be undergoing a training analysis at the same time and will, therefore, have an inbuilt August break. In such circumstances, virtually every single member of the staff team wishes to go on holiday in August, thus leaving the clinic potentially deserted. And managers may not always authorise this. So, occasionally, young psychologists and psychiatrists will have to juggle their summer holidays from year to year. But whenever possible, we should try to be as consistent as possible.

Younger colleagues without institutional restrictions will, however, often make the mistake of taking off the month of August one year, but then arrange a summer break in either June or July during the following year. This will assuredly cause difficulties. When I begin work with a new patient, I discuss the annual timetable in great detail, and I explain that the holiday periods will be *invariable* from year to year, with a two-week break each Easter, a two-week break each Christmas, and a longer summer break covering the entire month of August. By adhering to this clear practice, my patients can plan their own holidays well in advance.

Occasionally, people will be shocked to discover that I, and many of my colleagues likewise, take off a full month, or longer, during the summertime. In fact, I will generally be away for the last week of July, as well as all four weeks in August. I do so because I *need* to do so. The clinical year exerts such a heavy toll on our minds and on our spines; therefore, I recommend that we treat ourselves to a sufficient period of rest and recuperation, whether we lounge on a beach or whether we undertake our own personal projects.

Thus, I deeply endorse long and frequent holidays for clinical practitioners and I also recommend that we preserve the yearly timetable as consistently and reliably as possible.

In order to be a truly responsible psychotherapist, each of us must be well rested but, also, we must be "on call" 365 days per year (and 366 days during a leap year), in case patients might need our assistance. Thus, whenever I go away on holiday, I always travel with a list of all the telephone numbers of my patients. I use a special coding system in order to preserve confidentiality, so I will never write down the actual name of any patient next to a particular phone number; instead, I will use a special disguise that I have devised and memorised. In the unlikely event that somebody should ever stumble across my contact sheet (which has never happened and, I trust, never will), at best that person will discover the name of "Mr. Q-14" or "Mrs. T-27", followed by a telephone number.

While on holiday, I always ring up my London answering machine *at least* twice each day in order to check for any messages from patients. Because I work so hard during the clinical year, attending to my patients' lives and minds, only in very, very rare circumstances—such as a bereavement, a diagnosis of cancer, or an Asian tsunami—will my analysands telephone out of term time. But each and every one of my patients knows that they will always be welcome to call me and that no matter where I might be in the world, I will always ring up in order to listen to my messages. I confess that I have never found this annoying. In fact, I sleep much better at night knowing that I have checked for messages on a round-the-year basis.

With such systems in place—regular structuring of holidays and regular checking of messages—we will enjoy the summers much more enthusiastically and will, in consequence, refresh our spines much more fully.

CHAPTER NINETEEN

Embracing Idiosyncrasy

Conquering Creative Entanglements

Once we have established ourselves as fully engaged psychotherapy practitioners, and once we have developed a reputation and a wide collegial network, we will not have to worry quite so much about referrals or about how to conjure up new projects. The socially adept and fully flourishing psychotherapist will, by this point, have a wide group of people to whom he or she can turn.

A close colleague recently completed a three-year tenure as chairperson of a major psychotherapy organisation, with a responsibility for the welfare of over 8,000 professional registrants. In order to undertake such an enormous task, this generous, good-hearted practitioner had to reduce the size of his own private practice, thereby making enough time for this important institutional role. Upon retirement from his national position, this man found himself with as many as ten vacancies in his practice, which he wished to fill. And so, very sensibly, he wrote to a small number of old colleagues, myself included, explaining the situation. In gratitude, we all responded immediately, and within a week, we filled all the gaps in his timetable. At senior level, this sort of group action works very well and very often.

Likewise, a short while ago, I decided to assist one of my professional organisations by launching a new publishing project with an international publishing house. Although I had to attend several meetings and write several lengthy documents, I already knew the relevant people, and they knew me; hence, the project materialised quite straightforwardly. Had I attempted something of this nature as a younger practitioner, I suspect that I would have failed miserably, as I had not yet established any track record.

So, the older, more experienced psychotherapist will have developed, by this point, tremendous capabilities and capacities, and will be able to function quite effectively in many different spheres.

Nonetheless, simply being older, more savvy, more skilled, better connected and, perhaps, a little smarter, will not guarantee that we can do everything we might wish. No matter how competent we may be, each and every psychotherapist still suffers from creative inhibitions. "Dr. G.", a brilliant psychoanalyst, has published about twenty-five books to date. I find her work extraordinary. But, as an old friend, I know that, in spite of the wonderful library of publications that she has produced, she still has not completed the book dearest to her heart, which she has discussed with me many times, and which she knows will be her most clinically important piece of work. A very insightful and self-aware woman, Dr. G. knows that she has not yet finished this potentially landmark tome because she finds herself suffering from a creative inhibition. As she explained, "It's not as though I need to research the subject any further; I've spent my whole life researching it. But I fear that when I write this—my final statement—I'll have nothing more important to say afterwards. So, I think that this book is activating all of my death anxieties."

Dr. G. spoke to me very honestly, and she certainly put into words a concern shared by many of us, for as we age, we must become increasingly thoughtful about which projects we undertake and which ones we park, due to the limitations of our lifespans, and this will certainly force us to contemplate mortality in a very direct manner.

In my experience, even the most fully psychoanalysed mental health practitioners still have to struggle with creative inhibitions in later life, and such neurotic restrictions will generally stem from early conflicts and anxieties which become enacted in our professional worlds.

Let us consider a brief vignette from my clinical work with a creative writer.

"Hubert", a highly successful author of screenplays for the cinema, entered psychotherapy in the wake of a deeply painful divorce. During sessions, he spoke extensively about his marriage, but he barely ever talked about his professional work, as he regarded that as quite straightforward. As Hubert explained, "I just get on with it. I have no conflicts with my job." But one day, several years later, Hubert began his session in tears, having failed miserably to complete a commissioned screenplay. He moaned, "This has never happened to me before. I usually just sit down and write the damn thing, but this new film is driving me crazy. I spent the last six days staring blankly at the computer screen."

I knew, of course, that, at the age of only two years, Hubert's alcoholic father had abandoned the family, and Hubert and his mother had to move in with his maternal grandparents. Hubert often minimised the impact of his father's disappearance, in spite of my efforts to investigate this potentially vital chapter of his personal history. Although I cannot describe the details of our work in this context, I soon discovered that Hubert's new film centred upon a young child who experienced a traumatic paternal bereavement at the age of two! One certainly need not be a Freudian psychoanalyst to appreciate the way in which an early experience, often of a painful nature, can exert a profound effect upon one's capacity to be productive in later life, and that particular creative inhibitions do not appear randomly, but can be traced to very specific traumata.

Such a clinical vignette has evident implications for those of us who endeavour to become creative, later-in-life psychotherapists. I would argue that most, if not all, of our restrictions stem from unprocessed, unexplored, undigested early infantile and childhood experiences. Thus, should we, as creative people, find ourselves struggling with a particular project or with a particular area which we hope to develop and cannot do so with ease, we have the opportunity to discuss such difficulties with our colleagues, who will understand the terrain only too well. Sometimes, older psychotherapists will return for more psychoanalysis or psychotherapy; and sometimes we will analyse ourselves. But whatever path we choose, we should embrace our creative inhibitions seriously, think about them, speak about them with trusted friends, and attempt to work them through.

I know from my own experience of having treated numerous mental health professionals over the years how often even the healthiest among us will become "stuck" in certain aspects of our work. Fortunately, with dedication and perseverance, creative inhibitions in otherwise mentally solid people can be resolved most efficaciously. Indeed, I would regard the unravelling of creative inhibitions as one of the easiest set of symptoms to resolve through traditional psychoanalytically orientated psychotherapy.

Often, our inhibitions will stem not only from childhood traumata but, also, from a deep fear of exposing our most intimate and idiosyncratic core. For instance, Dr. G., my colleague who had written twenty-five books with ease but who struggled with what she hoped would be her *magnum opus*, had no difficulty producing an ordinary textbook in her specialist field. But when she sat down to write something more intimate, expressive of her personal credo and her original views on a certain clinical subject, she became quite stuck. Thus, part of the resolution of creative inhibitions in otherwise sturdy practitioners will consist in the embracing of one's own individuality—one's own idiosyncrasy.

Mourning Unfulfilled Dreams

As young practitioners, we all nurse thousands of dreams about what we might one day achieve. But many of those dreams will, in all likelihood, have to be transformed, renegotiated, or even buried as our lives progress. Thus, in order to flourish, the psychotherapist must engage in a considerable amount of mourning.

One of my colleagues, who has made an important set of contributions to world mental health, has always hoped that he would be nominated for a seat in the House of Lords; alas, this dream has not yet materialised. He and I have had numerous conversations about his sadness, as he has not received the full recognition of which he has fantasised. Another colleague always yearned for a professorship—a position which she richly deserves. However, in spite of numerous lobbying campaigns from fellow colleagues, this wish has not yet come true. We must all endure comparable disappointments, and each of us, no matter how successful, will have to find ways of mourning the loss of certain professional, as well as personal, aspirations.

Even Sigmund Freud had to forego his wish of winning a Nobel Prize. Although he had received nominations for such an international accolade (e.g., Abraham, 1916; Jones, 1928, 1955, 1957), the Swedish monarch never shook Freud's hands.

I know that there will be many, many projects about which I had fantasised over the decades which will never come to fruition during my lifetime. But I have not become as vexed about these unfulfilled dreams as some of my friends have done, perhaps, in part, because I spent a lot of time on the couch during my own psychoanalysis, exploring all of the infantile and childhood dreams which did not come true, and that proved to be a very helpful mourning experience. Moreover, although some of the projects about which I fantasised as a younger man have not come to life, many others *have* done—often some quite unexpected ones—and this has nurtured and fortified me. Thus, if one prioritises the development of one's creativities, it matters less *which* specific projects materialise, as long as one retains the capacity to use one's mind fully to facilitate the birth of rich endeavours.

Not everyone will be quite so fortunate, and it seems likely that, one day, as I age, there will come a time when I cannot deploy my abilities as I do today. Let us consider the case of "Dr. J.", an elderly psychotherapist of long standing who, in addition to her formidable career in mental health also enjoyed a successful "sideline" as a sculptress. When not in the consulting room, and when not attending to her family, Dr. J. made beautiful statues which she often distributed among her friends and colleagues as very treasured gifts. But during her late sixties, Dr. J. developed a truly crippling arthritis in her hands, which prevented her from moulding clay without considerable pain. The suffering became so intense that, although she could, with difficulty, still mould little statuettes, the arthritis spoiled the experience for Dr. J. and she eventually had to give up her sculpting work entirely. "Even though I still have my hands, I feel as though I have been amputated," she lamented. As Dr. J. explained, "I must now mourn my dream of a retirement filled with pleasurable hours of making art—a delight to which I have been looking forward for years."

With encouragement and assistance from friends and colleagues, Dr. J. succeeded in mounting an exhibition of her sculptures, something that she had not dared to do previously, and this brought her great pleasure. Dr. J., an emotionally strong personality, also decided that, if she could not sculpt, she could still practise psychotherapy, as that did not involve the use of the hands, and thus, she postponed her retirement from clinical work and found renewed joy in helping her patients to lead fuller lives.

Each of us, no matter how skilled, how sturdy, or how fortunate, will have to navigate the ageing process and will have to mourn not only the spines of our youth but, also, other losses, whether of a physical or psychological nature. Psychotherapists, especially those who have invested much in our careers and in our professional work, may be in a more blessed state because, although we cannot stave off age, disability, and death, we can take comfort in the fact that, over a long lifetime, we have engaged in many rich experiences and achievements, which we have internalised, and such an archive of private or public accomplishments will provide much nourishment.

No two of us, however, will manage this chapter of development in quite the same way. Resolving creative inhibitions, while also mourning dreams, will always be a unique and idiosyncratic process. But happily, at this stage, we have many fine comrades and intimates to whom we can turn, including our students and supervisees, who, like good children, become potent expressions of our impact and of our fantasised professional survivability.

As we attempt to manage our creativities and their inhibitions, and as we endeavour to bury our lost dreams while also enjoying some new and unexpected ones, the successful psychotherapist must, above all, embrace his or her own individuality and idiosyncrasy and must find a way to delight in being a maverick.

The Maverick in Mental Health

In considering my own journey and, also, those of my colleagues, I believe that I can identify at least two types of professional developmental pathways: the profoundly traditional and the delightfully maverick. Although one cannot always differentiate easily between the two, I shall endeavour to explicate these two trajectories in broad brushstrokes.

The traditionalists tend to be people who have often completed a solid training in one or more of the branches of psychotherapy and then progress up a predetermined track. For instance, I can think of one particular colleague, "Dr. T."—a lovely person—who studied medicine, and then trained as a psychoanalyst, and subsequently took a job in a National Health Service clinic, rising to the post of Consultant Psychiatrist in Psychotherapy and then, eventually, to that of Director of her institution. Throughout this whole time, Dr. T. maintained a small, but successful, private psychotherapeutic practice between the hours of 7.00 a.m. and 9.00 a.m., and then, again, from 6.00 p.m. until 8.00 p.m., squeezing her N.H.S. work in between.

In many respects, this very traditional route—the gold standard in Great Britain during the 1950s and 1960s and 1970s—provides the practitioner with tremendous respectability, a tenured position, and a good government pension upon retirement.

But this career path has a great shadow side. Dr. T. has often complained to me that she suffers from "N.H.S.-itis", as she must spend an increasingly large proportion of her long and exhausting day shuffling papers, responding to innumerable emails, entering confidential patient notes onto an ever more complex computer system, attending budget meetings, and preparing clinical reports. As she has risen higher and higher in the health care system, she has had much less time to spend with patients. Furthermore, this colleague—quite a smart person—has had virtually no time to develop her skills as a writer or as a public speaker, and, thus, has struggled to feel creative. Although Dr. T. enjoys the solidity of her career, she does not feel as though she has made any original contribution in her own voice.

Mavericks will also have completed one or more solid trainings, but they generally work for themselves. Many, though not all, mavericks have come from prior professional backgrounds. Indeed, over the years, I have trained students who began their working lives as policemen, oncologists, statisticians, academics, television producers, ballet dancers, novelists, drug and alcohol counsellors and, even, as taxi drivers. Some, upon qualification, managed to receive appointments in the National Health Service, but very few ever became directors of clinical services (although some have done so … and have hated the job). The mavericks will often follow their own specialist interests and will, in my experience, be more likely to create innovative community projects, write more interesting books, undertake more impactful consultations with organisations, and work psychotherapeutically with a wider range of patients.

I realise that this classification of traditionalists and mavericks might be grossly inaccurate or simplistic but, to me, it does encapsulate the difference between what social commentators from the 1960s might have referred to as the "company man" versus the "individual".

I have respect and admiration for both pathways; indeed, my own career might best be described as a blend of the two, because by having worked in various N.H.S. institutions and by having completed some of the "older" trainings, I have earned my traditionalist badge. But by having presented psychological concepts on radio and television, by having written books for the general public, by having talked at numerous cultural institutions, and by having worked increasingly for myself, I have, I believe, also earned my maverick stripes.

Each trajectory has its advantages and its disadvantages, but, reading between the lines, one can sense that I do have my particular concerns about the ways in which the traditionalists often suffer because of the many restrictions that they must endure, while the mavericks might be more likely to flourish in a less restricted fashion.

Of course, every single practitioner must forge a career in his or her own special way. But for those who do adopt the more idiosyncratic or maverick route, I would encourage such up-and-coming colleagues to embrace being maverick wholeheartedly and without shame.

Sigmund Freud began his career as an aspiring traditionalist. He attended medical school at the Universität zu Wien [University of Vienna] and then became the apprentice to some of the most distinguished physicians in late nineteenth-century Europe, but he never managed to obtain a formal, salaried professorship within the university, perhaps, in part, due to anti-Semitism, but, also, as a result of his own extremely wide range of interests which could not be quite so easily contained within the confines of a more traditional posting.

I doubt that most, if any, of us will ever attain the paradigm-shifting heights of Sigmund Freud, but, in my estimation, his maverick qualities permitted him to follow his own thoughts and create his own pathways. Indeed, from 1886 until 1939, Freud engaged in private practice and held only honorary institutional positions, rather than paid ones; and throughout that time, he worked only for himself and had no boss and no institutional hierarchy to constrain him. Such a free canvas, I believe, burdened Freud with considerable financial anxiety during the early years but, ultimately, afforded him the complete independence required to be his own person.

I can think of no better role model for idiosyncratic mavericks than the architect of the modern talking cure, namely, Sigmund Freud.

To flourish in the psychological arena, we need a great foundation of substantial training, undertaken with diligence; furthermore, we must cultivate inspiring colleagues over the course of a lifetime. We must pursue a range of interesting and engaging projects; and we must apply ourselves with the highest ethical standards imaginable. Moreover, we must survive the envy of those who might be less creative. Finally, we must mourn our own unfulfilled dreams and ambitions. But in order to prepare most fully for retirement and, ultimately, death, I propose that, above all, one needs to enjoy being a maverick and not feel that we ought to identify with a predetermined template.

CHAPTER TWENTY

Preparing for Death

The Appointment of Clinical Executors

When I first began to work psychotherapeutically with patients, I thought very little about death. As a very young man in my twenties, in essentially fine health, and with very little experience of bereavement in my personal life, death did not feature in such a direct way at that time.

I may not be the only person who struggled to learn about death. Many of the grandees of our profession have done so as well.

Donald Winnicott, perhaps the most famous British-born psychoanalyst of all time, smoked cigarettes compulsively throughout his adult life. Sadly, in early 1949, at the age of only fifty-two years, he suffered the first of several coronaries (Kahr, 1996, 2011b, 2019b). Nearly twenty years later, in 1968, at the age of seventy-two years, Winnicott succumbed to the most sinister of his many heart attacks and nearly died. Fortunately, by early 1969, he resumed clinical practice with some of his long-standing patients and he even took on new ones.

In 1995, while researching my biography of Winnicott (Kahr, 1996), I had the privilege of conducting a lengthy interview with Mrs. Isabel Menzies Lyth, an elderly psychoanalyst who, as a younger woman, had known Winnicott and who graciously shared her memories with me. Mrs. Lyth, known more commonly to colleagues as Miss Menzies (having married late in life), explained that, while serving on the Education Committee at the Institute of Psycho-Analysis, she and colleagues discovered that Winnicott had, in the wake of his 1968 coronary, agreed to treat a new candidate undergoing training. At that point, very few organisations had established upper age limits for training analysts, and many extremely elderly practitioners continued to work with patients while in their seventies, eighties, and nineties. Apparently, Menzies and her colleagues became very concerned that Winnicott had offered to provide an analysis to this student, knowing that he might die at any time, and thus, she had the daunting task of visiting him at his home in Belgravia, not far from Buckingham Palace, to suggest that he might wish to send this candidate to a younger training analyst. According to Menzies, the great Winnicott understood these collegial concerns, and he responded graciously and withdrew from analysing that patient (Kahr, 1995).

Interestingly, during our interview, Isabel Menzies Lyth told me that not only did Donald Winnicott cause anxiety for the Education Committee but so did Anna Freud, as she, too, had continued to treat psychoanalytical candidates well into her old age. Apparently, a long-standing colleague, Dr. Ilse Hellman, expressed a worry on behalf of the committee, whereupon Miss Freud exclaimed sardonically, "'So you think I'm senile?'" (quoted in Kahr, 1995).

In an effort to avoid accusations of ageism, few professional organisations have issued warnings about the risks of taking on new patients in one's older years, and I know of many septuagenarians and octogenarians and even one nonagenarian who maintain full-time private clinical practices. Obviously, should the elderly practitioner still be in good health, advanced age might not pose a problem.

But, in more recent years, we have become increasingly concerned about the possibilities of sudden illness and death, and we have now put certain protective structures in place. Indeed, during my lifetime, professional bodies have implemented an important change, which did not exist formally in earlier times, namely, that each registered practitioner must appoint one, and often two, clinical executors as a matter of priority.

A clinical executor (the official male version) or a clinical executrix (the official female version), sometimes known as a clinical trustee, might best be defined as a colleague of sufficient seniority who agrees to assume full or partial responsibility for one's current patients in the event that said practitioner becomes disabled—temporarily or permanently—or dies. In other words, the executor serves as a protective shield for our patients should we, as clinicians, become unable to do so for ourselves.

Professional organisations now require that each of us must maintain a formal list of patients with appropriate contact details and that we must deposit such a carefully sealed document with one or, more usually, two colleagues—our clinical trustees—who will be able to provide coverage should we become impaired. For instance, some years ago, long before the development of email, one of my fellow psychotherapists had to undergo surgery on the throat and became unable to speak out loud for several weeks. This woman thus had to authorise one of her trustees to telephone her patients in order to apprise them of the situation, informing them that their psychotherapist would not return to the office until such-and-such a date. Sometimes, the clinical executor or clinical executrix will have the more daunting task of contacting patients by telephone to inform them that their psychotherapist has died. These executors will then have the responsibility of meeting with the patients of the deceased colleague or talking to them on the telephone in order to discuss the situation and to help them find a new psychotherapist, should that be required.

Patients must be reassured that the lists which we deposit with our clinical trustees will be opened *only* in the event of a dire emergency.

Although it may not be pleasant to think about such matters, those of us who practise really do need to have a team of colleagues in place as executors or executrixes. Our clinical trustees will not only provide a safe cordon of responsible coverage for our patients should we become grossly unwell or should we die in the saddle but, also, they will help to protect our families. If I should die unexpectedly, prior to my retirement, while still treating patients, I do not want my spouse to have to bear the responsibility of liaising with patients, and I suspect that my patients would not necessarily wish to speak to a grieving widow. A professional, clinical call from an appropriately sad, but emotionally contained, colleague would certainly be preferable under such circumstances.

Practitioners must choose their clinical trustees with great care. As a young man, I selected two of my elder mentors for this task, because I knew these people extremely well and held them in the highest professional esteem. At that point, my more junior colleagues had not yet proven themselves to me as having sufficient gravitas for the job. Fortunately, my two original trustees—though both much older—still remain in good health. But, as they may predecease me, I have since appointed a further executrix—a younger colleague whom I have known for many years and whom I have come to trust completely.

It brings me great relief to know that I have a system in place, just in case something untoward should befall me. But, all being well, it would be far better to retire first, rather than to die in the middle of one's practice.

So, let us now consider the ways in which a busy, full-time clinician might begin to plan for a healthy and, if possible, gradual retirement from psychotherapeutic practice.

How to Retire Properly

As we enter our fifties, we should begin to think about the notion of retirement in a much more systematic fashion. Do we want to work into our sixties, and if so, should we pause in our early sixties, or mid-sixties, or late sixties? Do we wish to remain in practice into our seventies, or eighties, or even into our nineties? Will we have the financial security to do so? And will we still have the physical and mental capacities to practise actively for such a lengthy period of time?

I do not know any two people in our profession who have approached retirement in precisely the same way. Every single colleague of my acquaintance has retired at a rather different age and in quite a different manner. For instance, one of my teachers—a venerable, elderly psychoanalyst—told me that he had never saved any money in a pension fund and that, therefore, as a full-time private practitioner, he would have to work until his death. He continued treating patients into his eighties, but then he developed dementia, and he had to stop his professional work rather abruptly, which some of his patients found quite burdensome. Another colleague practised into her nineties. Although I had often questioned her about this and wondered whether she might not wish to enjoy some retirement, she told me that she felt sufficiently agile to continue treating patients and that her work brought her much joy and meaningfulness and helped her to navigate being an elderly widow. But in her mid-nineties, she, too, developed a form of dementia and also had to end her practice abruptly.

Although everyone has unique needs and desires, I strongly recommend that, if possible, we should endeavour to retire *before* we become permanently disabled or fatally ill and certainly *before* we die. That strikes me as far more thoughtful, both to ourselves and to our patients.

At the time of writing this chapter, I remain actively engaged in full-time private practice with no immediate plans to retire, although I remain aware of the possibility that I might have to modify such intentions at any time.

In the hope that I remain physically well for the foreseeable future, I have begun to craft a plan. Although I work full-time now, I cannot promise that, in years to come, I shall always be able to do so, and therefore I suspect that I will probably begin to stage my retirement, first by reducing my workload from five days per week to four. A dear friend, now in her late sixties, had treated patients for ten or more hours every single weekday across the whole of her career. But when she turned sixty-five years of age, she decided to forego working on Fridays, and so she juggled her diary and stopped taking on new patients for the time being, so that she could restrict herself to Mondays, Tuesdays, Wednesdays, and Thursdays. The four-day week made a huge difference to this woman, and she felt renewed and refreshed. She and her husband purchased a house in the country and revelled in the luxury of precious three-day weekends, which began late on Thursday evening and ended on Sunday evening. Two years later, my colleague became a grandmother for the first time, and she found that she enjoyed the experience so much that she began to devote more time to the care of the new baby; thus, at sixty-seven years of age, this colleague stopped her Monday sessions as well and reduced her workload to a three-day week: Tuesdays, Wednesdays, and Thursdays.

Such a plan, if manageable from a health perspective and from a financial perspective, strikes me as an ideal one. Because, by working a four-day week and, then, a three-day week, one has the opportunity to remain professionally engaged, and to continue treating one's ongoing long-term patients, while also being kind to one's increasingly elderly mind and body.

Many of my colleagues in their seventies still continue to treat patients but they, too, have made changes to their practice. "Dr. M.", a seventy-one-year-old psychotherapist, works five days per week, but she does not take on new clients any longer. "Mr. N.", a seventy-four-year-old psychotherapist, travels to his office on only three days a week, but he restricts himself entirely to short-term psychotherapy and to clinical supervision and will not take on any new, potentially long-term patients. "Mrs. O.", a seventy-year-old psychotherapist, offers only "one-off" assessment sessions to prospective patients, whom she then places with younger colleagues. Thus, we have many, many different models of how to conduct our clinical lives in later years.

I warmly recommend that, with good self-care, with a team of executors or executrixes in place, and with a range of retirement possibilities to consider, the competent psychotherapeutic practitioner can still flourish well into old age and can still be of great use. Some patients will, of course, crave a young clinician who might be available on a long-term basis, but many patients much prefer a wise old man or a wise old woman to help them on their journey.

One of my older colleagues told me a most interesting story. He had, of course, undertaken a very lengthy and successful personal psychoanalysis as part of his training. Some years later, after a painful divorce, this chap wished to embark upon further psychotherapy. His own analyst had, alas, died by this point, so this colleague needed to find someone else. As a mental health professional, he had met virtually everybody within the London community, and he knew which colleagues he respected and which he did not. After careful consideration, he decided that he would undergo psychotherapy only with a certain very elderly Kleinian analyst whose work he had admired over many years. My colleague approached this old psychoanalyst and asked for treatment, whereupon the Kleinian analyst explained, "I don't think I can take you on, because I am now eighty years old, and I have decided to close my clinical practice in exactly one year's time." My colleague replied, "I would rather have one year of very good analysis with you than many years of very mediocre analysis with someone else." In the end, the two men agreed to work together for twelve months, after which, the Kleinian clinician did, in fact, retire permanently. Afterwards, my colleague told me, "It was certainly the best year of psychoanalysis that I ever had."

Thus, the aged, retiring clinician can still be of great use and can still work very helpfully and very effectively, irrespective of the number of candles on one's cake!

On the Shaping of a Legacy

I do appreciate that we have covered a very wide canvas in the previous chapters and I suspect that readers may welcome an opportunity to digest the multiple challenges that I have addressed thus far, ranging from how we assess our sanity in the first place to how we appoint trustees who can care for our patients during the post-mortem period. In order to flourish as psychotherapists, we must attend to quite a bit.

I would not consider my little discourse complete, however, if I did not offer some brief and final thoughts about a matter of great importance, namely, the creation of a legacy. Do we wish to be remembered after our passing? Do we hope to have made a lasting impact upon our field, however small or large? Or will we be content simply to drift off into the afterlife with nary a care?

Speaking bluntly, I cannot imagine a more difficult section to write or, indeed, to read.

Colleagues have often asked me what sort of legacy I might wish to leave. As a clinical practitioner who has also trained as an historian, and as someone who has researched psychological treatments during the medieval era and the early modern period, as well as those of the nineteenth and twentieth centuries, I have no illusions about the fate of most mental health professionals. Virtually everybody who has ever lived and practised, with the possible exception of figures such as Sigmund Freud, Carl Gustav Jung, Melanie Klein, Donald Winnicott, and John Bowlby, will, ultimately, evaporate into obscurity. Almost nobody remembers Max Kahane or Rudolf Reitler—two men who held the distinction of being among the very first psychoanalytical practitioners in world history. Likewise, few will recognise the name of Margarete Hilferding—the first female ever to hold membership in a psychoanalytical society. And which of my readers can declare in all honesty that they have read the works of Gustav Bychowski, Felix Deutsch, Paul Federn, Max Graf, Tatjana Rosenthal, Isidor Sadger, and others too numerous to mention—all celebrity authors in their lifetime, but now mere footnotes?

As someone steeped in history, I do appreciate that most of us will end up quite forgotten over time. I know that, before too long, I, and most of my readers as well, will be eviscerated entirely from memory.

Having said that, it would be a source of satisfaction to think that we might still have the capacity to shape a legacy in some fashion.

First and foremost, I hope that, by having worked psychotherapeutically with several thousands of patients across my career, I will have made a significant improvement to the quality of life experienced by these individuals and that, by association, I will also have helped, thereby, their spouses, children, parents, siblings, neighbours, colleagues, and fellow citizens. We must never underestimate the impact that we make as psychotherapists, because, by curing a patient, we also have the potentiality to improve the worlds of those who live with them or near them.

Knowing that I will have helped a number of people will be legacy enough.

Thereafter, it might be pleasant to think that my writings may come to have a shelf-life beyond my death and that some of the organisational contributions that I have made across the years will enhance the professional lives of future generations of colleagues.

Of special personal importance, I hope that somebody might be able to do something with my very extensive library of books and journals. It would be rather nice to think that my carefully acquired and meticulously maintained collection might remain intact and might serve as the basis of a really useful mental health library which could educate practitioners in the decades to come. It might also be a source of comfort to think that one of my clinical executors might be able to donate my many boxes of papers and computer files to an archive so that my unpublished writings could still be of some small value to researchers. And it would be nice to think that one or two of my clinical-theoretical contributions, particularly those on the role of death wishes in the genesis of psychotic states, might be of assistance to mental health professionals in years to come (e.g., Kahr, 1993, 2007b, 2012, 2016, 2019c).

Most psychotherapists do not subscribe to a formal religion which privileges the afterlife. In my experience, the vast majority of practitioners would describe themselves as atheists. For those of us who do not believe in heaven or hell, our legacy may be less important than how we lead our lives, both personally and professionally, right now.

But for those who still wish to make a mark, please do take a moment to think about what creative inhibitions might still be worked through, what resistances could be profitably unpacked, what fears may be dispelled, and what wrongs should be righted. We have a chance to shape our legacy, even if we will not be here to enjoy it.

My Parting Thoughts

I recently had the opportunity to reread a marvellous textbook on *Psychoanalytic Diagnosis: Understanding Personality Structure in the Clinical Process*, written by the very adept and insightful Professor Nancy McWilliams, whose work I recommend most highly. In describing her professional life, McWilliams (1994, p. xii) has observed, quite movingly, that, "To be a psychoanalytic therapist is the closest approximation I have found to gratifying my wish to live more than one life in a single, very short lifetime. Not only have I learned something of what it is like to be alcoholic or depressive or bulimic; I have glimpsed what it is like to be a divorce lawyer, a scientist, a rabbi, a cardiologist, a gay activist, a preschool teacher, a mechanic, a police officer, an intensive-care nurse, a mother on welfare, an actor, a medical student, a politician, an artist, and many other kinds of people."

I agree with McWilliams's wonderful description of the ways in which we can learn about so many different lives, and I would underscore that, in addition to meeting alcoholics and bulimics and depressives, we also encounter schizophrenics, hysterics, psychopaths, anxiety neurotics, obsessive–compulsives, the disabled, the brain-damaged, and so many more. And as well as having worked with divorce lawyers, scientists, and rabbis, we also treat aristocrats and manual labourers, as well as philanthropists and paedophiles.

Whether we work with criminals or with law-abiding members of the public, I would describe the vast majority of my patients as loving and honourable men and women and children who simply wish to have a space to work through some of the fears and terrors and conflicts and struggles of being human.

In practising psychotherapy, we do have a truly extraordinary opportunity to experience something intimate and intense about the most private lives of others, and we have the honour and the privilege of helping to heal many deeply entrenched wounds. That constitutes, perhaps, the very heart of working psychotherapeutically.

But let us not forget that we must also enjoy our own lives, first and foremost, and that simply *surviving* this gratifying, though challenging, career may not be quite enough. I hope that all my psychotherapeutic colleagues will embrace the experience of *flourishing*, both professionally and personally, and will, over time, develop some marvellously creative ways in which to do so.

Acknowledgements

I owe the greatest of thanks to Mrs. Kate Pearce and Mr. Fernando Marques, the directors of the newly established Phoenix Publishing House, for welcoming me into their fold. I had the delight of having worked with both Kate and Fernando over many long years, during their tenure at Karnac Books. I appreciate their warm encouragement of this project, and I have every confidence that they will deploy all of their very best efforts and creativities so that their new enterprise will not only survive but will, also, flourish, and will help to disseminate important psychological knowledge worldwide. I also offer my appreciation to Mr. James Darley for his extremely felicitous work as copy-editor.

I extend my deepest appreciation to the many kind colleagues—old and young—who read this typescript prior to publication. In particular, I benefited from the helpful observations of several dear friends and comrades, including, Dr. Susie Orbach, Dr. Valerie Sinason, and Professor Estela Welldon, each of whom scoured the text with great vigilance and made many helpful suggestions, lavishing me with their wisdom.

My former student Raffaella Hilty—now a much-admired colleague—read the draft with extreme care and offered many truly cogent insights, for which I remain most grateful. David O'Driscoll, one of my first students, and now a leader in the field of disability psychotherapy, likewise provided very rich feedback in his characteristically generous manner. Both Mark

Archer and Dr. Anna Marshall bestowed warm encouragement. And my old friend Beric Livingstone read the typescript with supreme consideration and provided me with much food for thought.

Bryony Davies, the Assistant Curator at the Freud Museum London, has, as ever, proved an indispensable bibliographical comrade, for which I extend my fondest thanks.

I hold the deepest admiration for my patients who have entrusted me to do my utmost to be of service.

I must also extend my profound gratitude to my students, who have permitted me to hone my thoughts and ideas over many long decades in the classroom. I wish to pay particular tribute to the wonderful Rosemary Campher, one of my most brilliant students of all time and a true "flourisher". Sadly, she died after a long illness during the writing of this book. I remember her with great affection and will continue to admire her visionary work with troubled children, which resulted in the publication of a book that she edited for the "Forensic Psychotherapy Monograph Series" (Campher, 2008a), which contains her own excellent chapter on "Neutralizing Terror" (Campher, 2008b).

And, of course, I embrace the members of my family, several of whom read the text and offered many judicious comments, for which I offer my appreciation and my devotion for their love and support and, also, for their good humour.

About the Author

Professor Brett Kahr has worked in the mental health profession for over forty years. He is Senior Fellow at the Tavistock Institute of Medical Psychology in London and, also, Senior Clinical Research Fellow in Psychotherapy and Mental Health at the Centre for Child Mental Health. He holds posts as Consultant to The Bowlby Centre and, also, as Consultant Psychotherapist to The Balint Consultancy. Having worked for many years in the National Health Service, he currently maintains a private practice in Hampstead, North London, for individuals and couples.

Kahr is a Trustee of the Freud Museum London and of Freud Museum Publications, and he is also a trained historian with a special concentration in the history of psychoanalysis. Author or editor of eleven books, his titles include, *D.W. Winnicott: A Biographical Portrait*, which received the Gradiva Award for Biography; *Sex and the Psyche*, which became a chosen title in the *Sunday Times* Book Club and which appeared in serial form in both *The Times* and *The Observer*; *Tea with Winnicott*, selected as one of the "Books of the Year" in *The Guardian* newspaper; *Coffee with Freud*; and, most recently, *New Horizons in Forensic Psychotherapy: Exploring the Work of Estela V. Welldon*, an edited Festschrift in honour of Dr. Welldon's eightieth birthday. He has served as series editor for over fifty-five further titles in his capacity as Series Editor of the "Forensic Psychotherapy Monograph Series" and, also, as Series Co-Editor for both the "History of Psychoanalysis

Series" and the "Library of Couple and Family Psychoanalysis", all published by Routledge.

He has also worked in the field of media psychology for many years and held the post of Resident Psychotherapist on B.B.C. Radio 2 and, also, that of Spokesperson for the B.B.C. mental health campaign "Life 2 Live". A former Special Media Adviser to the United Kingdom Council for Psychotherapy, he currently serves as Chair of the Media Advisory Group for the British Psychoanalytic Council. In recognition of his work on the intersection between psychoanalysis and the media, he received an Honorary Visiting Professorship in the Department of Media, Culture and Language in the School of Arts at the University of Roehampton and, more recently, a Visiting Professorship in the Faculty of Media and Communication at Bournemouth University.

References

Abraham, Karl (1916). Letter to Sigmund Freud. 10th December. In Sigmund Freud and Karl Abraham (2009). *Briefwechsel 1907–1925: Vollständige Ausgabe. Band 2: 1915–1925*. Ernst Falzeder and Ludger M. Hermanns (Eds.), pp. 536–537. Vienna: Verlag Turia und Kant.

Abraham, Karl (1917a). Über Ejaculatio praecox. *Internationale Zeitschrift für ärztliche Psychoanalyse, 4*, 171–186.

Abraham, Karl (1917b). Ejaculatio Praecox. In Karl Abraham (1927). *Selected Papers of Karl Abraham M.D.* Douglas Bryan and Alix Strachey (Transls.), pp. 280–298. London: Leonard and Virginia Woolf at the Hogarth Press.

Abse, Susanna (2012). Commentary on Chapter Two. In Andrew Balfour, Mary Morgan, and Christopher Vincent (Eds.). *How Couple Relationships Shape Our World: Clinical Practice, Research, and Policy Perspectives*, pp. 57–70. London: Karnac Books.

Abse, Susanna (2014). Psychoanalysis, the Secure Society and the Role of Relationships. *Psychoanalytic Psychotherapy, 28*, 295–303.

Abse, Susanna (2015). Why This Review? In *What Works in Relationship Support: An Evidence Review*, pp. 1–5. London: Tavistock Centre for Couple Relationships.

Abse, Susanna (2018). More Doing and Less Being: Why We Need to Encourage and Authorise Our Leaders. *New Associations, 25*, pp. 1–2, 4.

Acquarone, Stella (2002). Mother-Infant Psychotherapy: A Classification of Eleven Psychoanalytic Treatment Strategies. In Brett Kahr (Ed.). *The Legacy of*

Winnicott: Essays on Infant and Child Mental Health, pp. 50–78. London: H. Karnac (Books)/Other Press.

Acquarone, Stella (2004). *Infant-Parent Psychotherapy: A Handbook*. London: H. Karnac (Books).

Aichhorn, August (1925). *Verwahrloste Jugend: Die Psychoanalyse in der Fürsorgeerziehung. Zehn Vorträge zur ersten Einführung*. Vienna: Internationaler Psychoanalytischer Verlag.

Aichhorn, August (1932). Treatment Versus Punishment in the Management of Juvenile Delinquents. Frederick M. Sallagar (Transl.). In *Proceedings of the First International Congress on Mental Hygiene: Volume One*, pp. 582–598. New York: International Committee for Mental Hygiene.

Alexander, Franz (1939a). Psychological Aspects of Medicine. *Psychosomatic Medicine, 1*, 7–18.

Alexander, Franz (1939b). Psychoanalytic Study of a Case of Essential Hypertension. *Psychosomatic Medicine, 1*, 139–152.

Alexander, Franz (1939c). Emotional Factors in Essential Hypertension: Presentation of a Tentative Hypothesis. *Psychosomatic Medicine, 1*, 173–179.

Alexander, Franz (1941). Statistical Dream Studies on Asthma Patients. In Thomas M. French, Franz Alexander, Catherine L. Bacon, Siegfried Bernfeld, Edwin Eisler, Eugene Falstein, Margaret Gerard, Helen Vincent McLean, George J. Mohr, Ben Z. Rappaport, Helen Ross, Leon J. Saul, Lucia E. Tower, and George W. Wilson. *Psychogenic Factors in Bronchial Asthma: Part I*, pp. 62–69. Washington, D.C.: National Research Council.

Alexander, Franz (1957). Psychosomatische Wechselbeziehungen. In Alexander Mitscherlich (Ed.). *Freud in der Gegenwart: Ein Vortragszyklus der Universitäten Frankfurt und Heidelberg zum hundertsten Geburtstag*, pp. 279–306. Frankfurt am Main: Europäische Verlagsanstalt.

Alexander, Franz G., and Selesnick, Sheldon T. (1966). *The History of Psychiatry: An Evaluation of Psychiatric Thought and Practice from Prehistoric Times to the Present*. New York: Harper and Row, Publishers.

Alexander, Franz, and Staub, Hugo (1929). *Der Verbrecher und seine Richter: Ein psychoanalytischer Einblick in die Welt der Paragraphen*. Vienna: Internationaler Psychoanalytischer Verlag.

American Academy of Neurology (2013). Does Being a Bookworm Boost Your Brainpower in Old Age? American Academy of Neurology. 3rd July. [https://www.aan.com/PressRoom/Home/PressRelease/1195]. [Accessed on 4th April, 2018].

American Psychiatric Association (2013). *Diagnostic and Statistical Manual of Mental Disorders: Fifth Edition. DSM-5™*. Washington, D.C.: American Psychiatric Publishing.

Anonymous [Sigmund Freud] (1914). Der Moses des Michelangelo. *Imago, 3*, 15–36.

Bainbridge, Caroline, and Yates, Candida (2007). Everything to Play for: Masculinity, Trauma and the Pleasures of DVD Technologies. In Caroline Bainbridge, Susannah Radstone, Michael Rustin, and Candida Yates (Eds.). *Culture and the Unconscious*, pp. 107–122. Houndmills, Basingstoke, Hampshire: Palgrave Macmillan/Palgrave Macmillan Division of St. Martin's Press.

Bainbridge, Caroline, and Yates, Candida (2014). *Media and the Inner World: Psycho-cultural Approaches to Emotion, Media and Popular Culture*. Houndmills, Basingstoke, Hampshire: Palgrave Macmillan/Macmillan Publishers.

Balfour, Andrew (2007). Facts, Phenomenology, and Psychoanalytic Contributions to Dementia Care. In Rachel Davenhill (Ed.). *Looking into Later Life: A Psychoanalytic Approach to Depression and Dementia in Old Age*, pp. 222–247. London: Karnac Books.

Balfour, Andrew (2014). Developing Therapeutic Couple Work in Dementia Care: The Living Together with Dementia Project. *Psychoanalytic Psychotherapy, 28*, 304–320.

Bateman, Anthony, and Fonagy, Peter (1999). Effectiveness of Partial Hospitalization in the Treatment of Borderline Personality Disorder: A Randomized Controlled Trial. *American Journal of Psychiatry, 156*, 1563–1569.

Bateman, Anthony, and Fonagy, Peter (2008). 8-Year Follow-Up of Patients Treated for Borderline Personality Disorder: Mentalization-Based Treatment Versus Treatment as Usual. *American Journal of Psychiatry, 165*, 631–638.

Bettelheim, Bruno (1982). Freud and the Soul. *The New Yorker*. 1st March, pp. 52–54, 57–58, 63–64, 66–67, 70–74, 79–93.

Bettelheim, Bruno (1983). *Freud and Man's Soul*. New York: Alfred A. Knopf.

Blanton, Smiley (1971). *Diary of My Analysis with Sigmund Freud*. New York: Hawthorn Books.

Boll, Theophilus E.M. (1962). May Sinclair and the Medico-Psychological Clinic of London. *Proceedings of the American Philosophical Society, 106*, 310–326.

Bowlby, John (1940). The Influence of Early Environment in the Development of Neurosis and Neurotic Character. *International Journal of Psycho-Analysis, 21*, 154–178.

Bowlby, John (1944a). Forty-Four Juvenile Thieves: Their Characters and Home-Life. *International Journal of Psycho-Analysis, 25*, 19–53.

Bowlby, John (1944b). Forty-Four Juvenile Thieves: Their Characters and Home-Life (II). *International Journal of Psycho-Analysis, 25*, 107–128.

Bowlby, John (1946). *Forty-Four Juvenile Thieves: Their Characters and Home-Life*. Covent Garden, London: Baillière, Tindall and Cox.

Bowlby, John; Miller, Emanuel, and Winnicott, Donald W. (1939). Evacuation of Small Children. *British Medical Journal.* 16th December, pp. 1202–1203.

Breuer, Josef (1895a). Beobachtung I. Frl. Anna O … In Josef Breuer and Sigmund Freud. *Studien über Hysterie*, pp. 15–37. Vienna: Franz Deuticke.

Breuer, Josef (1895b). Fräulein Anna O., pp. 21–47. In Josef Breuer and Sigmund Freud. *Studies on Hysteria.* James Strachey and Alix Strachey (Transls.). In Sigmund Freud (1955). *The Standard Edition of the Complete Psychological Works of Sigmund Freud: Volume II. (1893–1895). Studies on Hysteria.* James Strachey, Anna Freud, Alix Strachey, and Alan Tyson (Eds. and Transls.), pp. xxix–305. London: Hogarth Press and the Institute of Psycho-Analysis.

Breuer, Josef, and Freud, Sigmund (1895a). *Studien über Hysterie.* Vienna: Franz Deuticke.

Breuer, Josef, and Freud, Sigmund (1895b). *Studies on Hysteria.* James Strachey and Alix Strachey (Transls.). In Sigmund Freud (1955). *The Standard Edition of the Complete Psychological Works of Sigmund Freud: Volume II. (1893–1895). Studies on Hysteria.* James Strachey, Anna Freud, Alix Strachey, and Alan Tyson (Eds. and Transls.), pp. xxix–305. London: Hogarth Press and the Institute of Psycho-Analysis.

British Psychoanalytic Council (2018). Email to Registrants. 7th March.

Brown, Isaac Baker (1866). *On the Curability of Certain Forms of Insanity, Epilepsy, Catalepsy, and Hysteria in Females.* London: Robert Hardwicke.

Campher, Rosemary (Ed.). (2008a). *Violence in Children: Understanding and Helping Those Who Harm.* London: Karnac Books.

Campher, Rosemary (2008b). Neutralizing Terror. In Rosemary Campher (Ed.). *Violence in Children: Understanding and Helping Those Who Harm*, pp. 185–209. London: Karnac Books.

Coe, Henry C. (1890). Gynecology. *American Journal of the Medical Sciences, 100*, 317–322.

Coltart, Nina (1993). *How to Survive as a Psychotherapist.* London: Sheldon Press.

Corbett, Alan (2016). *Psychotherapy with Male Survivors of Sexual Abuse: The Invisible Men.* London: Karnac Books.

Danto, Elizabeth Ann (2005). *Freud's Free Clinics: Psychoanalysis and Social Justice, 1918–1938.* New York: Columbia University Press.

Davies, James Conway (1918). *The Baronial Opposition to Edward II: Its Character and Policy. A Study in Administrative History.* Cambridge: University Press, and London: Cambridge University Press.

deMause, Lloyd (1974). The Evolution of Childhood. In Lloyd deMause (Ed.). *The History of Childhood*, pp. 1–73. New York: Psychohistory Press.

Doctor, Ronald (Ed.). (2008). *Murder: A Psychotherapeutic Investigation.* London: Karnac Books.

Ellenberger, Henri F. (1970). *The Discovery of the Unconscious: The History and Evolution of Dynamic Psychiatry*. New York: Basic Books.

Erikson, Erik H. (1950). *Childhood and Society*. New York: W.W. Norton and Company.

Etchegoyen, R. Horacio (1986). *Los fundamentos de la técnica psicoanalítica*. Buenos Aires: Amorrortu editores.

Etchegoyen, R. Horacio (1991). *The Fundamentals of Psychoanalytic Technique*. Patricia Pitchon (Transl.). London: H. Karnac (Books).

Falzeder, Ernst (2015). *Psychoanalytic Filiations: Mapping the Psychoanalytic Movement*. London: Karnac Books.

Farber, Stephen, and Green, Marc (1993). *Hollywood on the Couch: A Candid Look at the Overheated Love Affair Between Psychiatrists and Moviemakers*. New York: William Morrow and Company.

Ffytche, Matt (2012). *The Foundation of the Unconscious: Schelling, Freud and the Birth of the Modern Psyche*. Cambridge: Cambridge University Press.

Flechsig, Paul (1884). Zur gynaekologischen Behandlung der Hysterie. [Part I]. *Neurologisches Centralblatt, 3*, 433–439.

Forsyth, David (1922). *The Technique of Psycho-Analysis*. London: Kegan Paul, Trench, Trubner and Company.

Freeman, Hugh (1992). In Conversation with Ismond Rosen: Hugh Freeman Interviewed Dr Rosen Recently. *Psychiatric Bulletin, 16*, 593–604.

Freeman, Lucy (1951). *Fight Against Fears*. New York: Crown Publishers.

Freeman, Lucy (1969). *Farewell to Fear*. New York: G.P. Putnam's Sons.

Freeman, Lucy (Ed.). (1970). *Celebrities on the Couch: Personal Adventures of Famous People in Psychoanalysis*. Los Angeles, California: Prince/Stern/Sloan Publishers/Ravenna Books.

Freeman, Lucy (1972). *The Story of Anna O*. New York: Walker and Company.

Freeman, Lucy (1980). *Freud Rediscovered*. New York: Arbor House/Arbor House Publishing Company.

Freeman, Lucy (1992). *Why Norma Jean Killed Marilyn Monroe*. Chicago, Illinois: Global Rights.

Freeman, Lucy, and Greenwald, Harold (1961). *Emotional Maturity in Love and Marriage*. New York: Harper Brothers.

Freeman, Lucy, and Strean, Herbert S. (1981). *Freud and Women*. New York: Frederick Ungar Publishing Company.

Freud, Anna (1927). *Einführung in die Technik der Psychoanalyse*. Vienna: Internationaler Psychoanalytischer Verlag.

Freud, Anna (1936). *Das Ich und die Abwehrmechanismen*. Vienna: Internationaler Psychoanalystischer Verlag.

Freud, Anna (1975). Letter to Humberto Nágera. 7th February. In Daniel Benveniste (Ed.). (2015). *Anna Freud in the Hampstead Clinic: Letters to Humberto Nágera*, pp. 195–196. Astoria, New York: IPBooks.net/International Psychoanalytic Books, and New York City, New York: A.I.P., American Institute for Psychoanalysis/American Psychodynamic Press Book Series.

Freud, Sigmund (1875). Letter to Eduard Silberstein. 30th January. In Sigmund Freud (1989). *Jugendbriefe an Eduard Silberstein: 1871–1881*. Walter Boehlich (Ed.), pp. 99–101. Frankfurt am Main: S. Fischer/S. Fischer Verlag.

Freud, Sigmund (1887a). Letter to Wilhelm Fliess. 24th November. In Sigmund Freud (1986). *Briefe an Wilhelm Fliess 1887–1904: Ungekürzte Ausgabe*. Jeffrey Moussaieff Masson and Michael Schröter (Eds.), pp. 3–4. Frankfurt am Main: S. Fischer/S. Fischer Verlag.

Freud, Sigmund (1887b). Letter to Wilhelm Fliess. 24th November. In Sigmund Freud (1985). *The Complete Letters of Sigmund Freud to Wilhelm Fliess: 1887–1904*. Jeffrey Moussaieff Masson (Ed.). Lottie Newman, Marianne Loring, and Jeffrey Moussaieff Masson (Transls.), pp. 15–16. Cambridge, Massachusetts: Belknap Press of Harvard University Press.

Freud, Sigmund (1895a). Katharina .... In Josef Breuer and Sigmund Freud. *Studien über Hysterie*, pp. 106–116. Vienna: Franz Deuticke.

Freud, Sigmund (1895b). Katharina—, pp. 125–134. In Josef Breuer and Sigmund Freud. *Studies on Hysteria*. James Strachey and Alix Strachey (Transls.). In Sigmund Freud (1955). *The Standard Edition of the Complete Psychological Works of Sigmund Freud: Volume II. (1893–1895). Studies on Hysteria*. James Strachey, Anna Freud, Alix Strachey, and Alan Tyson (Eds. and Transls.), pp. xxix–305. London: Hogarth Press and the Institute of Psycho-Analysis.

Freud, Sigmund (1895c). Zur Psychotherapie der Hysterie. In Josef Breuer and Sigmund Freud. *Studien über Hysterie*, pp. 222–269. Vienna: Franz Deuticke.

Freud, Sigmund (1900a). *Die Traumdeutung*. Vienna: Franz Deuticke.

Freud, Sigmund (1900b). *The Interpretation of Dreams*. James Strachey (Transl.). In Sigmund Freud (1953). *The Standard Edition of the Complete Psychological Works of Sigmund Freud: Volume IV. (1900). The Interpretation of Dreams. (First Part)*. James Strachey, Anna Freud, Alix Strachey, and Alan Tyson (Eds. and Transls.), pp. xxiii–338. London: Hogarth Press and the Institute of Psycho-Analysis.

Freud, Sigmund (1900c). *The Interpretation of Dreams*. James Strachey (Transl.). In Sigmund Freud (1953). *The Standard Edition of the Complete Psychological Works of Sigmund Freud: Volume V. (1900–1901). The Interpretation of Dreams. (Second Part) and On Dreams*. James Strachey, Anna Freud, Alix Strachey, and

Alan Tyson (Eds. and Transls.), pp. 339–621. London: Hogarth Press and the Institute of Psycho-Analysis.

Freud, Sigmund (1900d). Letter to Wilhelm Fliess. 1st February. In Sigmund Freud (1986). *Briefe an Wilhelm Fliess 1887–1904: Ungekürzte Ausgabe.* Jeffrey Moussaieff Masson and Michael Schröter (Eds.), pp. 436–438. Frankfurt am Main: S. Fischer/S. Fischer Verlag.

Freud, Sigmund (1901a). Zur Psychopathologie des Alltagslebens: (Vergessen, Versprechen, Vergreifen) nebst Bemerkungen über eine Wurzel des Aberglaubens. [Part One]. *Monatsschrift für Psychiatrie und Neurologie, 10,* 1–32.

Freud, Sigmund (1901b). Zur Psychopathologie des Alltagslebens: (Vergessen, Versprechen, Vergreifen) nebst Bemerkungen über eine Wurzel des Aberglaubens. [Part Two]. *Monatsschrift für Psychiatrie und Neurologie, 10,* 95–143.

Freud, Sigmund (1901c). *The Psychopathology of Everyday Life: Forgetting, Slips of the Tongue, Bungled Actions, Superstitions and Errors.* Alan Tyson (Transl.). In Sigmund Freud (1960). *The Standard Edition of the Complete Psychological Works of Sigmund Freud: Volume VI. (1901). The Psychopathology of Everyday Life.* James Strachey, Anna Freud, Alix Strachey, and Alan Tyson (Eds. and Transls.), pp. 1–279. London: Hogarth Press and the Institute of Psycho-Analysis.

Freud, Sigmund (1909). Analyse der Phobie eines 5jährigen Knaben. *Jahrbuch für psychoanalytische und psychopathologische Forschungen, 1,* 1–109.

Freud, Sigmund (1911). Psychoanalytische Bemerkungen über einen autobiographisch beschriebenen Fall von Paranoia (Dementia Paranoides). *Jahrbuch für psychoanalytische und psychopathologische Forschungen, 3,* 9–68.

Freud, Sigmund (1912a). Letter to Ludwig Binswanger. 16th December. In Sigmund Freud and Ludwig Binswanger (1992). *Briefwechsel: 1908–1938.* Gerhard Fichtner (Ed.), pp. 119–120. Frankfurt am Main: S. Fischer/S. Fischer Verlag.

Freud, Sigmund (1912b). Letter to Ludwig Binswanger. 16th December. In Sigmund Freud and Ludwig Binswanger (2003). *The Sigmund Freud—Ludwig Binswanger Correspondence: 1908–1938.* Gerhard Fichtner (Ed.). Arnold J. Pomerans (Transl.), p. 107. London: Open Gate Press.

Freud, Sigmund (1914a). Zur Einführung des Narzißmus. *Jahrbuch der Psychoanalyse, 6,* 1–24.

Freud, Sigmund (1914b). The Moses of Michelangelo. In Sigmund Freud (1953). *The Standard Edition of the Complete Psychological Works of Sigmund Freud: Volume XIII. (1913–1914). Totem and Taboo and Other Works.* James Strachey, Anna Freud, Alix Strachey, and Alan Tyson (Eds. and Transls.), pp. 211–236. London: Hogarth Press and the Institute of Psycho-Analysis.

Freud, Sigmund (1916). Einige Charaktertypen aus der psychoanalytischen Arbeit. *Imago, 4*, 317–336.

Freud, Sigmund (1918). Aus der Geschichte einer infantilen Neurose. In *Sammlung kleiner Schriften zur Neurosenlehre: Vierte Folge*, pp. 578–717. Vienna: Hugo Heller und Compagnie.

Freud, Sigmund (1926). *Hemmung, Symptom und Angst*. Vienna: Internationaler Psychoanalytischer Verlag.

Freud, Sigmund (1927). *Die Zukunft einer Illusion*. Vienna: Internationaler Psycho-analytischer Verlag.

Freud, Sigmund (1928a). Letter to István Hollós. 10th April. Box 15. Freud Museum London, Swiss Cottage, London.

Freud, Sigmund (1928b). Letter to István Hollós. 10th April. Peter Gay (Transl.). Cited in Peter Gay (1988). *Freud: A Life for Our Time*. New York: W.W. Norton and Company.

Freud, Sigmund (1931). Über die weibliche Sexualität. *Internationale Zeitschrift für Psychoanalyse, 17*, 317–332.

Freud, Sigmund (1937). Die endliche und die unendliche Analyse. *Internationale Zeitschrift für Psychoanalyse, 23*, 209–240.

Freud, Sigmund (1950). *Aus den Anfängen der Psychoanalyse: Briefe an Wilhelm Fliess, Abhandlungen und Notizen aus den Jahren 1887–1902*. Marie Bonaparte, Anna Freud, and Ernst Kris (Eds.). London: Imago Publishing Company.

Freud, Sigmund (1953a). *The Standard Edition of the Complete Psychological Works of Sigmund Freud: Volume IV. (1900). The Interpretation of Dreams (First Part)*. James Strachey, Anna Freud, Alix Strachey, and Alan Tyson (Eds. and Transls.). London: Hogarth Press and the Institute of Psycho-Analysis.

Freud, Sigmund (1953b). *The Standard Edition of the Complete Psychological Works of Sigmund Freud: Volume V. (1900–1901). The Interpretation of Dreams (Second Part) and On Dreams*. James Strachey, Anna Freud, Alix Strachey, and Alan Tyson (Eds. and Transls.). London: Hogarth Press and the Institute of Psycho-Analysis.

Freud, Sigmund (1953c). *The Standard Edition of the Complete Psychological Works of Sigmund Freud: Volume VII. (1901–1905). A Case of Hysteria. Three Essays on Sexuality and Other Works*. James Strachey, Anna Freud, Alix Strachey, and Alan Tyson (Eds. and Transls.). London: Hogarth Press and the Institute of Psycho-Analysis.

Freud, Sigmund (1953d). *The Standard Edition of the Complete Psychological Works of Sigmund Freud: Volume XIII. (1913–1914). Totem and Taboo and Other Works*. James Strachey, Anna Freud, Alix Strachey, and Alan Tyson (Eds. and Transls.). London: Hogarth Press and the Institute of Psycho-Analysis.

Freud, Sigmund (1955a). *The Standard Edition of the Complete Psychological Works of Sigmund Freud: Volume II. (1893–1895). Studies on Hysteria.* James Strachey, Anna Freud, Alix Strachey, and Alan Tyson (Eds. and Transls.). London: Hogarth Press and the Institute of Psycho-Analysis.

Freud, Sigmund (1955b). *The Standard Edition of the Complete Psychological Works of Sigmund Freud: Volume X. (1909). Two Case Histories ('Little Hans' and the 'Rat Man').* James Strachey, Anna Freud, Alix Strachey, and Alan Tyson (Eds. and Transls.). London: Hogarth Press and the Institute of Psycho-Analysis.

Freud, Sigmund (1955c). *The Standard Edition of the Complete Psychological Works of Sigmund Freud: Volume XVII. (1917–1919). An Infantile Neurosis and Other Works.* James Strachey, Anna Freud, Alix Strachey, and Alan Tyson (Eds. and Transls.). London: Hogarth Press and the Institute of Psycho-Analysis.

Freud, Sigmund (1955d). *The Standard Edition of the Complete Psychological Works of Sigmund Freud: Volume XVIII. (1920–1922). Beyond the Pleasure Principle. Group Psychology and Other Works.* James Strachey, Anna Freud, Alix Strachey, and Alan Tyson (Eds. and Transls.). London: Hogarth Press and the Institute of Psycho-Analysis.

Freud, Sigmund (1957a). *The Standard Edition of the Complete Psychological Works of Sigmund Freud: Volume XI. (1910). Five Lectures on Psycho-Analysis, Leonardo da Vinci and Other Works.* James Strachey, Anna Freud, Alix Strachey, and Alan Tyson (Eds. and Transls.). London: Hogarth Press and the Institute of Psycho-Analysis.

Freud, Sigmund (1957b). *The Standard Edition of the Complete Psychological Works of Sigmund Freud: Volume XIV. (1914–1916). On the History of the Psycho-Analytic Movement, Papers on Metapsychology and Other Works.* James Strachey, Anna Freud, Alix Strachey, and Alan Tyson (Eds. and Transls.). London: Hogarth Press and the Institute of Psycho-Analysis.

Freud, Sigmund (1958). *The Standard Edition of the Complete Psychological Works of Sigmund Freud: Volume XII. (1911–1913). The Case of Schreber. Papers on Technique and Other Works.* James Strachey, Anna Freud, Alix Strachey, and Alan Tyson (Eds. and Transls.). London: Hogarth Press and the Institute of Psycho-Analysis.

Freud, Sigmund (1959a). *The Standard Edition of the Complete Psychological Works of Sigmund Freud: Volume IX. (1906–1908). Jensen's 'Gradiva' and Other Works.* James Strachey, Anna Freud, Alix Strachey, and Alan Tyson (Eds. and Transls.). London: Hogarth Press and the Institute of Psycho-Analysis.

Freud, Sigmund (1959b). *The Standard Edition of the Complete Psychological Works of Sigmund Freud: Volume XX. (1925–1926). An Autobiographical Study, Inhibitions, Symptoms and Anxiety, The Question of Lay Analysis and Other Works.*

James Strachey, Anna Freud, Alix Strachey, and Alan Tyson (Eds. and Transls.). London: Hogarth Press and the Institute of Psycho-Analysis.

Freud, Sigmund (1960a). *The Standard Edition of the Complete Psychological Works of Sigmund Freud: Volume VI. (1901). The Psychopathology of Everyday Life.* James Strachey, Anna Freud, Alix Strachey, and Alan Tyson (Eds. and Transls.). London: Hogarth Press and the Institute of Psycho-Analysis.

Freud, Sigmund (1960b). *The Standard Edition of the Complete Psychological Works of Sigmund Freud: Volume VIII. (1905). Jokes and Their Relation to the Unconscious.* James Strachey, Anna Freud, Alix Strachey, and Alan Tyson (Eds. and Transls.). London: Hogarth Press and the Institute of Psycho-Analysis.

Freud, Sigmund (1961a). *The Standard Edition of the Complete Psychological Works of Sigmund Freud: Volume XIX. (1923–1925). The Ego and the Id and Other Works.* James Strachey, Anna Freud, Alix Strachey, and Alan Tyson (Eds. and Transls.). London: Hogarth Press and the Institute of Psycho-Analysis.

Freud, Sigmund (1961b). *The Standard Edition of the Complete Psychological Works of Sigmund Freud: Volume XXI. (1927–1931). The Future of an Illusion. Civilization and its Discontents and Other Works.* James Strachey, Anna Freud, Alix Strachey, and Alan Tyson (Eds. and Transls.). London: Hogarth Press and the Institute of Psycho-Analysis.

Freud, Sigmund (1962). *The Standard Edition of the Complete Psychological Works of Sigmund Freud: Volume III. (1893–1899). Early Psycho-Analytic Publications.* James Strachey, Anna Freud, Alix Strachey, and Alan Tyson (Eds. and Transls.). London: Hogarth Press and the Institute of Psycho-Analysis.

Freud, Sigmund (1963a). *The Standard Edition of the Complete Psychological Works of Sigmund Freud: Volume XV. (1915–1916). Introductory Lectures on Psycho-Analysis. (Parts I and II).* James Strachey, Anna Freud, Alix Strachey, and Alan Tyson (Eds. and Transls.). London: Hogarth Press and the Institute of Psycho-Analysis.

Freud, Sigmund (1963b). *The Standard Edition of the Complete Psychological Works of Sigmund Freud: Volume XVI. (1916–1917). Introductory Lectures on Psycho-Analysis. (Part III).* James Strachey, Anna Freud, Alix Strachey, and Alan Tyson (Eds. and Transls.). London: Hogarth Press and the Institute of Psycho-Analysis.

Freud, Sigmund (1964a). *The Standard Edition of the Complete Psychological Works of Sigmund Freud: Volume XXII. (1932–36). New Introductory Lectures on Psycho-Analysis and Other Works.* James Strachey, Anna Freud, Alix Strachey, and Alan Tyson (Eds. and Transls.). London: Hogarth Press and the Institute of Psycho-Analysis.

Freud, Sigmund (1964b). *The Standard Edition of the Complete Psychological Works of Sigmund Freud: Volume XXIII. (1937–1939). Moses and Monotheism. An Outline of Psycho-Analysis and Other Works.* James Strachey, Anna Freud, Alix Strachey, and Alan Tyson (Eds. and Transls.). London: Hogarth Press and the Institute of Psycho-Analysis.

Freud, Sigmund (1966). *The Standard Edition of the Complete Psychological Works of Sigmund Freud: Volume I. (1886–1899). Pre-Psycho-Analytic Publications and Unpublished Drafts.* James Strachey, Anna Freud, Alix Strachey, and Alan Tyson (Eds. and Transls.). London: Hogarth Press and the Institute of Psycho-Analysis.

Freud, Sigmund (1974). *The Standard Edition of the Complete Psychological Works of Sigmund Freud: Volume XXIV. Indexes and Bibliographies.* James Strachey, Anna Freud, Alix Strachey, Alan Tyson, and Angela Richards (Eds.). London: Hogarth Press and the Institute of Psycho-Analysis.

Freud, Sigmund (1986). *Briefe an Wilhelm Fliess 1887–1904: Ungekürzte Ausgabe.* Jeffrey Moussaieff Masson and Michael Schröter (Eds.). Frankfurt am Main: S. Fischer/S. Fischer Verlag.

Freud, Sigmund, and Weiss, Edoardo (1973). *Briefe zur psychoanalytischen Praxis: Mit den Erinnerungen eines Pioniers der Psychoanalyse.* Martin Grotjahn (Ed.). Frankfurt am Main: S. Fischer/S. Fischer Verlag.

Friedjung, Josef K. (1931). *Die Fehlerziehung in der Pathologie des Kindes.* Vienna: Verlag von Julius Springer.

Gay, Peter (1988). *Freud: A Life for Our Time.* New York: W.W. Norton and Company.

Gelder, Michael; Gath, Dennis, and Mayou, Richard (1983). *Oxford Textbook of Psychiatry.* Oxford: Oxford University Press.

Greenson, Ralph R. (1967). *The Technique and Practice of Psychoanalysis: Volume 1.* New York: International Universities Press.

Greenson, Ralph R. (1968). Dis-Identifying from Mother: Its Special Importance for the Boy. *International Journal of Psycho-Analysis, 49,* 370–374.

Grinker, Roy R. (1940). Reminiscences of a Personal Contact with Freud. *American Journal of Orthopsychiatry, 10,* 850–854.

Grosskurth, Phyllis (1981). Interview with Clare Winnicott. 18th September. Cited in Phyllis Grosskurth (1986). *Melanie Klein: Her World and Her Work.* New York: Alfred A. Knopf.

Grosskurth, Phyllis (1986). *Melanie Klein: Her World and Her Work.* New York: Alfred A. Knopf.

Grosskurth, Phyllis (1987). An Interview with Herbert Rosenfeld. *Free Associations, 10,* 23–31.

Hinshelwood, Robert D. (1989). *A Dictionary of Kleinian Thought*. London: Free Association Books.

Hollins, Sheila (1997). Counselling and Psychotherapy. In Oliver Russell (Ed.). *Seminars in the Psychiatry of Learning Disabilities*, pp. 245–258. London: Gaskell/Royal College of Psychiatrists.

Hug-Hellmuth, Hermine (1921). Zur Technik der Kinderanalyse. *Internationale Zeitschrift für Psychoanalyse, 7*, 179–197.

James, Oliver (2002). *They F*** You Up: How to Survive Family Life*. London: Bloomsbury Publishing.

James, Oliver (2016). *Not in Your Genes: The Real Reasons Children Are Like Their Parents*. London: Vermilion/Ebury Publishing, Penguin Random House UK.

Jones, Ernest (1928). Letter to Sigmund Freud. 13th February. In Sigmund Freud and Ernest Jones (1993). *The Complete Correspondence of Sigmund Freud and Ernest Jones: 1908–1939*. R. Andrew Paskauskas (Ed.). Frauke Voss (Transl.), p. 639. Cambridge, Massachusetts: Belknap Press of Harvard University Press.

Jones, Ernest (1953). *The Life and Work of Sigmund Freud: Volume 1. The Formative Years and the Great Discoveries. 1856–1900*. New York: Basic Books.

Jones, Ernest (1955). *The Life and Work of Sigmund Freud: Volume 2. Years of Maturity. 1901–1919*. New York: Basic Books.

Jones, Ernest (1957). *The Life and Work of Sigmund Freud: Volume 3. The Last Phase. 1919–1939*. New York: Basic Books.

Jung, Carl Gustav (1933). Letter to Gustav Richard Heyer. 20th December. C.G. Jung-Arbeitsarchiv. E.T.H. Zürich, Zürich, Switzerland. Cited in William Schoenl and Linda Schoenl (2016). *Jung's Evolving Views of Nazi Germany: From the Nazi Takeover to the End of World War II*. Asheville, North Carolina: Chiron Publications.

Kahr, Brett (1993). Ancient Infanticide and Modern Schizophrenia: The Clinical Uses of Psychohistorical Research. *Journal of Psychohistory, 20*, 267–273.

Kahr, Brett (1995). Interview with Isabel Menzies Lyth. 12th February.

Kahr, Brett (1996). *D.W. Winnicott: A Biographical Portrait*. London: H. Karnac (Books).

Kahr, Brett (1999a). The Adventures of a Psychotherapist: Lucy Freeman and Her Fight Against Fear. *Psychotherapy Review, 1*, 199.

Kahr, Brett (1999b). The Adventures of a Psychotherapist: Lucy Freeman's Pioneering Contributions to the Study of Mental Health Journalism. *Psychotherapy Review, 1*, 244–248.

Kahr, Brett (2001). *Exhibitionism*. Duxford, Cambridge: Icon Books.

Kahr, Brett (2002). Multiple Personality Disorder and Schizophrenia: An Interview with Professor Flora Rheta Schreiber. In Valerie Sinason (Ed.). *Attachment, Trauma and Multiplicity: Working with Dissociative Identity Disorder*, pp. 240–264. Hove, East Sussex: Brunner-Routledge/Taylor and Francis Group.

Kahr, Brett (2005). I Suffer from Karnacitis. *Karnac Review*, May, 14–15.

Kahr, Brett (2006a). I Suffer from Karnacitis. *American Imago, 63*, 81–85.

Kahr, Brett (2006b). The Handshake. *American Imago, 63*, 359–369.

Kahr, Brett (2007a). *Sex and the Psyche*. London: Allen Lane/Penguin Books, Penguin Group.

Kahr, Brett (2007b). The Infanticidal Attachment. *Attachment: New Directions in Psychotherapy and Relational Psychoanalysis, 1*, 117–132.

Kahr, Brett (2007c). A Night at the Opera: The Freudians at Covent Garden. *American Imago, 64*, 261–272.

Kahr, Brett (2007d). The Ten-Minute Gap. *American Imago, 64*, 567–574.

Kahr, Brett (2008). *Who's Been Sleeping in Your Head?: The Secret World of Sexual Fantasies*. New York: Basic Books/Perseus Books Group.

Kahr, Brett (2011a). Multiple Personality Disorder and Schizophrenia: An Interview with Professor Flora Rheta Schreiber. [Revised Version]. In Valerie Sinason (Ed.). *Attachment, Trauma and Multiplicity: Second Edition. Working with Dissociative Identity Disorder*, pp. 204–214. London: Routledge/Taylor and Francis Group, and Hove, East Sussex: Routledge/Taylor and Francis Group.

Kahr, Brett (2011b). Winnicott's *"Anni Horribiles"*: The Biographical Roots of "Hate in the Counter-Transference". *American Imago, 68*, 173–211.

Kahr, Brett (2012). The Infanticidal Origins of Psychosis: The Role of Trauma in Schizophrenia. In Judy Yellin and Kate White (Eds.). *Shattered States: Disorganised Attachment and its Repair. The John Bowlby Memorial Conference Monograph 2007*, pp. 7–126. London: Karnac Books.

Kahr, Brett (2013a). *Life Lessons from Freud*. London: Macmillan/Pan Macmillan, Macmillan Publishers.

Kahr, Brett (2013b). All-Party Parliamentary Group for Strengthening Couple Relationships. Tavistock Centre for Couple Relationships, Tavistock Institute of Medical Psychology, London. [http://www.tccr.ac.uk/policy/appg/661–previous-meetings-7].

Kahr, Brett (2013c). Lecture on "Psychotherapeutic Work with Couples". All Party Parliamentary Group for Strengthening Couple Relationships. Committee Room 6, House of Commons and House of Lords, Houses of Parliament, Palace of Westminster, Westminster, London. 15th July.

Kahr, Brett (2014). Harry Karnac: A Memorial Tribute. *New Associations, 15*, p. 15.

Kahr, Brett (2015a). Winnicott's *Anni Horribiles*: The Biographical Roots of "Hate in the Counter-Transference". In Margaret Boyle Spelman and Frances Thomson-Salo (Eds.). *The Winnicott Tradition: Lines of Development—Evolution of Theory and Practice Over the Decades*, pp. 69–84. London: Karnac Books.

Kahr, Brett (2015b). Lecture on "The Roots of Mental Health Broadcasting". Afternoon Workshop on "Donald Winnicott, the Public Psychoanalyst: Broadcasting Beyond the Consulting Room". International Conference on "Donald Winnicott and the History of the Present: A Celebration of the Collected Works of D.W. Winnicott". The Winnicott Trust, London, in association with the British Psychoanalytical Society, Byron House, Maida Vale, London, and the British Psychoanalytic Association, British Psychotherapy Foundation, London, and the Association of Independent Psychoanalysts, London, at the Board Room, Mary Ward House Conference and Exhibition Centre, Holborn, London. 21st November.

Kahr, Brett (2016). "Happy Birthdeath to Me": Surviving Death Wishes in Early Infancy. In Stella Acquarone (Ed.). *Surviving the Early Years: The Importance of Early Intervention with Babies at Risk*, pp. 57–84. London: Karnac Books.

Kahr, Brett (2017a). *Coffee with Freud*. London: Karnac Books.

Kahr, Brett (2017b). [*Darshaayeh Freud baraayé zendegi*]. Second Printing. Saleh Najafi (Transl.). Tehran: Hanooz Pub.

Kahr, Brett (2017c). From the Treatment of a Compulsive Spitter: A Psychoanalytical Approach to Profound Disability. *British Journal of Psychotherapy, 33*, 31–47.

Kahr, Brett (2017d). Oliver Rathbone and the Staff of Karnac Books: An Affectionate Valediction. *New Associations, 24*, pp. 12–13.

Kahr, Brett (Ed.). (2018a). *New Horizons in Forensic Psychotherapy: Exploring the Work of Estela V. Welldon*. London: Karnac Books.

Kahr, Brett (2018b). The Public Psychoanalyst: Donald Winnicott as Broadcaster. In Angela Joyce (Ed.). *Donald W. Winnicott and the History of the Present: Understanding the Man and His Work*, pp. 111–121. London: Karnac Books.

Kahr, Brett (2018c). Sigmund Freud's Revolution in Psychiatry. *Friends News. Freud Museum London*, pp. 14–16.

Kahr, Brett (2019a). *Bombs in the Consulting Room: Surviving Psychological Shrapnel*. London: Routledge/Taylor and Francis Group, and Abingdon, Oxfordshire: Routledge/Taylor and Francis Group. [In Press].

Kahr, Brett (2019b). *Winnicott's Anni Horribiles: The Creation of 'Hate in the Counter-Transference'*. London: Routledge/Taylor and Francis Group, and Abingdon, Oxfordshire: Routledge/Taylor and Francis Group. [In Preparation].

Kahr, Brett (2019c). *The Traumatic Roots of Schizophrenia*. London: Routledge/ Taylor and Francis Group, and Abingdon, Oxfordshire: Routledge/Taylor and Francis Group. [In Preparation].

Kardiner, Abram (1977). *My Analysis with Freud: Reminiscences*. New York: W.W. Norton and Company.

Karon, Bertram P., and VandenBos, Gary R. (1981). *Psychotherapy of Schizophrenia: The Treatment of Choice*. New York: Jason Aronson.

Kelley, Kitty (1984). Interview with Hildi Greenson. 27th April. Cited in Kitty Kelley (1986). *His Way: The Unauthorized Biography of Frank Sinatra*. New York: Bantam Books.

Kelley, Kitty (1986). *His Way: The Unauthorized Biography of Frank Sinatra*. New York: Bantam Books.

Klein, Melanie (1925a). Zur Genese des Tics. *Internationale Zeitschrift für Psychoanalyse, 11*, 332–349.

Klein, Melanie (1925b). A Contribution to the Psychogenesis of Tics. Melanie Klein and D.J. Barnett (Transls.). In Melanie Klein (1948). *Contributions to Psycho-Analysis: 1921–1945*, pp. 117–139. London: Hogarth Press and the Institute of Psycho-Analysis.

Klein, Melanie (1932a). *Die Psychoanalyse des Kindes*. Vienna: Internationaler Psychoanalytischer Verlag.

Klein, Melanie (1932b). *The Psycho-Analysis of Children*. Alix Strachey (Transl.). London: Hogarth Press and the Institute of Psycho-Analysis.

Klein, Melanie (1948). *Contributions to Psycho-Analysis: 1921–1945*. London: Hogarth Press and the Institute of Psycho-Analysis.

Klein, Melanie (1957). *Envy and Gratitude: A Study of Unconscious Sources*. London: Tavistock Publications.

Klein, Melanie (1961). *Narrative of a Child Analysis: The Conduct of the Psycho-Analysis of Children as Seen in the Treatment of a Ten Year Old Boy*. London: Hogarth Press and the Institute of Psycho-Analysis.

Leichsenring, Falk (2005). Are Psychodynamic and Psychoanalytic Therapies Effective?: A Review of Empirical Data. *International Journal of Psychoanalysis, 86*, 841–868.

Leichsenring, Falk, and Rabung, Sven (2004). The Efficacy of Short-term Psychodynamic Psychotherapy in Specific Psychiatric Disorders: A Meta-analysis. *Archives of General Psychiatry, 61*, 1208–1216.

Leichsenring, Falk, and Rabung, Sven (2008). Effectiveness of Long-term Psychodynamic Psychotherapy: A Meta-analysis. *Journal of the American Medical Association*. 1st October, pp. 1551–1565.

Leichsenring, Falk, and Rabung, Sven (2011). Long-term Psychodynamic Psychotherapy in Complex Mental Disorders: Update of a Meta-analysis. *British Journal of Psychiatry, 199*, 15–22.

MacCarthy, Brendan (2002a). Personal Communication to the Author. 29th May.

MacCarthy, Brendan (2002b). Personal Communication to the Author. 27th September.

Makari, George (2008). *Revolution in Mind: The Creation of Psychoanalysis.* New York: Harper/HarperCollins Publishers.

Masserman, Jules H., and Balken, Eva R. (1939). The Psychoanalytic and Psychiatric Significance of Phantasy. *Psychoanalytic Review, 26*, 343–379.

McWilliams, Nancy (1994). *Psychoanalytic Diagnosis: Understanding Personality Structure in the Clinical Process.* New York: Guilford Press/Guilford Publications.

Menaker, Esther (1989). *Appointment in Vienna: An American Psychoanalyst Recalls Her Student Days in Pre-War Austria.* New York: St. Martin's Press.

Menninger, Karl (1968). *The Crime of Punishment.* New York: Viking Press.

Minne, Carine, and Kassman, Paul (2018). Working with Gangs and within Gang Culture: A Pilot for Changing the Game. In Brett Kahr (Ed.). *New Horizons in Forensic Psychotherapy: Exploring the Work of Estela V. Welldon*, pp. 183–201. London: Karnac Books.

Molnar, Michael (1992). Notes and References. In Sigmund Freud. *The Diary of Sigmund Freud: 1929–1939. A Record of the Final Decade.* Michael Molnar (Ed. and Transl.), pp. 271–308. London: Hogarth Press.

Murimuth, Adae [Adam Murimuth] (n.d.). Continuatio Chronicarum: [Incipit Continuatio Chronicarum Regum Angliae, cum interpositione quorundam casuum contingentium in curia Romana et regno Franciae, sicut eidem scribenti suis temporibus occurrebant.]. In Edward Maunde Thompson (Ed.). (1889). Adae Murimuth [Adam Murimuth]. *Continuatio Chronicarum*, and Robertus de Avesbury [Robert of Avesbury]. *De Gestis Mirabilibus Regis Edwardi Tertii*, pp. 3–219. London: Eyre and Spottiswoode.

Orbach, Susie (1986). *Hunger Strike: The Anorectic's Struggle as a Metaphor for Our Age.* London: Faber and Faber.

Orbach, Susie (1999). *The Impossibility of Sex.* London: Allen Lane/Penguin Press, Penguin Books, Penguin Group.

Orbach, Susie (2002). The False Self and the False Body. In Brett Kahr (Ed.). *The Legacy of Winnicott: Essays on Infant and Child Mental Health*, pp. 124–134. London: H. Karnac (Books)/Other Press.

Orbach, Susie (2009). *Bodies.* London: Profile Books.

Orbach, Susie (2016). *In Therapy: How Conversations with Psychotherapists Really Work.* London: Profile Books.

Orbach, Susie (2018). *In Therapy: The Unfolding Story*. London: Profile Books/ Wellcome Collection.

Ornston, Darius (1982). Strachey's Influence: A Preliminary Report. *International Journal of Psycho-Analysis, 63,* 409–426.

Ornston, Darius Gray (1985a). The Invention of 'Cathexis' and Strachey's Strategy. *International Review of Psycho-Analysis, 12,* 391–399.

Ornston, Darius (1985b). Freud's Conception is Different from Strachey's. *Journal of the American Psychoanalytic Association, 33,* 379–412.

Ornston, Darius Gray, Jr. (1988). How Standard is the 'Standard Edition'? In Edward Timms and Naomi Segal (Eds.). *Freud in Exile: Psychoanalysis and its Vicissitudes,* pp. 196–209. New Haven, Connecticut: Yale University Press.

Ornston, Darius Gray, Jr. (1992a). Improving Strachey's Freud. In Darius Gray Ornston, Jr. (Ed.). *Translating Freud,* pp. 1–23. New Haven, Connecticut: Yale University Press.

Ornston, Darius Gray, Jr. (1992b). Alternatives to a Standard Edition. In Darius Gray Ornston, Jr. (Ed.). *Translating Freud,* pp. 97–113. New Haven, Connecticut: Yale University Press.

Ornston, Darius Gray, Jr. (1992c). Obstacles to Improving Strachey's Freud. In Darius Gray Ornston, Jr. (Ed.). *Translating Freud,* pp. 191–222. New Haven, Connecticut: Yale University Press.

Phillips, Seymour (2010). *Edward II*. New Haven, Connecticut: Yale University Press.

Raitt, Suzanne (2004). Early British Psychoanalysis and the Medico-Psychological Clinic. *History Workshop Journal, 58,* 63–85.

Raphael-Leff, Joan (2002). Presence of Mind and Body. In Joan Raphael-Leff (Ed.). *Between Sessions and Beyond the Couch,* pp. 269–290. Colchester, Essex: CPS Psychoanalytic Publications/University of Essex.

Read, John, and Gumley, Andrew (2008). Can Attachment Theory Help Explain the Relationship Between Childhood Adversity and Psychosis? *Attachment: New Directions in Psychotherapy and Relational Psychoanalysis, 2,* 1–35.

Read, John, and Hammersley, Paul (2005). Child Sexual Abuse and Schizophrenia. *British Journal of Psychiatry, 186,* 76.

Reich, Wilhelm (1932). *Der sexuelle Kampf der Jugend*. Berlin: Verlag für Sexualpolitik.

Rifkind, Gabrielle (2007). *A Standing Conference Table: A Process for a Sustainable Peace in the Palestinian-Israeli Conflict*. London: Oxford Research Group.

Rifkind, Gabrielle (2008). *The Arab Peace Initiative: Why Now? One Year on from Annapolis—The Need for a Regional Frame for Negotiations. Report Following an Oxford Research Group Meeting on 'The Arab Peace Initiative as a Possible*

Exit from the Current Impasse: What Needs to happen'. 15–17 October 2008, Oxfordshire, UK. London: Oxford Research Group.

Rifkind, Gabrielle (2009). Seminar on "Psychopolitics, Fear and Trauma in the Middle East: Gabrielle Rifkind in Conversation with Brett Kahr". Freud Museum, Swiss Cottage, London, at The Library, Anna Freud Centre, Swiss Cottage, London. 30th June.

Rifkind, Gabrielle (2018). *The Psychology of Political Extremism: What Would Sigmund Freud Have Thought About Islamic State?* London: Routledge/Taylor and Francis Group, and Abingdon, Oxfordshire: Routledge/Taylor and Francis Group.

Rifkind, Gabrielle, and Picco, Giandomenico (2014). *The Fog of Peace: The Human Face of Conflict Resolution.* London: I.B. Tauris/I.B. Tauris and Company.

Ritholz, Benjamin D. (1938). Letter to Sigmund Freud. 23rd June. Box 24. Freud Museum London, Swiss Cottage, London.

Roazen, Paul (1969). *Brother Animal: The Story of Freud and Tausk.* New York: Alfred A. Knopf.

Roazen, Paul (1975). *Freud and His Followers.* New York: Alfred A. Knopf.

Roazen, Paul (1990). *Encountering Freud: The Politics and Histories of Psychoanalysis.* New Brunswick, New Jersey: Transaction Publishers.

Roazen, Paul (1993). *Meeting Freud's Family.* Amherst, Massachusetts: University of Massachusetts Press.

Roazen, Paul (1995). *How Freud Worked: First-Hand Accounts of Patients.* Northvale, New Jersey: Jason Aronson.

Roazen, Paul (2001). *The Historiography of Psychoanalysis.* New Brunswick, New Jersey: Transaction Publishers.

Rosen, Ruth (2016). Personal Communication to the Author. 23rd September.

Samuels, Andrew (2015). *A New Therapy for Politics?* London: Karnac Books.

Schreiber, Flora Rheta (1973). *Sybil.* Chicago, Illinois: Henry Regnery Company.

Schreiber, Flora Rheta (1983). *The Shoemaker: The Anatomy of a Psychotic.* New York: Simon and Schuster.

Segal, Hanna (1964). *Introduction to the Work of Melanie Klein.* London: William Heinemann Medical Books.

Segal, Hanna (1973). *Introduction to the Work of Melanie Klein: New, Enlarged Edition.* London: Hogarth Press and the Institute of Psycho-Analysis.

Sharaf, Myron (1983). *Fury on Earth: A Biography of Wilhelm Reich.* New York: St. Martin's Press/Marek.

Shorter, Edward (1987). *A History of Psychiatry: From the Era of the Asylum to the Age of Prozac.* New York: John Wiley and Sons.

Sinason, Valerie (1992). *Mental Handicap and the Human Condition: New Approaches from the Tavistock*. London: Free Association Books.

Sinason, Valerie (2010). *Mental Handicap and the Human Condition: An Analytic Approach to Intellectual Disability*. Revised Edition. London: Free Association Books.

Socarides, Charles, and Loeb, Loretta R. Loeb (Eds.). (2004). *The Mind of the Paedophile: Psychoanalytic Perspectives*. London: H. Karnac (Books).

Sondheim, Stephen (1981). Franklin Shepard, Inc. In Stephen Sondheim (2010). *Finishing the Hat: Collected Lyrics (1954–1981) with Attendant Comments, Principles, Heresies, Grudges, Whines and Anecdotes*, pp. 391–392. New York: Alfred A. Knopf.

Spoto, Donald (1993). *Marilyn Monroe: The Biography*. New York: HarperCollins Publishers.

Volkan, Vamik D. (1988). *The Need to Have Enemies and Allies: From Clinical Practice to International Relationships*. Northvale, New Jersey: Jason Aronson.

Volkan, Vamik (1997). *Bloodlines: From Ethnic Pride to Ethnic Terrorism*. New York: Farrar, Straus and Giroux.

Volkan, Vamik D. (2013). *Enemies on the Couch: A Psychopolitical Journey Through War and Peace*. Durham, North Carolina: Pitchstone Publishing.

Volkan, Vamik D. (2014a). *Animal Killer: Transmission of War Trauma from One Generation to the Next*. London: Karnac Books.

Volkan, Vamik D. (2014b). *Psychoanalysis, International Relations, and Diplomacy: A Sourcebook on Large-Group Psychology*. London: Karnac Books.

Warner, Kathryn (2016). *Isabella of France: The Rebel Queen. The Story of the Queen Who Deposed Her Husband Edward II*. Stroud, Gloucestershire: Amberley/ Amberley Publishing.

Weiss, Edoardo (1970). The Letters: With Commentary by Edoardo Weiss. In *Sigmund Freud as a Consultant: Recollections of a Pioneer in Psychoanalysis*. Etelka Grotjahn and Martin Grotjahn (Transls.), pp. 23–82. New York: Intercontinental Medical Book Corporation.

White, Kate (2019). An Attachment Approach to Understanding and Living Well with Dementia. In Kate White, Angela Cotter, and Hazel Leventhal (Eds.). *Dementia: An Attachment Approach*, pp. 13–42. London: Routledge / Taylor and Francis Group, and Abingdon, Oxfordshire: Routledge / Taylor and Francis Group.

Wilson, Robert S., Boyle, Patricia A., Yu, Lei; Barnes, Lisa L., Schneider, Julie A., and Bennett, David A. (2013). Life-span Cognitive Activity, Neuropsychologic Burden, and Cognitive Aging. *Neurology, 81*, 314–321.

Wilson, Robert S., Krueger, Kristin R., Arnold, Steven E., Schneider, Julie A., Kelly, Jeremiah F., Barnes, Lisa L., Tang, Yuxiao, and Bennett, David A. (2007). Loneliness and Risk of Alzheimer Disease. *Archives of General Psychiatry, 64*, 234–240.

Winnicott, Donald W. (1930a). Enuresis. *Proceedings of the Royal Society of Medicine, 23*, 255.

Winnicott, Donald W. (1930b). Short Communication on Enuresis. *St. Bartholomew's Hospital Journal, 37*, 125–127.

Winnicott, Donald W. (1931a). *Clinical Notes on Disorders of Childhood*. London: William Heinemann (Medical Books).

Winnicott, Donald W. (1931b). A Clinical Note on Convulsions, p. 257. In Anonymous. British Paediatric Association: Proceedings of the Fourth Annual General Meeting. *Archives of Disease in Childhood, 6*, 255–258.

Winnicott, Donald W. (1932). Growing Pains; the Problem of Their Relation to Acute Rheumatism, p. 227. In Anonymous. British Paediatric Association: Proceedings of the Fifth Annual General Meeting. *Archives of Disease in Childhood, 7*, 225–229.

Winnicott, Donald W. (1933a). Short Communication on Enuresis. *British Journal of Children's Diseases, 30*, 41–42.

Winnicott, Donald W. (1933b). Pathological Sleeping. *British Journal of Children's Diseases, 30*, 205–206.

Winnicott, Donald W. (1949). Hate in the Counter-Transference. *International Journal of Psycho-Analysis, 30*, 69–74.

Winnicott, Donald W. (1958). *Collected Papers: Through Paediatrics to Psycho-Analysis*. London: Tavistock Publications.

Winnicott, Donald W. (1963). Communicating and Not Communicating Leading to a Study of Certain Opposites. In Donald W. Winnicott (1965). *The Maturational Processes and the Facilitating Environment: Studies in the Theory of Emotional Development*, pp. 179–192. London: Hogarth Press and the Institute of Psycho-Analysis.

Winnicott, Donald W. (1965). *The Maturational Processes and the Facilitating Environment: Studies in the Theory of Emotional Development*. London: Hogarth Press and the Institute of Psycho-Analysis.

Winnicott, Donald W. (1968). Clinical Regression Compared with Defense Organization. In Stanley H. Eldred and Maurice Vanderpol (Eds.). *Psychotherapy in the Designed Therapeutic Milieu*, pp. 3–11. Boston, Massachusetts: Little, Brown and Company.

Winnicott, Donald W. (1970). Cure. In Donald W. Winnicott (1986). *Home is Where We Start From: Essays by a Psychoanalyst*. Clare Winnicott, Ray Shepherd, and Madeleine Davis (Eds.), pp. 112–120. Harmondsworth, Middlesex: Penguin Books/Pelican Books.

Yates, Candida (2014). Psychoanalysis and Television: Notes Towards a Psycho-Cultural Approach. In Caroline Bainbridge, Ivan Ward, and Candida Yates (Eds.). *Television and Psychoanalysis: Psycho-Cultural Perspectives*, pp. 1–28. London: Karnac Books.

Yates, Candida (2015). *The Play of Political Culture, Emotion and Identity*. Houndmills, Basingstoke, Hampshire: Palgrave Macmillan/Macmillan Publishers.

Yates, Candida (2018). On the Psychodynamics of Boris Johnson and Brexit. *New Associations*, *25*, pp. 4–5.

Zilboorg, Gregory, and Henry, George W. (1941). *A History of Medical Psychology*. New York: W.W. Norton and Company.

Index